153

'Suzannah Lipscomb shows vividly how the events of a single tumultuous year, from marital betrayal to mass rebellion, crystallized Henry's personal fears, religious priorities, political style and visual image, shaping the tyranny of his last years, the idiosyncrasies of his Reformation and the lasting myth of the wilful colossus.'

Steven Gunn, Lecturer in Modern History, University of Oxford

'An enlightening and comprehensive analysis of a pivotal year in Henry VIII's reign.'

Tracy Borman, author of King's Mistress, Queen's Servant: Henrietta Howard

'*1536* is a lucid and evocative account of Henry VIII in his times, and a finely judged portrait of the pomp, envy, fury and melancholy of kingship. It is also an object lesson in male vainglory, and the precipitous decline even the most gilded life can lurch into: of how the best-known and most naturally gifted monarch in British history succumbed to the strange, familiar passions of age, arrogance and insecurity.'

Tom Chatfield, Arts & Books Editor, Prospect

'At once scholarly and a joy to read.'

Thomas Betteridge, Reader in Early Modern English Literature, Oxford Brookes University

1536

The Year that Changed Henry VIII

Suzannah Lipscomb

LION

A Lion Book
an imprint of
Lion Hudson plc
Wilkinson House, Jordan Hill Road,
Oxford OX2 8DR, England
www.lionhudson.com

UK hardback ISBN 978 0 7459 5365 6
US hardback ISBN 978 0 8254 7938 0
UK paperback ISBN 978 0 7459 5332 8
US paperback ISBN 978 0 8254 7922 9

Distributed by:
UK: Marston Book Services, PO Box 269, Abingdon, Oxon, OX14 4YN
USA: Trafalgar Square Publishing, 814 N. Franklin Street, Chicago, IL 60610
USA Christian Market: Kregel Publications, PO Box 2607, Grand Rapids,
Michigan 49501

First edition 2009
10 9 8 7 6 5 4 3 2 1 0
All rights reserved

Text Acknowledgments
Scripture taken from the New King James Version®. Copyright © 1982 by
Thomas Nelson, Inc. Used by permission. All rights reserved.

Picture Acknowledgments
pp. i, vi (tl), vi (br): Thyssen, Jane Seymour, Cranmer – The London Art Archive
/ Alamy; rp. ii, iv, vii:1520 Henry, Cartoon and Cromwell © National Portrait
Gallery, London; pp. iii, vi (tl), vi (bl) Mural, Anne Boleyn, Henry Fitzroy The
Royal Collection © 2009 Her Majesty Queen Elizabeth II; p. v Walker – The
Bridgeman Art Library / Getty; p. viii Frontispiece – Classic Image / Alamy

This book has been printed on paper independently certified as having been
produced from sustainable forests.
A catalogue record for this book is available
from the British Library

Typeset in 10.5/14 Caxton BT
Printed and bound in Malta

For my father and mother, Nick and Marguerite,
my great-aunt, Sylvia,
and in loving memory of my grandad, Charlie,
all of whom were proud of the book before
a word of it had been written.

Contents

1536

Acknowledgments

This book would not have been possible had I not been offered the post of Associate in the Knowledge Transfer Partnership between Historic Royal Palaces and Kingston University, which is part-funded by the Arts and Humanities Research Council. I am very grateful for the wonderful opportunities this role has opened up to me, this book included.

I would like to express my gratitude to Historic Royal Palaces for kindly agreeing to release copyright on the research I had carried out as part of my duties as the Research Curator on the Henry VIII project, and especially would like to thank Lucy Worsley, Polly Schomberg, Erica Longfellow and Kent Rawlinson for their support and friendship. My thanks also go to Benedetta Tiana for being the first person to be enthused by the 1536 idea!

I am grateful to the many scholarly giants on whose shoulders I have stood. I would particularly like to acknowledge my debt to the work of George Bernard, Susan Brigden, Xanthe Brooke and David Crombie, Michael Bush and David Bownes, C. S. L. Davies, G. R. Elton, Christopher Haigh, R. W. Hoyle, Eric Ives, Stanford E. Lehmberg, Diarmaid MacCulloch, Peter Marshall, Alec Ryrie, David Starkey, Tania String and Greg Walker. I thank Tania String for giving me a copy of a forthcoming article in draft. I am very grateful to my peer-reviewer, Eric Ives, for his thoughtful comments on the text. As always, the errors that remain are mine alone.

On a personal note, I would like to thank Tom Betteridge, my wonderful DPhil supervisor Robin Briggs, Lyndal Roper and the Balliol history workshop, and Susan Brigden, my undergraduate tutor, inspiration and friend – the person who first introduced me to the words 'you loke for ded men's showys'. I'd also like to thank John Cairns for taking a great author's photo and Miranda Powell for improving the book immeasurably with her

1536

thoughtful copy-editing. Thank you to the friends and family who have encouraged and supported me as I wrote this book. I am enormously grateful to Kate Kirkpatrick, my excellent editor, and to my mother, Marguerite Lipscomb, who's been my splendid and untiring first reader and critic, and the source of much encouragement. Thank you.

Illustrations

Bust portrait of Henry VIII c.1536–37, Hans Holbein (oil on oak panel, 28 x 20 cm). Thyssen-Bornemisza Collection, Madrid

Henry VIII by an unknown artist c.1520, panel 50.8 x 38.1 cm, National Portrait Gallery, London

Remigius van Leemput, *Copy after Holbein's Whitehall mural*, 1667 (oil on canvas, 88.9 x 98.7 cm), The Royal Collection, Hampton Court Palace

Hans Holbein, *Cartoon Showing Henry VIII and Henry VII*, 1537 (ink and wash on paper sheets mounted on canvas), 257.8 x 137.1 cm, National Portrait Gallery, London

The Walker – *Henry VIII*, artist unknown, painted between 1537 and 1562? (oil on six oak panels, 238.2 x 134.2 cm), The Board of Trustees of NMGM., The Walker, Liverpool, no.1033

Anne Boleyn (?), Hans Holbein, The Royal Collection

Jane Seymour, oil on oak 65.4 x 40.7 cm, Kunsthistorisches Museum, Vienna, Gemaeldegalerie

Portrait miniature of *Henry Fitzroy* by Lucas Horenbout, 1534–35, The Royal Collection

Archbishop Thomas Cranmer, 1546, Gerlach Flicke, National Portrait Gallery

Thomas Cromwell, 1533–34, after Hans Holbein the Younger, National Portrait Gallery

_1536_

Title page of the *Great Bible*, published 1539, 35.5 x 24 cm, Windsor Castle, The Royal Library

Preface

My publishers and I quibbled over the word 'changed' in the title. I had put forward the extraordinary litany of events that occurred in 1536, all with huge repercussions for Henry VIII, those around him and his kingdom in general, and marshalled the evidence of his behaviour after this point, noting how markedly it differed from the early years of his reign. But 'changed'? Was it not too dogmatic, too emphatic? I worried about the confines of a year, especially as the Tudors understood their years to start and end at different points to our 1 January – 31 December axis. I also worried about the apparent conceit of positing the seismic shifts of Henry VIII's thinking within this one (Gregorian) calendar year that occurred after his 'divorce' from Katherine of Aragon, his marriage to Anne Boleyn, the Acts of Supremacy and Succession and the deaths of Thomas More and Bishop John Fisher.

And yet, the more I researched, studied, and pondered the facts, the more convinced I've become that this year really *did* change Henry VIII. He did move from being the much fêted, glorious, and fun young monarch of the 1510s and 1520s, into the overweight, suspicious, ruthless tyrant who is commonly depicted as in popular culture. In some ways, of course, this was the result of a cumulative process, but the events of 1536 catalyzed, fostered and entrenched this change. Whether looking at Henry VIII's character, health, religion, image, reputation or legacy, it is possible to talk of 'before' and 'after' 1536.

This book really explores how Henry VIII became Henry VIII – and who Henry VIII really was. As such, it sets itself up to tackle what Eric Ives has called 'the ultimate unresolvable paradox of Tudor history: Henry VIII's psychology'.[1] There are evident difficulties with doing this. The available evidence gives us limited access to Henry VIII's thoughts, motivations and emotions – there are, for example, no helpful personal diaries or confessional letters that tell us his thoughts and feelings over, say, the period of Anne Boleyn's arrest and execution.[1]

A number of commentators have put Henry VIII on the psychiatrist's couch. Psychologist J. C. Flügel considered Henry VIII with reference to the Oedipus complex. In doing so, he suggested that Henry was driven by conflicting tendencies in his 'psychosexual life'; that is, the simultaneous desire for, and repulsion by, sexual rivals, incestuous liaisons and chastity in his wives. Miles F. Shore suggested Henry VIII's childhood separations from his parents, and alternating adulation and brutality, contributed to a mid-life 'crisis of generativity', extreme narcissism, grandiose fantasies, and transience in relationships. With these serious analyses by psychologists at one end of the scale, at the other is the pop psychology that has informed the production of the myriad films about Henry VIII. The scriptwriter of ITV's 2003 Henry VIII, Peter Morgan, described Henry as a 'neglected second son... there's a vulnerability to him... [he's] impulsive, powerful, not a complete oaf, a wounded character'. Ray Winstone, who played the title role, reflected, 'Once [Henry] got rid of his first wife, who was his brother's widow, he lost a bit of his soul. Once you do that, you can't get it back. And each [wife] became easier to get rid of. That's what I was trying to portray. A man who, at the beginning, was a young man in love, but had been left this legacy by his father: have a son. And that would consume him.' Henry VIII can appear to be, as Lacey Baldwin Smith described him, 'a baffling composite of shifting shadows'.[2]

My experience at Hampton Court Palace has shown me that

what visitors want to know about people in the past above all is 'how they felt'. Yet, it can be difficult enough knowing what one feels oneself, let alone understanding the feelings of another person at a 500-year remove. There are numerous ways to read Henry VIII's character, but it is important to be confined by the available evidence. This book attempts to recreate and understand the pressures on, and convictions of, Henry VIII, and it does so by analyzing contemporary reports of his behaviour and speech, material produced by Henry VIII himself including his letters, theological treatises, royal proclamations and other state papers, and the context of the culture and attitudes of the period. It does this cautiously, however, and refrains, I hope, from wild speculation or unreasonable conjecture. It is sometimes necessary to infer and extrapolate from available evidence, but my inference has been trammelled by existing evidence and reasoning. The picture one can form of Henry, the man and monarch, is one composed of fragments – be they his letters to the rebels of the Pilgrimage of Grace, the artwork he commissioned, the marginal annotations in his psalter or the gossip reported by the Imperial ambassador, Eustace Chapuys. From this we can make reasoned, intelligent guesses, but this must always be in line with what we actually know.

To readers familiar with Tudor history, much of what follows will be commonplace; as Lacey Baldwin Smith once wrote, 'most of the ideas have been knocking about the historical attic for years'. I do think, however, that there is a new perspective to be gained from the historical method of examining the events of a year in conjunction with each other. Connections can be made between, for instance, Anne Boleyn's alleged adultery and the art history narrative of Holbein's Henry, or between Reginald Pole's *De Unitate* and Thomas Cromwell's appointment as vicegerent in spirituals over all ecclesiastical affairs. Links can also be made between even apparently contradictory behaviour, like Henry's partying with Jane Seymour and the ladies of the court during Anne's imprisonment, and his later telling Chapuys that he felt himself growing old. Set in the context of the reign as a whole, the analysis of 1536 and its repercussions can shape a deeper understanding of this most fascinating and elusive of monarchs – an understanding that both humanizes him and looks unflinchingly at his flaws. The Henry VIII who emerges is one whose reactions to betrayal negatively determined the fates of many.[3]

Please note all dates have been modernized, as has spelling for the most part. As this book is intended for a general readership, references are fewer than in an equivalent academic work. Similarly, the calendared state papers are references, not the original manuscripts. Notes relating to cited source material can be found at the end of each paragraph, and their references in the 'Notes' section.

PART ONE
Setting the Scene

The past is a foreign country: they do things
differently there.

L. P. Hartley, *The Go-Between*[1]

Prologue

For those living in 1536, the world could be a frightening place. To make sense of it, there were certain principles, values and beliefs to which people held – many of which require a great stretch of the imagination for the twenty-first century observer to understand. Yet, without grasping them, it is impossible even to begin to enter into the mind of our protagonist, Henry VIII himself.

Above all, this was a world that believed in the existence of a divinely created order. The disruption of this order was widely expected to bring the terrifying prospect of chaos on a cosmic scale. As Shakespeare wrote in *Troilus and Cressida*:

> Take but degree away, untune that string,
> And hark, what discord follows.

This order needed to be reflected in society, by rank, status and hierarchy. Everyone had their place and station; all men were not created equal. This fact was displayed even in what people wore. Sumptuary laws governed the dress of each rank of society: no man under the degree of a lord could wear cloth of gold or silver, or sable (the brown fur of the arctic fox). Only Knights of the Garter and above could wear crimson or blue velvet. No person under a knight could wear gowns or doublets of velvet. Those who owned land yielding £20 a year might wear satin or damask in their doublets, while husbandry servants, shepherds and labourers were forbidden to wear cloth costing more than two shillings a yard. The penalty for the latter was three days in the stocks. The threat of such a punishment represented the belief that dissatisfaction with one's lot could engender disorder, injustice and anarchy. In practice, however, the social structure was accommodating enough to allow some superlative men, Thomas Wolsey and Thomas Cromwell included, to rise above the position of their birth. The corollary of hierarchy was the idea of patronage – that those of superior status would advance those of lower status who could be useful to them.[2]

At the top of the hierarchy was the king, who, it was believed, had been appointed by God. To be a king was therefore a high calling and a sacred duty. It was his role and responsibility to rule in a way that ensured peace, prosperity, stability and security in the realm. Kingship by divine right meant that, in theory, kings were answerable to God alone. They could not legitimately be removed from their position, nor was disobedience to them permissible. The role of the subject was to obey them as God. In practice, such absolute power was modified by the need to maintain the cooperation of the populace, but even that cooperation was wedded to the idea that the 'commonwealth' was produced by living in harmony in line with the divine ordering of society.[3]

For everyone in sixteenth-century society knew that there was a God in heaven and a devil in hell, and that every decision in their lives moved them closer to one or other of them. Everyone conceived of the world in religious terms, and religion was part of the natural warp and weave of everyday life. Everyone believed that one day they would face judgment and that the decisions they made on earth would determine their eternity. It has been suggested that it was not even conceptually possible to be an atheist in the sixteenth century. Some historians have suggested that the religion of the sixteenth century was so potent because it was an epoch dominated by fear, and religious belief offered a means of apparent control. This might be too reductionist, but either way, the depth and sincerity of religious conviction meant that decisions in Tudor times about what people today might see as the finer points of theology could have life and death consequences. How one conducted one's religious life was of the utmost importance.[4]

This prevalence of religious belief meant that crime was conceived of as evidence of sin and not the consequence of social circumstances. As such, painful and spectacular punishment was thought necessary both to deter others and to cleanse society from the disorder and pollution of the criminal's sin. The public – and often brutal – discipline of wrongdoers restored order through exemplary justice, and prevented God's wrath on society as a whole. It was therefore divinely sanctioned. The violence of the times was not restricted to the lower classes of society: 'polite society was almost as violent, almost as crowded and credulous, almost as brutal'.[5]

A final, obvious observation to make of sixteenth-century English society is that women were considered to be inferior to men, weaker in mind and body and more prone to sin. Medical theory held that women's bodies were imperfectly formed (inverted) males, and were cold and moist, to men's superior qualities of hot and dry. Women were also thought to be naturally more lustful than men, and therefore, the source and cause of sexual sin. Honour, for both men and women, was linked to ensuring women's chastity, before and within marriage. Such beliefs were to have major repercussions in the life of Henry VIII in 1536.[6]

CHAPTER 1

The Change

We are a bit like cocky adolescents when it comes to Henry VIII – we all think that we know him and all about him. We can define him in an instant. In a column in *The Observer* in 2007, Victoria Coren wrote, 'if you type "wife-killing" into Google, the first listing is a reference to Henry VIII, of wife-killing notoriety. Oh, that Henry VIII.' At around the same time as I read this, I overheard two men in Christ Church Cathedral, Oxford, commenting on a damaged tomb whose heads of female figurines had broken off or worn away. One said to the other, 'Henry VIII has a lot to answer for, hasn't he?' Market research by Historic Royal Palaces has shown that the popular perception of Henry VIII is that he was a fat guy who had six, or maybe eight, wives and killed a lot of them. The appearance of Henry in films over the years, whether played by Charles Laughton, Richard Burton, Keith Michell, Sid James, Ray Winstone, Jonathan Rhys-Meyers or Eric Bana, has given us our script – Henry VIII is seen as a misogynistic, ruthless, egotistical, fickle, predatory, infantile and sex-obsessed glutton. This is not to say that he wasn't some of these things, but they are certainly not all, or even chiefly, what Henry VIII was.[1]

Indeed, for more than twenty years after he came to the throne in 1509, his contemporaries used the words gifted, courageous, gentle, noble, brilliant and accomplished to describe him. Even after this point (in 1539), one courtier could describe Henry's nature as 'so benign and pleasant that I think till this day no man hath heard many angry words pass his mouth' (though this speaker knew Henry VIII would read his comments). Another could wax, in 1545, that to hear the king speak 'so sententiously, so kingly, or rather fatherly… was such a joy and marvellous comfort as I reckon this day one of the happiest of my life'. Henry VIII was evidently extremely charismatic. Thomas More had commented on the king's 'way of making every man feel that he is enjoying his special favour'. He was also surprisingly intelligent, devout, serious, moralistic and legalistic.[2]

Yet, Henry VIII was also prone to rage and cruelty – certainly in the later years of his reign. From being the glorious young prince of his accession, Henry changed to become a man who was markedly dour, irritable, mistrustful and repressively brutal towards his enemies. This was matched by his physical degeneration, from a handsome, athletic youth, into an obese old man, plagued by ill-health. Even before he died, people were starting to call him by the dreaded epithet 'tyrant'.

So, it seems that at some point Henry VIII changed. This is not a new idea. Many historians have recognized this character shift, but there has been less of a consensus on when Henry reached this important psychological turning point. Miles F. Shore, a professor of psychiatry at Harvard Medical School, suggests the years 1525–27. After this point, he noted, Henry had more than four wives, turned on his closest male friends and advisers, demonstrated 'distinct behavioural changes' and experienced at least one major episode of depression. The turning point was a 'crisis of generativity' – when the reality of middle age failed to live up to Henry's youthful narcissistic fantasies of omnipotence, resulting in 'abrupt decompression', disappointment and depression. Sir Arthur Salisbury MacNulty,

MD, studied Henry VIII's medical history, and he also concludes that the turning point came around 1527. He links this to a head injury sustained by Henry in 1524, resulting in severe headaches which worsened around 1527, and cautiously suggested that a cerebral injury could be linked to the alteration in Henry VIII's behaviour and character. 'From being a kindly and jovial monarch...' he writes, 'he gradually became an irritable, suspicious and selfish tyrant'. He was a 'double personality, a Jekyll and Hyde', with the Jekyll predominant in the first half of his reign, Hyde in the second. Historian Greg Walker concurs with this timing. He suggests that for the first eighteen years of his reign – that is, until 1527 – Henry did deliver on the promise he had earlier displayed.[3]

Others have positioned the change in Henry's personality a little bit later. Psychologist J. C. Flügel notes that Henry's character 'underwent a marked transformation' after the split with Rome, that is, around 1533, after which point Henry became 'vastly more despotic'. Historian Lacey Baldwin Smith does not explicitly assign a date, but explores Henry's behaviour from around 1542 by reflecting that geriatric studies suggest that during the final stages of life a man 'casts off a portion of the protective shield hammered out during childhood and adolescence and reveals the raw personality beneath'.[4]

Some, however, unable to identify a turning-point, conclude that Henry VIII's character was constant (that is, constantly unpleasant). J. J. Scarisbrick, in his important 1968 biography entitled *Henry VIII*, does not believe that there was ever a great change in Henry's character. He rejects suggestions that Henry had been brain-damaged either by the accident of 1524 or by a fall from his horse in January 1536 (a theory put forward by Frederick Chamberlin in 1932). He writes 'whether it [the 1536 fall] caused any brain damage is doubtful, not least because it is difficult to see the deterioration of character which, as has sometimes been argued, set in thereafter. Henry was not notably more cruel afterwards than he had been before'. Yet, the arguments set forward by this book will suggest otherwise. Even Alison Weir who, following J. J. Scarisbrick, says there is no evidence of a sudden change in Henry's character, later contrasts the Henry who had 'once been open-handed, liberal and idealistic', with the older king who was 'now contrary, secretive, dogmatic, and unpredictably changeable'.[5]

This book suggests that Henry VIII did undergo a change, and that although this was in part a cumulative process, it was greatly accelerated by the events of 1536. The damage that this year made to Henry's physical, and less tangibly, his psychological, health, appears to have started a chain-reaction, tapping into his propensity for high self-regard, and exaggerating it into a brutal, egotistical obduracy that had terrible consequences.

But he had not always been like this.

Chapter 2

Young Henry

Prince Henry, later Henry VIII, was born on 28 June 1491 at Greenwich Palace. He was one of seven children born to Henry VII and Elizabeth of York, although only four survived infancy. As the second son, he was not destined for the throne. That honour and responsibility fell to his elder brother, Arthur, Prince of Wales. Yet, the renowned Desiderius Erasmus later wrote glowingly of Henry in these years, stating that even 'when the King was no more than a child... he had a vivid and active mind, above measure to execute whatever tasks he undertook... you would say that he was a universal genius'.[1]

In May 1502, Arthur, who had recently married and taken on a position of responsibility in the Welsh Marches, died at the age of fifteen. As a result, the spotlight suddenly turned on the ten-year-old Henry, the next heir-apparent. Unlike Arthur, however, Henry was given no opportunity to practise ruling – the only surviving heir needed to be protected. His life remained the confined, secluded lifestyle of a lesser royal child, both indulged and frustratingly sheltered, and so when Henry came to the throne, he was unrehearsed in the art of sovereignty. The loss of his mother quickly followed that of his brother. In February 1503, Elizabeth of York died as a result of childbirth when Henry was eleven years old, and Henry's later correspondence shows he took her death badly. In June, Henry also effectively lost his sister Margaret, who moved to Edinburgh to marry James IV.[2]

In June 1503, a year after Arthur's death, Henry was betrothed to his brother's widow, the seventeen-year-old Katherine of Aragon. In receipt of a papal dispensation to overcome the obstacle of the couple's consanguinity (after Katherine's marriage to Arthur), Henry and Katherine were scheduled to marry when Henry attained his fifteenth birthday. A condition of the marriage was that Katherine's father, Ferdinand of Spain, should provide in advance 100,000 crowns in plate, jewels and coin as a marriage portion. Yet by 1505, this had not been received, and so the date for the wedding came and went; the solemnization of the marriage appeared to be indefinitely postponed. Henry VII began to toy with making another alliance for his son with Eleanor of Austria, Katherine of Aragon's niece. In fact, the negotiations for a marriage between Henry and Eleanor were only stopped by Henry VII's death on 21 April 1509 (later Eleanor would marry Henry's rival, Francis I of France).[3]

So, on 22 April 1509, aged seventeen, Henry was proclaimed King Henry VIII. His coronation was greeted with rapture. William Blount, Lord Mountjoy wrote to Erasmus on 27 May:

> When you know what a hero [the king] now shows himself, how wisely he behaves, what a lover he is of justice and goodness, what affection he bears to the learned, I will venture that you will need no wings to make you fly to behold this new and auspicious star. If you could see how all the world here is rejoicing in the possession of so great a prince, how his life is all their desire, you could not contain your tears of joy. The

heavens laugh, the earth exults, all things are full of milk,
of honey, of nectar. Avarice is expelled from the country.
Liberality scatters wealth with bounteous hand. Our King
does not desire gold or gems or precious metals, but
virtue, glory and immortality.

One of his first acts as king was to marry Katherine on 11 June in
the Franciscan church at Greenwich Palace. While it is possible
that in doing so Henry was fulfilling his father's deathbed
wish, it seems likely to have been a match primarily based on
affection. The sources state that Henry wrote to his father-in-
law in 1513 saying 'the love he bears Katherine is such, that if
he were still free he would choose her in preference to all others'.
Other men may have commented that Katherine was 'rather
ugly than otherwise' and 'not handsome, though she had a very
beautiful complexion', but Henry chose her. The couple were
jointly crowned in Westminster Abbey on Midsummer's Day, 24
June 1509, four days before Henry's eighteenth birthday.[4]

It is clear that in these early years, and indeed, for the first
twenty years of his reign, Henry was truly quite brilliant, having
been blessed by nature with all the attributes and qualities he
might desire. The chronicler Edward Hall said as much:

The features of his body, his goodly personage, his
amiable visage, princely countenance, with the noble
qualities of his royal estate, to every man known, needs
no rehearsal, considering that, for lack of cunning, I
cannot express the gifts of grace and of nature that God
has endowed him with all.

Reports from foreign observers at his court run into hyperbole.
In 1515, Henry VIII was described as 'not only very expert in
arms and of great valour, and most excellent in his personal
endowments, but... likewise so gifted and adorned with mental
accomplishments of every sort that we believe him to have few

equals in the world'. Two years later, Francesco Chieregato wrote that Henry was a 'most invincible King, whose acquirements and qualities are so many and excellent that I consider him to excel all who ever wore a crown'. And in his final report on four years spent at Henry's court between 1515 and 1519, the Venetian ambassador Sebastian Giustinian concluded that Henry was 'much handsomer than any other Sovereign in Christendom… [and] the best dressed sovereign in the world'.[5]

The grounds for all this praise were that besides being exceedingly good-looking, Henry VIII appeared to be accomplished in every way. He was a talented linguist – he spoke French, Spanish and Latin, the latter to the point of being able to reply spontaneously to an oration in elegant Latin. He loved music and was a skilled musician and composer: when an embassy from France arrived in 1517, Henry entertained the visitors himself by 'singing and playing on every musical instrument' quite excellently. He danced beautifully, surpassed all the archers of his guard with his bowmanship ('as', adds this commentator, 'he surpasses them in stature and personal graces'), and was 'a capital horseman and a fine jouster'.[6]

From contemporary sources we can build up a composite picture of Henry's character. He was full of spirit, vigour and energy, 'young, lusty and courageous… [and] disposed to all mirth and pleasure'. As a man in his teens, twenties and thirties, he pursued pleasure – he loved entertainments, masques, banquets, hunting, dancing and other diversions. For example, on May Day 1515, the king and all his guard gathered in a wood near Greenwich to play at being Robin Hood and his merry men. Dressed all in green, with bows in their hands, and attended by 100 noblemen on horseback 'gorgeously arrayed', Henry and his court enjoyed an open-air banquet. Singers and musicians played from bowers, which had been purposely filled with sweetly-singing birds. Afterwards, they processed back to Greenwich, where a joust was held in very great pomp. Ambassadors often noted, perhaps with some frustration, that the king was off 'taking his pleasure', which normally meant hunting, a sport at which Henry would ride out all day, tiring eight or ten horses before retiring. Such exuberance was also displayed at the tiltyard. He was often reported as outshining all his noblemen at the joust. It was impossible for this athletic, ebullient and extrovert young man not occasionally to be something of a show-off. In 1517, at a great joust in honour of the French ambassadors, the king wanted to joust against all fourteen competitors, 'but this was forbidden by the Council, which moreover decreed that each jouster was to run six courses and no more, so that the entertainment might be ended on that day'. Nonetheless, when he 'presented himself before the Queens and the ladies', he made 'a thousand jumps in the air', and after tiring out his horse, mounted one of those ridden by his pages, a pattern he repeated constantly over the course of the day until the end of the joust.[7]

The greatest example of such athletic extravagance, albeit with a serious diplomatic purpose, was Henry VIII's meeting with the French king, Francis I, at the Field of the Cloth of Gold from 7 to 20 June 1520. This extraordinary summit between the two kings and their entire courts was a magnificent festival of feasting, jousting, dancing and entertainment held on the border between the two countries, in between the English village of Guines (in English Calais) and the French village of Ardres. For the occasion, a town was temporarily constructed, including a temporary palace of stone and timber, and a multitude of tents and pavilions made from cloth of gold (hence the name). The English retinue alone was 5,172 persons. For the 48-day trip, the quantities of food and drink consumed are astonishing – with a total cost of £8,839 2s 4d, the list included 2,014 mutton, 51 pigs, 82 pheasants, 9,100 plaice, 7,836 whiting, 30,700 eggs and 114,000 litres of wine, enough to fuel wine fountains that flowed freely for hours at a time.[8]

Such flamboyance and excess on special occasions was matched daily by the extraordinary sumptuousness with which

Henry surrounded himself. One example is the constant finery of his clothing. There was great extravagance and not a little vanity in Henry's glorious displays of magnificence, wearing one day royal robes of gold brocade lined with ermine, another a doublet of crimson and white satin with slashed scarlet hose and a mantle of purple velvet. He adorned himself in jewels: on one occasion, he was described as wearing a gold collar, from which hung a round cut diamond 'the size of the largest walnut I ever saw', and suspended from this, a very large round pearl, while his fingers were 'one mass of jewelled rings'. His attachment to luxurious clothing would remain with him throughout his life. He carried off such opulence because of his considerable stage-presence and charisma. He received one ambassador while standing under his canopy of cloth of gold, and leaning against his gilt throne, almost as if the moment were posed simply so that the ambassador could marvel at his magnificence. His famous exchange with a Venetian ambassador, in which he asked after the height and figure of the king of France before boasting that he also had a good calf to his leg, suggests his own beauty led him to at least a little conceit. But such vainglory was compensated for by the young Henry's warm and benevolent nature. Erasmus described him in 1529 as 'a man of gentle friendliness, and gentle in debate; he acts more like a companion than a king'. Henry seems to have been light-hearted, merry and easily given to laughter. He could be upbeat, kindly and encouraging – a diarist records how, after rain had soaked the English troops near Calais in July 1513, the king rode round at three o'clock in the morning comforting the watch – saying, 'Well, comrades, now that we have suffered in the beginning, fortune promises us better things, God willing.' He was described in 1519 as 'affable and gracious; [a man who] harmed no one…'; he was exceedingly generous in gifts and very affectionate – when Giustinian left his court after four years, Henry told him that 'he had ever loved him as a father'.[9]

Although Henry assured his father-in-law that his love of

jousting and hunting did not mean he neglected affairs of state, others demurred. It was said that while the king was away seeking amusement, 'he did not choose to be troubled by anybody or to be saddled with any business' and that he wanted only 'to follow his desire and appetite, nothing minded to travail in the busy affairs of this realm'. Instead, until 1529, he delegated much power and responsibility for state affairs to Thomas Wolsey, who, from 1515, had been a cardinal and the king's chief minister. Some therefore concluded the cardinal 'governs everything alone'. Yet, while Wolsey was incredibly powerful, Henry VIII, if uninterested in the administrative detail of running the country, had strong views on many matters of state policy. Chiefly, in the first half of his reign, besides being preoccupied with fun and diversion, he was interested in foreign affairs, and above all, martial glory. The example of the great monarchs he had known of as a boy – Richard the Lionheart, Edward I, and especially, Henry V, and his early contemporaries, his father-in-law, Ferdinand of Aragon, Louis XII of France and Maximilian of Hapsburg – urged him to earn a reputation on the field of battle. He wanted to be a warrior and a hero, a knight of old, according to the ideals of chivalry and valour that his culture exalted. In this, he contrasted with the peaceful ambitions of his father: Henry VIII wanted a new age of virile, energetic, ambitious conquest. He launched a war against France in 1512, fighting at sea and in 1513, laying siege to the towns of Thérouanne and Tournai (a battle later dubbed the Battle of the Spurs, and commemorated in the 1540s with a glorious painting of the occasion). These battles won him glory, but little of lasting value. Although peace with France was negotiated in 1514 (a peace celebrated at the Field of the Cloth of Gold), Henry was at war with France once again between 1522 and 1525. His armies also fought against the Scots, most notably in the massacre at Flodden Field in 1513.[10]

Yet, despite all this evidence of pleasure-seeking, martial ambition and youthful zest, it would be wrong to conclude that this exuberant and boisterous young king was always happy-go-lucky. He could at times, even in his early years, be wilful, stubborn and obstinate. Wolsey wrote of Henry that 'rather than... miss or want any part of his will or appetite, [the king] will put the loss of one half of his realm in danger', and warned a potential member of the privy council to 'be well advised and assured what matter ye put in his head; for ye shall never pull it out again'. He testified to having spent hours on knees pleading with Henry to dissuade him from one or other course of action, to no avail. Ironically in light of later events, one issue on which Henry was dogmatic in this period was orthodox Roman Catholic religion. In 1521, in response to Martin Luther's *De Captivitate Babylonica*, Henry VIII, undoubtedly with some help, wrote a polemical book called *Assertio Septum Sacramentorum* (*In Defence of the Seven Sacraments*) defending papal authority and condemning Luther. This book, which sold remarkably well, earned him the title *Defensor Fidei* or Defender of the Faith.[11]

Perhaps Henry's tendency towards obstinacy was partly a result of his ideas about how a king should be. Despite relying on his ministers, Henry seems to have believed that he should rule as well as reign. He once told Giustinian that 'things uncertain ought not to escape the lips of a king', and later was reported as saying that 'if I thought my cap knew my counsel, I would cast it into the fire and burn it' – indications that he believed he should be firm, decisive and self-reliant. While it was not a common occurrence during his youth, he also was at times reported to 'wax wrath', suggesting that the obduracy and temper of his elder years were latent, though not catalyzed nor fully developed at this stage. Another quality that would be exaggerated with his passing years was his pronounced sense of his own importance, even in the context of far greater European powers. In 1516, he bragged to Giustinian that 'I have now more money and greater force and authority than I myself or my ancestors ever had; so that what I will [wish] of other princes, I can obtain'. Interestingly, what does not seem to be apparent in these years is the 'strong streak of cruelty' that at least one historian has suggested as a constant quality to Henry VIII: such cruelty was only really exhibited from around the mid-1530s, especially in and after 1536.[12]

CHAPTER 3

The Divorce

Despite his earlier love for her, from around 1527, Henry VIII sought to separate from Katherine of Aragon after nearly twenty years of marriage. This was in large part because, although Katherine had been pregnant six times, the couple had suffered a series of heartbreaking miscarriages, stillbirths and cot deaths, and only one daughter, Princess Mary, had survived. Although Henry had an illegitimate son by his former mistress, Elizabeth Blount, in 1519, he had good reason to want a legitimate heir. Henry – and most people at the time – believed that one of his principal responsibilities as king was to produce an adult male heir, that is, a boy of at least fifteen years old, who could succeed peacefully when Henry died, to secure the dynasty. It was feared that if one of his daughters became queen then their marriage to another king or prince would mean England would be ruled, or dominated, by a foreign power. Children could not rule as monarchs themselves; their powers were given to individual regents or groups of councillors, and disputes over a regency could be very bloody, endangering the security, peace and prosperity of a country. The Tudor dynasty was still very new and far from securely rooted, having been established by Henry VII's victory at the Battle of Bosworth in 1485. Henry VIII – and the country – wanted a secure line of princes to ensure that the turmoil of a contested throne did not occur again. He worried that if he didn't have one or more legitimate sons by his early thirties, then he might easily die in his fifties without an adult male heir (he had good reason to worry – his grandfathers had died at twenty-six and forty-one; his own father at fifty-two). And even one son was no guarantee of a smooth succession, as the death of Henry's elder brother, had shown.[1]

This very real anxiety about the lack of a male heir suggests that Henry was genuine in his conviction that his lack of a surviving legitimate male heir meant that he was, in some way, being punished by God, and that the Pope should never have given him the dispensation that allowed him to marry his brother's widow. This realization coincided with the discovery of the witty, captivating Anne Boleyn. Although not particularly beautiful, Anne had unusual dark hair, fine eyes, a certain grace and seemed sophisticated because of her time at the French court. Before long, Henry 'began to kindle the brand of amours, which was not known to any person'.[2]

Henry probably first noticed Anne around Easter 1526, and he began seeking a divorce in 1527. It is important to note that Henry wanted to marry Anne, and would not accept any alternative. The traditional explanation for why Henry was determined to marry her, rather than take her as his mistress, is that Anne refused to consummate their relationship before marriage. The evidence of their letters suggests that there was some level of sexual play between the couple, but it is very likely that they did wait six or seven years before having intercourse. In an age before any reliable contraception, the fact that Anne did not give birth until September 1533 suggests that they had simply abstained for many years. Yet the decision to marry Anne was prompted by more than Anne withholding sex (the abstinence may even have been mutual). Henry, throughout his life, liked things to conform to the letter of the law. He wanted the world to be recast as he saw it. In this, he wanted it to be declared that it had never been right for him to marry Katherine of Aragon, and that it was therefore right for him to marry Anne Boleyn. He wanted, above all, legitimacy and exoneration. According to his own testimony, he did not wish to take another wife 'for any carnal concupiscence, nor for any displeasure or mislike of the Queen's person or age', but because of a 'certain scrupulosity that pricked my conscience'.[3]

Henry staked his challenge to the validity of his marriage to Katherine on two arguments:

* That the union of a man and the wife of his brother was contrary to the law of God, according to Leviticus 18:16 and 20:21, and that no papal dispensation was sufficient to permit it.

* That the specific dispensation granted by Pope Julius II was invalid because of certain technical irregularities, especially where the deliberate insertion of the word *forsan* (perhaps) made it unclear whether or not the marriage between Katherine and Arthur had been consummated.

There were a few minor problems – such as the fact Henry and Katherine weren't actually childless, just had not had a surviving male child, and above all, that Deuteronomy 25:5 stated the polar opposite of Leviticus: that if a man died without children, 'the wife of the dead shall not marry without unto a stranger: her husband's brother shall go in unto her, and take her to him to wife, and perform the duty of an husband's brother unto her.' The real crux of the matter rested on whether or not Katherine had been a virgin, as she claimed, when she remarried, a fact impossible to verify either way. So Henry gathered a team of theological experts, led by Thomas Cranmer, to study the scriptures for him, bolster his position and garner the support of the universities of Europe. Nevertheless, the theological ambiguities of his case meant it could never be watertight, and anyway, Pope Clement VII was not a free agent. The response he could give depended a lot on his relationship with Charles V, the Holy Roman Emperor, Katherine's nephew.[4]

Henry needed an alternative strategy, and that strategy could be found in the increasing warmth Henry felt towards the ideas of royal supremacy and divine-right kingship. Historian J. J. Scarisbrick was so convinced that Henry's growing commitment to the principle of the royal supremacy paralleled the divorce crisis that he asserted: 'if there had been no divorce Henry might yet have taken issue with the Church'. The English crown had always subscribed to the notion of the divine right of kings to rule, as their motto since 1413, *Dieu et mon droit,* emphasized. Henry's assumption of the title of Supreme Head of the Church of England took this a stage further. Henry grew convinced of his unique position as God's anointed deputy on earth, believing that the Supreme Headship was his birthright, and expecting others to believe it too. Even before the 1530s, Henry showed signs of believing in his position directly under God: in November 1515 at Baynard's Castle, he declared that 'by the ordinance and sufferance of God we are king of England, and the kings of England in time past have never had any superior but God alone'. Then, at some point after 1528, Anne Boleyn had given him a copy of William Tyndale's *The Obedience of a Christian Man,* an evangelical work which asserted that it was shameful for princes to submit to the power of the church and an inversion of divine order. Tyndale stressed it was the king, and not the pope, who was ordained by God to have no superior on earth, and kings must be obeyed, for they give account to God alone. Henry said it was 'the book for me and all kings to read'. It is vital to realize that for Henry, the royal supremacy, and his direct position under God became a firm conviction, and like all his firm convictions, it was not easily moved.[5]

The scholars examining the case for divorce reached the conclusion that England was an empire, which, in the language of the time, meant that English kings had always enjoyed spiritual supremacy in their dominions and possessed a sacral kingship. The first indication of Henry's belief in his rightful role as Supreme Head in his own country came in August 1530 when Henry asserted that no English man could be summoned out of his homeland to a foreign jurisdiction (in other words, to a divorce court in Rome). It was also in 1530 at Hampton Court that Henry, having summoned a council to discuss his divorce, decided to inform the Pope that he had no jurisdiction in the case, though it took another three or four years for the royal supremacy to be completed. The logical result of this came in April 1533 when parliament passed the Act of Restraint in Appeals forbidding appeals to Rome, which stated that 'this realm of England is an empire, and so hath been accepted in the world, governed by one supreme head and king'. In May 1533, convocation of the English clergy and Thomas Cranmer, newly appointed archbishop of Canterbury, declared Henry's union with Katherine of Aragon null. But Henry had in fact already married Anne Boleyn – twice – officially in January 1533 and secretly before that, in November 1532. On 11 July 1533, the Pope condemned Henry's separation from Katherine and gave him until September to take her back under threat of excommunication. Henry ignored this, and in September, Anne gave birth to a healthy girl, whom they named Elizabeth, after their mothers.

Meanwhile, progress towards the royal supremacy continued. In early 1534, an act of parliament halted all payments to Rome and granted the king permission to appoint bishops, and most importantly of all, the 1534 Act of Supremacy finally declared that Henry was and *had always been* the Supreme Head of the Church of England. The Anglican Church had been created. A public persuasion campaign was mounted through the pulpit and printing press, and from June 1535, bishops were ordered to preach on the royal supremacy each Sunday.[6]

But this was not enough to satisfy Henry. The whole nation

was required to be complicit in the king's decision. The Act of Succession, also passed in 1534, stated the lawfulness of Henry's marriage to Anne Boleyn and that their children would be true heirs to the throne and all English subjects were required to swear an oath agreeing this. The oath read: 'to be true to Queen Anne, and to believe and take her for the lawful wife of the King and rightful Queen of England, and utterly to think the Lady Mary daughter to the King by Queen Katherine, but as a bastard, and thus to do without any scrupulosity of conscience'. Among the laity and episcopacy, only Sir Thomas More and John Fisher, bishop of Rochester, refused to swear. Henry's overarching commitment to the principle of royal supremacy must explain the vehemence of his response: both were sent to the Tower of London and Henry deliberately passed the Act of Treason, which came into effect in early 1535 and promised death for anyone 'maliciously denying the royal supremacy'. As a result of this act, in June 1535 Fisher and More were both beheaded. Their execution, particularly Fisher's (as a bishop), shocked the world. The separation from Rome was complete.[7]

For Henry, there was a significant degree of 'religion' in his decision to break with Rome. It was manifested in the way he saw his relationship with Katherine, as one punished by God for living outside the law. It was also apparent in his dedication to the notion of the royal supremacy and to his divine-right kingship, under God, which committed him to the righting of religious abuses in the church, and the 'cure' of his people. With Anne Boleyn at his side, Henry had been exposed to evangelical thought, especially that which gave primacy to princes over prelates, and had, perhaps inadvertently, opened the door to the reformed ideas of continental Europe. For Anne Boleyn deserves a little more mention in this story. As we have seen with her apparent refusal to sleep with the king, by her gift to Henry of important evangelical works such as Tyndale's *The Obedience of a Christian Man*, and not least by her charm and attractiveness, Anne Boleyn's influence on the king was great. Influence on the king meant influence in the country. Anne used her position to become an ardent patron of the evangelical cause. She was a major importer of evangelical books and she had 'the perfect opportunity to promote evangelical activists after an extraordinary crop of deaths of distinguished elderly bishops who might have proved awkward obstacles for the evangelical cause.' Between 1532 and 1536, nine bishops died, eight of which were apparently due to natural causes (Fisher, as we have noted, was beheaded); and there were also two resignations. Many of their replacements were Anne's evangelical clients. Her power was such that the imperial ambassador, Eustace Chapuys, declared her displacement by Jane Seymour would be 'a remedy for the heretical doctrines and practices of the concubine – the principal cause of the spread of Lutheranism in this country'.[8]

Yet, on the eve of 1536, Anne Boleyn's star was in the ascendant, and Henry VIII enjoyed a powerful position, full of hope for the future. He had been on the throne twenty-seven years, and for much of that time, he had been highly and fulsomely praised. His wife, who had two and a half years before given birth to a healthy little girl, was three months pregnant, and Henry had strong hopes that this time, Anne would bear him a son and heir. Six months earlier, Henry had eradicated opposition to his new position of Supreme Head of the Church of England, by silencing permanently those who refused to acquiesce, such as John Fisher and Sir Thomas More. His illegitimate son, Henry Fitzroy, Duke of Richmond and Somerset, was a strong lad of seventeen in whom Henry took much joy. The only fly in the ointment was that his ex-wife, Katherine of Aragon, the Princess Dowager, lingered at Kimbolton Castle in Cambridgeshire. As a result of her degraded position, her nephew, Charles V, emperor of the Holy Roman Empire, was a constant, if latent, threat to the security of England. Yet, in 1536, Henry VIII would have had good reason to hope that all things would finally be well. In actual fact the opposite was true; this year would, in many ways, be his undoing.

CHAPTER 4

1536 and All That

*H*istorians have noted that that 1536 was a particularly awful year for Henry. Derek Wilson calls it Henry's *'annus horribilis'*, R. W. Hoyle refers to it as 'the year of three queens', and Sir Arthur Salisbury MacNulty concludes that, in reaching forty-five, 'it is justifiable to regard the year 1536 as marking the approach of Henry's old age'. Few, though, have connected this turbulent and important year with Henry VIII's changing character. Only Derek Wilson has noted that 'most of the reign's acts of sanguinary statecraft' occurred after this point, and that 'it was in 1536 that bloodletting of those close to the Crown became frequent'.[1]

A brief chronological overview, however, of the many tumultuous events in the life of Henry VIII in 1536 begins to suggest the significance of this one year.

The year began, from Henry's perspective, well. On 7 January, Katherine of Aragon, Henry's estranged (and denied) first wife, died. Yet, only a couple of weeks later, a series of less propitious acts occurred. Henry fell from his horse while jousting. He was unconscious for two hours and observers feared the worst.

Despite the official pronouncements of his rude health, the fall appears to have burst open an old injury which would never properly heal and meant that this great athlete of the tiltyard would never joust again.

Anne Boleyn attributed her shock at the king's fall to the next major event of 1536. She miscarried on the day of Katherine of Aragon's funeral – and it had been a boy. This was a huge disappointment to the king, and threatened the stability of the realm at a time when English security was already in jeopardy. In early 1536, an edict issued by the Pope that would have deprived Henry of his right to rule was circulating in Europe, and only needed to be formally published for the invasion and overthrow of Henry's throne to become legitimate.

In March 1536, parliament passed an act that was to have enormous repercussions – the Act for the Dissolution of the Smaller Monasteries. At the same time, Henry received a book, written by Reginald Pole, his own cousin, which viciously attacked Henry's role as the Supreme Head of the Church of England.

The most shocking incident of the spring was, however, the 'discovery' of Anne Boleyn's apparent adultery with a number of men of the King's Privy Chamber, and her arrest, trial and, finally, execution on 19 May. The king lost no time in remarrying: on the day of Anne's death, Archbishop Cranmer issued a dispensation for Henry to marry Jane Seymour; the couple were engaged the following day and married ten days later, on 30 May. Perhaps to mark their union, around this time, Hans Holbein the younger painted portraits of the pair. The one of Henry, known as the Thyssen portrait, is a stunning departure from previous portraits of the king; the power and magnificence exuded by Henry in the image is striking, starkly contrasting with the reality of the fact that Henry turned forty-five on 28 June 1536 – an age reckoned by the standards of the sixteenth century to represent old age.

At the time of Anne's death, parliament passed the Second Succession Act, which declared Henry's marriage to Anne invalid and their daughter Elizabeth illegitimate, and removed her from the line of succession – leaving Henry with no direct legitimate heir to the throne. This was buttressed by Henry's insistence that Mary, after two years of resistance, should now sign an oath declaring her father's royal supremacy and her own illegitimacy. In addition, the king's niece, now second in line to the throne, chose this moment to marry without the king's consent – a deed which now amounted to treason because it lined up her husband to be the future king. She was imprisoned with extraordinary timing, as just at that moment the king's illegitimate but much-beloved son, Henry Fitzroy, died at the age of seventeen. Henry no longer even had the option of legitimizing his bastard.

In July 1536, Henry responded to all these challenges by making his first minister, Thomas Cromwell, vicegerent over all ecclesiastical affairs, and issued the Church of England's first doctrinal statement – a clear indication that as far as Henry was concerned, his royal supremacy did not merely make him a figurehead. The king also issued two important proclamations dealing with religious issues – one designed to stop extremist preachers, another to cut the number of holy days that would be celebrated in the country. As the new vicegerent, in August 1536, Cromwell issued a set of royal injunctions or orders to enforce this new doctrine, and presided over the beginning of the dissolution of the monasteries.

In October, these new religious commands, and especially the suppression of the monasteries, led to a large uprising against the king in Lincolnshire, which was quickly followed by a massive armed rebellion, starting in Yorkshire, which became known as the Pilgrimage of Grace. This was the largest peacetime rebellion ever raised against an English monarch – and what is worse, Henry did not have sufficient troops to meet the rebels in the field if it came to battle. It was the single greatest crisis of his reign. An indication that the watching world expected Henry's downfall is suggested by the fact that the Pope, at this juncture, made Reginald Pole a cardinal for his opposition to Henry's rule. Incredibly, the rebels were persuaded to stand down, and the year ended with Henry curiously inviting the rebels' leader, Robert Aske, to court. It was truly an *annus horribilis*.

It was a year of threats – both external and internal – of things going horribly wrong, of betrayal, rebellion, grief, age, and ill health. But it was also a year of reaction – of Henry asserting his power through his supremacy, his image, his rapid remarriage and the festivities, through his bluster to the rebels. The impact of the year can be seen immediately in the course of 1537 when Henry cracked down on those who had rebelled against him, oversaw further dissolution of the monasteries and commissioned from Holbein the Whitehall mural, an important projection of his masculinity and power. This was truly a year that defined, changed and created the character we think of as Henry VIII.

PART TWO
The Crisis of Masculinity

Oh my heart and O my heart,
My heart it is so sore,
Since I must needs
From my love depart
And know no cause wherefore.

Henry VIII[1]

*I*n 1536, a series of events cut right to the core of how Henry VIII saw himself as a man. This might seem something of a grand assertion, given that many of the sources most coveted by historians – those that reveal the deep, inner-workings of a man's mind – are simply not available for this enigmatic king. Yet, we can gain insight from the way Henry VIII acted, from the cultural worldview of his time, and from remarks those around him reported him as making. With all these in mind, it requires only a little careful psychological inference to reconstruct and analyse the impact of the events of 1536.

The events that most require our attention occurred over the course of a harrowing six months, between January and July 1536. The cumulative impact of these traumas is made all the more striking if one realizes, as what follows will suggest, that Henry only allowed Anne Boleyn's execution because he truly believed Anne was guilty of adultery and had horribly betrayed him. It is small wonder that this succession of events challenged his very manhood and changed him from a virile man in his prime, to a man who suddenly perceived he was 'growing old', and tried to fight this in ways that made him 'a caricature of virility'.[2]

CHAPTER 5

A Wife's Death

*H*enry VIII's response to the first major event of 1536 betrays little sign that he yet sensed this approaching weakness, even if, in practice, this first pivotal event shaped the way he responded to everything that followed. At 2 p.m. on 7 January 1536, Katherine of Aragon died. Hers had been a relatively short illness, which modern commentators have deduced to be stomach cancer. She had been in very great pain over the course of five weeks, having first been reported sick in early December 1535. It was thought serious enough to call the Spanish ambassador, Eustace Chapuys, to her side in mid-December. By late December, her apothecary, Philip Grenacre, wrote that she couldn't eat or drink anything without being sick, couldn't sleep for more than an hour and a half because of the pain in her stomach, and had lost all her strength. Chapuys was shocked to discover at the turn of the year that Katherine 'was so wasted that she could not support herself either on her feet or sitting in bed', but she obviously had a remission before she died, because after four days at her bedside, Chapuys was convinced enough that she was out of danger to leave her in the evening of Tuesday 4

January 1536, in 'good hope of her health', and was desolate at news of her death three days later.[1]

For Katherine, life had been thoroughly unpleasant for many years – Diarmaid MacCulloch calls them 'years of dignified misery'. This had been particularly apparent since August 1531, when Henry had sent Katherine away from court to live at The More, close to St Albans, and the princess Mary to Richmond. This was the last time Katherine saw her daughter: Henry even refused to let Mary see her mother in her dying days. By the time of her death, Katherine had not left her chamber at her new house of Kimbalton Castle for two years, and her supporters regarded the men that Henry had placed in her household – all except her confessor, apothecary and physician – as 'guards and spies, not servants'. She had always stayed true to Henry. In June 1533, Katherine had movingly written of her feelings for him, citing 'the great love that hath been betwixt him and me ere this... the which love in me is as faithful and true to him... as ever it was'.[2]

Henry's feelings for her were quite different. Before Chapuys rode to be at Katherine's deathbed, Henry had called him for a meeting. There he told Chapuys that he believed Katherine would not live long, and when they spoke a little later, that she was *in extremis* and he would hardly find her alive. After each of these comments, Henry immediately directed Chapuys' attention to foreign affairs. He emphasized the strained relationship between Charles V, the Holy Roman Emperor, and England, reiterating his hope that Katherine's death would remove all the difficulties between them, so that 'if she died you would have no cause to trouble yourself about the affairs of this kingdom'. This apparent callousness on Henry's behalf, to which Chapuys responded in terse, shocked staccato that her death could do no good, did have some basis in legitimate fears about the safety of the kingdom. At this time, a papal bull[3] had been prepared which would allow Henry's kingdom to be given to anyone who could take it, and English subjects to be absolved from their duty of allegiance to the king. Although the bull was not actually published until 1538, in late 1535 and early 1536 its publication – and the legitimated treason and chaos it would unleash – appeared to rest upon a knife-edge. Simultaneously, Francis I of France was being asked if he were willing to make war on England. It is in light of this substantial threat being made upon his kingdom because of Henry's divorce from Katherine and union with Anne Boleyn that we should interpret Henry's immediate reaction to hearing of Katherine's death on Saturday 8 January. He exclaimed 'God be praised that we are free from all suspicion of war'![4]

Yet, even this defence does not make the rest of the king's conduct more palatable. He and Anne showed great joy, and appear to have celebrated the occasion. Anne gave a 'handsome present' to the messenger who brought her news of Katherine's death. Henry, dressed 'all over in yellow, from top to toe, except the white feather he had on his bonnet', went to Mass accompanied by trumpets. Afterwards, he danced with the ladies, where, having sent for Elizabeth, who was almost two and a half (Chapuys calls her 'his Little Bastard'), Henry showed her off, parading her from one lady to the next, 'like one transported with joy'. He also organized an informal joust at Greenwich in which he participated, the significance of which will become apparent later. It is perhaps wise to be a little cautious about Chapuys' report – coming as it did from a partial observer who was very much on Katherine's side. The chronicler Edward Hall reports that it was Anne who was dressed in yellow, and another report suggests Henry was dressed in purple silk with a white plume. These seemingly garish colours, which are normally represented as an exhibition of unbecoming glee, may have had a different symbolism to the wearers. Hall specifically notes that Anne 'wore yellow for the mourning' – it was the colour of royal mourning in Spain at that time, and purple has traditionally been the colour of royalty (although Henry's other actions make clear it would have been his own royalty, rather than Katherine's, except as Princess Dowager, that he was marking), and had traditional associations with public mourning.[5]

Nevertheless, Henry and Anne were very obviously exceedingly happy, in a way that some considered unseemly. Apart from Henry's anxieties about foreign affairs, his other concerns, as David Starkey has noted, were to use the style of Katherine's funeral to indicate his continuing belief that she had never been his wife nor a queen, and to acquire her belongings. Ralph Sadler, Cromwell's clerk, wrote to Cromwell that he had questioned Henry's decision not to have a hearse at St Paul's, as had been the custom at the death of Henry's sister, Mary, in 1533. Henry had replied that 'she was a Queen' (Mary was the dowager queen of France, as well as duchess of Suffolk) and that for Katherine it would not be 'either requisite or needful', though he intended she would be buried at Peterborough with great solemnization. His approach to Katherine's possessions is darker. If Katherine had not been queen, then she died a widow, and a 'woman sole' with the right to dispose of her goods as she wished (they would not automatically go to Henry). Yet, on 19 January, Richard Rich, the solicitor-general, the man whose word had sent Thomas More to his death, wrote to Henry about this tricky legal situation suggesting that Henry 'might seize her goods by another means', without admitting her to be his wife.[6]

Henry's behaviour – his almost unmitigated joy and capacity for self-deception – suggests the youthful ebullience, confidence and conviction he felt at the turn of 1536. One might have thought that the death of his first wife, the wife of his youth, would have had a greater effect on him. He was, however, so thoroughly persuaded of the legitimacy of his position as Supreme Head of the Church of England – of his marriage to Anne Boleyn who was expecting his son and heir – that it doesn't seem to be until later that his experience of Katherine's death had a consequential effect on his sense of his own mortality. Henry was not to know at this stage that Katherine's was the first, and least emotionally draining, of the three deaths of those close to him in this year. Rather his reaction to this event paints a picture of Henry's mental state before the cataclysmic events of 1536 had really begun to unfold. When they did, it was precisely his buoyant, youthful exuberance that came under attack.

CHAPTER 6

The King's Honour

$\mathcal{O}$ne way of understanding the effect of the events of 1536 is to realize that they threatened Henry VIII's honour, with which he was greatly preoccupied. He commented as much in August 1544 in a letter to Francis I, king of France 'thus touching our honour, which, as you know, we have hitherto guarded and will not have stained in our old age'. He was not alone. Men at this time were 'intoxicated' with honour, and with maintaining their reputations and good names. Men and women in the sixteenth century used the concept of 'honour' to talk about their gender roles: male honour was bound up with masculinity, upholding patriarchy, controlling women and defending one's good name.[1]

The characteristics of masculinity, or 'manhood' as it was referred to in the sixteenth century, were marriage and the patriarchal control of a household, the exercise of reason, sexual prowess, physical strength, especially demonstrated through violence, and courage. In the noble and chivalric world in which Henry VIII operated, the paramount place for demonstrating physical strength and manly courage was in the joust, and until 1536, this was where Henry's untroubled sense of masculinity had most glorified itself. The joust was the central event of a tournament, which normally also included other forms of mock combat. There would have been groups of knights fighting each other on horseback (called the tourney) as well as combat at barriers – opponents fighting on foot with swords or long staves across waist-high barriers. In the joust, two armoured riders would charge at each other on either side of a wooden barrier called the tilt, holding a lance in their right hands with the barrier to their left. Points were awarded for striking, and especially for breaking their lance against the body of the opposing knight. By the early sixteenth century, blunted lances, or lances made safe by a tip fixed to their point, were in general use. Nevertheless, the jousts were still wildly violent and dangerous. When kings participated, they fought for real. In 1559, Henri II, the king of France, was fatally wounded in a tournament when his opponent's lance shattered and splinters pierced his visor, entering his head above his left eye. Henry VIII had narrowly escaped therefore, when in 1524, tilting against Charles Brandon, Duke of Suffolk, he charged without remembering to lower his visor, and the duke's spear broke on the king's helmet and filled his headpiece full of splinters.[2]

By Henry VIII's day, tournaments had become lavish occasions for pomp and magnificence. Despite the huge cost of tournaments and their associated masques and banquets (one estimate is that Henry VIII spent £4,000 on the Westminster tournament of 1511, almost twice the cost of his 900-ton warship, the *Great Elizabeth*), these were not mere entertainment, nor were they decadent, self-indulgent or wasteful binges in expenditure. For a start, in the sixteenth century, there was really no such thing as 'inconspicuous consumption' – anything of value was showy and obvious – and it was proper and necessary for a monarch to appear magnanimous and majestic. Baldesar Castiglione in his manual for courtiers published in 1528, summarizes contemporary thought when he wrote that the ideal ruler 'should be a prince of great splendour and generosity… he should hold magnificent banquets, festivals, games and public shows'. Monarchical magnificence was an essential part of good lordship and kingly honour. The tournament thus served the important political goal of demonstrating the wealth and prestige of the monarch to his subjects and, especially, to foreign diplomats. Tournaments were, symbolically, also regarded as important peacetime training for war, and served as chivalrous alternatives, even if by this point they bore little resemblance to real warfare. Before a tournament in May 1540, the challenge framed itself in these terms, stating how 'in the idleness of peace there is danger that noble men may themselves fall into idleness', so now, 'as, in the past, feats of arms have raised men to honour, both in God's service against his infidel enemies and in serving their princes'. Sir Thomas Elyot, in his 1531 *The Book Named the Governor*, spoke of exercises, including wrestling, hunting and combat of arms, which are 'apt to the furniture of a gentleman's personage, adapting his body to hardness, strength and agility, and to help therewith himself in peril, which may happen in wars'.[3]

In the joust, individual knights competed against each other, so there were also opportunities for great personal glory. Henry VIII was a fine athlete and one of the champions of the joust. Sebastian Giustinian, the Venetian ambassador at Henry VIII's court between 1515 and 1519, was suitably impressed: 'after dinner, a stately joust took place, at which His Majesty jousted with many others, strenuously and valorously... this most serene King is not only very expert in arms, and of great valour, and most excellent in his personal endowments'. His secretary, Nicolo Sagudino, also noted that 'King excel[led] all the others, shivering many lances, and unhorsing one of his opponents'. From January 1510, when Henry made his first public appearance in the tiltyard as king, until January 1536, he was a splendid, passionate, skilful and brave participant in the joust. Miles F. Shore has commented that 'Henry's narcissism was strongly attached to masculine activities', and the joust was pre-eminently an arena in which Henry VIII could display his superior physical strength, his 'prowess' and 'the nobility of his courage' (according to the contemporary *Book of the Order of Chivalry*) – all of which differentiated him from the weaker sex and established his credentials as a consummate man.[4]

Until 1536 then, Henry disported himself as a young athletic man, attracting the praise and admiration of onlookers. In 1536, this was all to change. On 24 January 1536, the 44-year-old Henry was unhorsed by an opponent and fell so heavily 'that everyone thought it a miracle he was not killed'. The speed of the gallop at the charge, his heavy armour, the height of Henry's great horse (and weight, if the large, mailed animal fell on him) and the blow of his opponent's lance combined to make this a very serious accident. Henry was unconscious for two hours, and one suggestion has been that he bruised his cerebral cortex. Given what later happened to Henri II, it is no wonder that people suddenly became concerned with his mortality. The official line appears to have been to make light of the event. Chapuys, the imperial ambassador, wrote that Henry had sustained no injury, and at the beginning of February, Thomas Cromwell, the king's chief minister, was reassuring people that 'the King is merry and in perfect health'. Yet, there are several indications that such a fall was thought to have consequences on a grand scale. The papal nuncio in France, Bishop Faenza, wrote to the Vatican on 17 February 'that since the King had this fall, there is some hope that he may return', that is, to the Catholic fold. In other words, he made a direct correlation between a momentous accident that would have made the king aware of his mortality, and Henry's concern for his own spiritual wellbeing (as the writer saw it) and that of his kingdom. The fall was felt to be so significant that it might just bring about such a momentous volte-face in Henry's religious and foreign policy. By 6 March, Catholic Europe had conceded that such a change has not occurred, 'the King has not improved in consequence of his fall', but the very hope of it indicates the importance of the event in the eyes of the watching world.[5]

Anne Boleyn claimed that king's fall was of even greater importance. On 29 January 1536, Anne miscarried, blaming the miscarriage on her shock at hearing the news of the king's fall five days earlier. It was Chapuys who reported this and he was scathing about her reasoning. But at least two other sources confirm this. The chronicler and Windsor herald, Charles Wriothesley, wrote that 'Queen Anne was brought abed and delivered of a man child... afore her time', because 'she took a fright, for the King ran that time at the ring and had a fall from his horse... and it caused her to fall in travail'. In addition, Lancelot de Carles, who was staying in London, composed a French poem on 2 June 1536. It reiterates how the king fell so severely from his horse that it was thought it would prove fatal, and that when the queen heard the news, it 'strongly offended' her stomach and advanced 'the fruit' of her womb, so that she gave birth prematurely to a stillborn son.[6]

It is almost certain that this fall had a major impact on Henry's health that would affect him ever after. During one of his royal progresses in 1527, Henry had suffered from a 'sore leg', which seems likely to have been a varicose ulcer on the thigh. It was, at least temporarily, successfully healed by Thomas Vicary, who was appointed the king's surgeon in 1528, no doubt in recognition of his services. The fall of 1536 probably caused the ulcer to burst open. This time, however, Vicary seems to have been unable to cure it, despite the fact that he was finally made Sergeant-Surgeon in this year, a timing which may have been more than mere coincidence. That this ulcer was to plague Henry chronically throughout the rest of his life is made clear in a letter from John Hussey to Lord Lisle in April 1537 which noted 'the King goes seldom abroad, because his leg is something sore', and in June that same year, Henry himself wrote to Thomas Howard, the Duke of Norfolk, that the real reason for postponing his trip to York was 'to be frank with you, which you must keep to yourself, a humour has fallen into our legs, and our physicians advise us not to go far in the heat of the day, even for this reason only'.

A year later, one of the fistulas in his leg became blocked, and the French ambassador, Louis de Perreau, Seigneur de Castillon, noted that 'for ten or twelve days the humours which had no outlet were like to have stifled him, so that he was sometime without speaking black in the face and in great danger'. Later that year, Sir Geoffrey Pole, in his examination under the charge of treason, said, 'that though the King gloried with the title to be Supreme Head next God, yet he had a sore leg that no poor man would be glad of, and that he should not live long for all his authority next to God'. After a similar attack in 1541, the new French ambassador, Charles de Marillac, made a passing reference that further confirms that the king's leg had put him in great peril from around 1536, although it seems not to have been much publicized at the time. Marillac wrote in March 1541 that there was a complication with the ulcer for 'one of his legs, formerly opened and kept open to maintain his health, suddenly closed to his great alarm, *for, five or six years ago*, *in like case, he thought to have died*'. The diagnosis of the exact nature of the ulcer has been debated. Early suggestions that it was a luetic – or syphilitic-ulcer, do not correspond well with the fact that the king showed no other signs of syphilis and that syphilitic ulcers are inclined to self-heal. Sir Arthur Salisbury MacNalty suggests that Henry suffered from osteomyelitis, a chronic septic infection of the thigh bone, and that the episode of 1541 may have been a thrombosis vein with detachment of the clot causing pulmonary embolism, with intermittent fevers thereafter as a result of septic absorption from the wound, as for example, in 1544. It is also possible that such an attack was the cause of Henry's death, although Sir Arthur indicates that 'uraemia due to chronic nephritis with a failing heart and dropsy cannot be excluded'.[7]

The ulcer produced increasingly frequent and severe pain, infections and fevers and discharges that let off an embarrassingly unpleasant smell. The combination of this recurrent and excruciating pain, together with the unprepossessing nature of his running sore, seems to have gradually manifested itself in the personality of the king. Henry became increasingly anxious and irascible, easily irritated and prone to rage. As we'll see, there were other factors in this shift in his character, but the impact of this draining and debilitating pain should not be underestimated.

Although Henry continued to hunt, the pain in his leg meant that he was never able to joust again. 1536 effectively spelled the end of his active life, and with it, the beginnings of his obesity. In 1536, Henry's waist measured 37 inches, and his chest 45 – an increase from his 23-year-old measurements of 35 and 42, but still a fine figure for a man in his mid-forties (and still keeping roughly the same waist-chest ratio as in 1514). Yet by 1541, only five years later, he had become enormous – with a waist measurement of 54 inches, and a chest measurement of 57. While this may not be exceptionally obese by modern standards, at six foot two, Henry already towered over his contemporaries (the average adult male was about 5 foot 7½ inches), and was now gross, compared with his peers. In a letter of October 1540 Richard Pate, the archdeacon of Lincoln, reported from Brussels the European gossip that the king had 'waxen fat' while Marillac in 1541 noted that Henry was very stout ('*bien fort replet*'). Eventually, his obesity was such that he had to be moved around his palaces in some form of carrying-chair. This was quite a come-down for one who had been eulogized as a young man for his athleticism and good looks. Giustinian wrote in 1515 that 'His Majesty is the handsomest potentate I ever set eyes on', and went on to rhapsodize that Henry was 'above the usual height, with an extremely fine calf to his leg, his complexion very fair and bright, with auburn hair combed straight and short, in the French fashion, and a round face so very beautiful, that it would become a pretty woman'. Thomas More remarked that, 'among a thousand noble companions, the King stands out the tallest, and his strength fits his majestic body. There is fiery power in his eyes, beauty in his face, and the colour of twin roses in his cheeks.' Henry, at this time, was the fulfilment of Castiglione's description of the appearance of the ideal courtier: 'I wish our courtier to be well built, with finely proportioned members, and I would have him demonstrate strength and lightness and suppleness and be good at all the physical exercises befitting a warrior'.[8]

The psychological impact of the fall is more difficult to measure than the physical, but it is not hard to imagine the effect that massive obesity might have had on one so formerly praised for his masculine beauty. In addition, if physical strength was understood by the sixteenth century to be a key yardstick of masculinity, then it is a fair assertion that for a man who had been so publicly acclaimed for his prowess at the tilt, his inability to pursue such activities after this point must have had a deep emotional impact. Until this time, 'he never attempted anything in which he did not succeed. He had such natural dexterity, that in the ordinary accomplishments of throwing the dart, he outstripped everyone', Erasmus noted in 1529. Now, he had met with disability. According to historian Lyndal Roper, sixteenth-century masculinity drew its power from 'rumbustious energy': the 'figure who epitomized masculinity' was the 'man of excess' in his strength, courage, display and riotousness. Henry had been such a man, and although, as we shall see, Henry compensated for his lost manhood in display, he no longer possessed any of the 'rumbustious energy' of his youth.[9]

Essentially, the fall marked, for Henry, the onset of old age. In the same year he turned forty-five. To understand the significance of this, it is important to realize that the sixteenth century conceived of ageing as a series of stages. The 'ages of man' moved from childhood to adolescence, from adolescent to youth, from youth to manhood and from manhood to old age. Different medical tracts assigned different ages to these stages: the most pessimistic considered 'the lusty stage of life' to last from twenty-five to thirty-five, followed by old age. Elyot's *Castle of Health*, published in 1561, was slightly more optimistic, stating that old age began at forty, but even the most upbeat categorization placed it no later than fifty. Turning forty-five certainly marked the onset of this new phase for Henry. Prospero, in Shakespeare's *The Tempest*, is in his mid-forties, but throughout the play, references are made to his advancing age and declining abilities.

It wasn't all bad, however. As scholar Keith Thomas points out, early modern society was gerontocratic – it was ruled by men in their forties and fifties. Such men were thought to possess the right measure of humours, which dried up their strength but made them calmer, more sedate and, therefore, more wise. But this society was also gerontophobic. There were lots of anxieties and insecurities around old age – chiefly to do with powerlessness, the stripping away of health and respect, and becoming the scorned stereotype of 'Old Adam', the 'doddering old man... being cuckolded by his lusty young wife'. Old age was universally regarded as 'itself a disease', 'a perpetual sickness', and 'the dregs... of a man's life'.[10]

One piece of evidence suggests that the diminishing effect of the events of 1536 on Henry's youth and manhood would have been magnified by latent concerns. In May 1535, Henry VIII had caused his beard 'to be knotted and no more shaven', and at the same time, he polled his head and commanded the court to adopt a similar fashion – a closely cropped style. The permanent adoption of a beard is very significant. In a fascinating article, Will Fisher suggests that 'in the Renaissance, facial hair often conferred masculinity: the beard made the man'. He points out that virtually every man depicted in portraits in the century after 1540 sported some kind of facial hair. Texts of the period corroborate the association of a beard with manliness. Again and again, treatises reiterate that a beard is 'a sign of manhood', 'the natural ensign of manhood', or as explained by Johan Valerian in 1533, 'nature hath made women with smooth faces, and men rough and full of hair', therefore 'it beseemeth men to have long beards, for [it is] chiefly by that token...[that] the vigorous strength of manhood is discerned from the tenderness of women'. Finally, facial hair, was in medical textbooks of the time strongly linked to the production of semen. In other words, a beard was a mark of 'procreative potential'. Henry VIII's decision to wear a beard and be 'no more shaven' was therefore a powerful assertion of his masculinity and ability to father children. It suggests that there were pre-existing anxieties about his manhood, naturally associated with his continuing lack of a legitimate son, that were ready to be activated into full-blown paranoia and reaction by the turn of events just one year later. Interestingly, at the same time, Henry VIII introduced laws on the wearing of beards by commoners. In April 1536, Henry VIII commanded the newly-conquered town of Galway that men's 'upper lips [were] to be shaven'. This colonial injunction suggests that Henry knew that there was a power in stripping a man of his beard. There has also been a suggestion that in 1535, Henry VIII ordered a tax on the wearing of beards, though this remains unverifiable. Nevertheless, the Irish law – and this alleged tax – indicate both Henry's latent insecurity and his assertion of his pre-eminent manliness.[11]

CHAPTER 7

The Fall of Anne Boleyn

Henry's fall from his horse thus provided the context, and according to Anne Boleyn, the catalyst, for the first of a further series of events in 1536 associated with Henry's family and marital life.

On 29 January, the day of Katherine of Aragon's funeral, Anne Boleyn miscarried of a male foetus. The significance of this miscarriage has been the subject of great discussion among historians. Many commentators have suggested that Anne's miscarriage inexorably led to her downfall – for only four months later, she was executed and the king remarried. Had she, in the words of Chapuys, 'miscarried of her saviour'? Was the miscarriage, as David Starkey suggests, 'the last straw'? Or was her undoing the result of a more complex set of causes?[1] Had, for example, Henry and Anne's relationship gone into terminal decline, and what was the role of Jane Seymour in this? Did Henry knowingly and monstrously invent the charges of adultery against Anne, or did he allow himself to be deceived? Was it Cromwell who was responsible for Anne's demise? Or was she simply guilty of the charges laid against her?

Anne's Miscarriage

We should first consider whether Anne's miscarriage marked the beginning of the end for the queen. The issue is confounded by the fact that Anne may or may not have miscarried two years earlier, in 1534. Anne had given birth to Elizabeth eight months after her official marriage to Henry in January 1533, and ten months after Anne and Henry's secret wedding, recorded by chronicler Edward Hall in mid-November 1532. Becoming pregnant so swiftly after beginning sexual intercourse and bearing a healthy child boded well. In 1534, there were again signs of a pregnancy and observers commented on it. Chapuys noted that Anne was pregnant in late January 1534 and George Taylor, in a letter to Lady Lisle in April, remarked that 'the Queen hath a goodly belly'. This comment implies Anne's pregnancy was visible, that is, she was at least four months pregnant by this time. Her pregnancy also featured in royal communications. Henry muttered to Chapuys in February that he had no other heir except his daughter Elizabeth, 'until he had a son, which he thought would happen soon'. There were also instructions issued to Anne's brother in early July to carry a missive to the French king postponing a meeting between the two monarchs until the following April because 'being so far gone with child, she [Anne] could not cross the sea with the King, and she would be deprived of his Highness's presence when it was most necessary'. Finally, a portrait medal of Anne Boleyn was cast, inscribed with Anne's motto 'The Most Happy', possibly to commemorate the expected arrival of a prince: this survives in the British Museum as the only agreed contemporary image of Anne.[2]

But no child was born. Then in late September 1534, Chapuys sent a strange letter to Charles V after he was reunited with the court after their summer progress. It reads 'since the King began to doubt whether his lady was *enceinte* [pregnant] or not, he has renewed and increased the love he formerly had for a very beautiful damsel of the Court'. Sir John Dewhurst, in a study of the miscarriages of Katherine of Aragon and Anne Boleyn, remarked that there was little reason for the king to doubt the queen's pregnancy unless she failed to go into labour and bear a child. Certainly, a pregnancy that was at four months by April would, in the normal course of things, have been due by late September. Sir John suggests that it was a case of pseudocyesis or phantom pregnancy, which occurs when the stomach swells because a woman is desperate to have a child, even though she is not actually pregnant. Henry's daughter, Mary, was later to experience exactly the same thing. The alternative is what many historians, including Anne's most recent biographer, Eric Ives, have concluded – that Anne secretly miscarried or had a stillbirth while the court was on royal progress in the summer months of 1534. Mystery shrouded it because Henry and Anne were keen to conceal it, and the reduced size of the court on progress made such secrecy possible. Yet, this is quite dissatisfying because it means arguing for a miscarriage on the very basis of an absence of evidence. And this is not the usual pattern for Henry's wives' miscarriages. For the whole sorry tale of Katherine of Aragon's miscarriages, and for Anne Boleyn's miscarriage of 1536, there appears to have been no attempt at concealment, and the court was awash with the gossip. Our primary sources for the 1536 miscarriage are Chapuys, Charles Wriothesley and Lancelot de Carles – in other words, all people who would have picked up the rumours at court. Neither could the royal couple have expected people to have simply forgotten about her rounded belly of the preceding months. Finally, a previous phantom pregnancy would explain the otherwise curious rumours across Europe in early 1536 that Anne's miscarriage had been a pretence. The bishop of Faenza, the papal nuncio in France, wrote in March 1536 that ' "that woman" pretended to have miscarried of a son, not really being with child, and, to keep up the deceit, would allow no one to attend on her but her sister.' These sentiments were reiterated elsewhere. We just don't have enough evidence to conclude this with confidence.[3]

Either way, the miscarriage of January 1536 – whether as the first shocking failure or a further nail in the coffin – was a great blow to both Henry and Anne. Wriothesley's *Chronicle* states that Anne 'reckoned herself at the time but fifteen weeks gone with child', which tallies roughly with Chapuys' estimate that Anne had carried the child for three and a half months: it seems to have been long enough either way to know that it was a son and heir that had been lost. Did it suggest to Henry, as some historians would have it, that Anne would never be able to bear him a male heir, and that the marriage was doomed? The king was known to have shown 'great distress' and 'great disappointment and sorrow' at the tragedy. Chapuys gives an account of the king's visit to Anne's chamber after hearing the news. He said very little to her, except, 'I see that God will not give me male children', and as an afterthought as he prepared to leave, 'When you are up, I will come and speak to you.' These sound like the words of one numb with grief. Anne then told him why she thought she had miscarried – that it had been the result of Henry's fall, and that his love for another woman broke her heart. At which Henry was greatly hurt – whether ashamed of his failings or bitter at her accusations depends on one's reading – and left her to convalesce at Greenwich while he went to mark the feast day of St Matthew at Whitehall. Chapuys rather maliciously reads into this that Henry had abandoned Anne, 'whereas in former times he could hardly be one hour without her'. Certainly, both Henry and Anne seem to have been painfully aware of the possibility that history might repeat itself. There is some evidence that Anne worried on the day of her miscarriage that Henry would dispose of her, as he had the last queen. There is also the story that Chapuys reported third-hand, having been told it by Anne's enemies, the Marquess and Marchioness of Exeter. They in turn had been informed by one of the principal courtiers, who said Henry had spoken to him in confidence. This was that Henry said to this anonymous courtier 'as if in confession' that he had made the marriage by being 'seduced and constrained by *sortilèges*', and that he considered the marriage to be null and void, seeing that God had shown his displeasure at it because he did not allow them any male children. Henry therefore believed he could take another wife, which he said he wished to do.[4]

The word apparently used by Henry, *sortilèges*, translates as 'sorcery, spells, charms', and has given rise to the suggestion that Anne Boleyn dabbled in witchcraft. This is regularly cited as one of the charges for which she was found guilty at her trial, even though on this latter point, there is no evidence at all – witchcraft is not mentioned in the trial records. Eric Ives has suggested that the use of this French word is misleading as while Chapuys' letters were in French, Henry, if he made this comment, would probably have been speaking in English. The primary English meaning of *sortilèges* at this time was 'divination', which potentially changes the meaning of this sentence. It could mean Henry was persuaded into the marriage by the premarital prophecies that Anne would bear sons. Equally, the use of the word could refer simply to Henry's earlier infatuation or 'bewitchment' by Anne. Recently, the sense of Henry being 'seduced by witchcraft' has become attached to another theory, which holds that the real reason for Anne's ruin was that she gave birth to a deformed foetus. According to Retha Warnicke's reading of sixteenth-century superstition, this evinced that Anne was both a witch and adulterously promiscuous. The evidence for this is one description during Elizabeth's reign by the Catholic sympathizer, Nicholas Sander, that Anne had miscarried of a 'shapeless mass of flesh'. Sander himself did not link this to Anne's fall, nor does his partisan opinion, written so long after the event, make him a reliable source. It seems highly improbable that such a fantastically damning piece of evidence would not have surfaced in 1536 if there were anything in it at all. Despite the fact there is no other evidence of any sort to add credence to the 'deformed foetus' theory, it has a salacious quality that has made it highly attractive and enduring.[5]

So, to return to the question of Henry's response to Anne after the miscarriage, if – and it is quite a big if – Henry said these things, they could be taken as powerful evidence of his reaction against Anne, especially if they had been followed by a backlash against her over the following months. But, as we shall see, the evidence of February–April 1536 does not sustain such a conclusion. Both Henry's stunned remarks to Anne in her chamber and this outburst, if it occurred, appear to have been made in moments of frank emotion in the immediate aftermath, full of the 'shock of grief and disappointment'. They do not represent Henry's resolved opinion once some stability had been regained. Both Henry and Anne were upbeat before long. Anne is recorded as telling her ladies soon after this that the miscarriage had been for the best, because she would soon conceive again, and that the legitimacy of this new son would be unquestionable, because he would have been conceived after Katherine's death.[6]

Jane Seymour

Yet, in February 1536, another character was thought important enough for Chapuys to mention her in his dispatches – Jane Seymour. An Elizabethan writer, George Wyatt, believed that Jane Seymour used Anne Boleyn's pregnancy to displace her in Henry's affections: 'she waxing great again and not so fit for dalliance, the time was taken to steal the king's affection from her, when most of all she was to have been cherished'. Henry had previously had affairs and flirtations, while married to both Katherine (notably with Elizabeth Blount, the mother of his illegitimate son, Henry Fitzroy, and with Anne's sister, Mary Boleyn) and Anne. When Jane Seymour is first mentioned by Chapuys in mid-February, it is in the context of Henry lavishing gifts upon her, as he would a potential mistress. Henry's attentions to her continued throughout March, and on 1 April, Chapuys wrote to the Holy Roman Emperor of Jane's reception of a purse full of sovereigns sent to her by Henry, accompanied by a letter. Rather than opening the letter, which Eric Ives suggests contained a summons to the royal bed, Jane kissed it, returned it unopened and asked the messenger to tell the king that 'she was a well-born damsel, the daughter of good and honourable parents, without blame or reproach... there was no treasure in this world that she valued as much as her honour, and on no account would she lose it, even if she were to die a thousand deaths'. She added that if the king wanted to make her a present of money, she begged that it might be at 'such a time as God would be pleased to send her some advantageous marriage'. In other words, a marriage to Henry himself.[7]

Such a calculated response is reminiscent of Anne in the days of her courtship, and in response to her coy elusiveness, Henry's love for Jane was said to have 'marvellously increased'. It was so clever that Chapuys (and historians since) thought she was being coached not to give in to him unless he made her his queen. Yet, even Chapuys, who gives us this information, says earlier in the same letter that 'there had been... talk of a new marriage for this king... which rumour agrees well with my own news from the court of France, where, according to letters [I have] received, courtiers maintain that this king has actually applied for the hand of Francis' daughter'. Chapuys himself therefore does not connect up the rumours of a 'new marriage' with Jane Seymour. In early April, Jane was still little more than a lady whom the king was pursuing. At best, in accordance with the conventions of courtly love, she was the lady whom 'he serves' – a telling phrase. At worst, she was a passing fancy, whom Henry may have hoped to make his mistress. Chapuys certainly didn't think much of Henry's choice. He described Jane the day before Anne's execution as 'no great beauty' and 'not a woman of great wit'; he implied that she was unlikely to be a virgin, and reported that people said she was inclined 'to be proud and haughty'. Yet, by this point, the world had changed, and with it, Henry's intentions towards Jane. It is highly improbable that before Anne was considered guilty of adultery, Henry had seriously begun to plan to make Jane his wife.[8]

The Still Before the Storm

If Anne's miscarriage and the arrival of Jane Seymour on the scene were not enough to justify Anne's downfall, a natural decline in Henry and Anne's relationship could hold the key. One line of argument has been that 'Anne's proud and abrasive character soon became intolerable to her husband'. J. J. Scarisbrick writes that 'what had once been devastating infatuation turned into bloodthirsty loathing, for reasons we will never completely know'. This, however, is a peculiar conclusion, because according to the psychological theory of dissonance, the opposite is likely to have been true. This theory of cognitive dissonance – the 'state of tension that occurs whenever a person holds two cognitions (ideas, attitudes, beliefs, opinions) that are psychologically inconsistent' – suggests that holding two such contradictory ideas is very uncomfortable, and as a result, humans will always seek to resolve the two and make sense of them. One of the consequences of this is that if people go through a great deal of pain, effort or discomfort to attain something, they'll generally be happier with that thing than they would have been if they'd won it easily, in order to resolve the sense of dissonance produced by working for something and then not enjoying it. The very fact that Henry had gone through such ordeals and difficulty to obtain Anne, should, according to dissonance theory, have made her a greater prize and more precious to him. The notion that he would rapidly lose interest is therefore neither psychologically plausible, nor in fact, historically accurate.[9]

There were, indeed, some observers who thought that Henry was sick and tired of Anne by early 1536, and had determined to abandon her. Chief among those reporting this was, though, the ever-hopeful Chapuys. It is hard not to read wish-fulfilment into the evidence of one who referred to Anne as 'the concubine' or 'the she-devil', and who had made similar bitter assertions about the doomed state of Henry and Anne's relationship at the height of their happiness, in August and September 1533. Even

Chapuys himself recognized that Henry and Anne had always been prone to 'lovers' quarrels', and that the king's character was very 'changeable'. Henry and Anne were direct with each other, got angry, shouted, sulked, got jealous – but they were also frequently described as being 'merry' together, including throughout the autumn of 1535 – and this epithet seems to be appended to their marriage more often than to any of Henry's other marriages. G. W. Bernard has correctly described theirs as a 'tumultuous relationship of sunshine and storms'. But, between February and April 1536, Henry's actions in support of his marriage to Anne speak louder than the rumours that she was out of favour.[10]

For, during this period, Henry increased his pressure on the Holy Roman Emperor, Charles V, to recognize Anne Boleyn as his wife, and admit his error in his past treatment of Henry over the annulment from Katherine of Aragon. A series of negotiations on this theme reached their climax on 18 April 1536, when Chapuys, the Imperial ambassador, was invited to the court to talk with the king. Events that day were very deliberately staged to provoke official recognition of Anne by the diplomat. On arrival, Chapuys was warmly welcomed by George Boleyn, Lord Rochford (Anne's brother), and Cromwell brought a message from Henry inviting Chapuys to visit Anne and kiss her hand. Chapuys politely declined, but the royal party had another trick up its sleeve. Rochford accompanied the ambassador to Mass, and as Henry and Anne descended from the royal pew to the chapel, Anne stopped before Chapuys, turned and bowed to him. Etiquette necessitated that he do likewise – a significant diplomatic coup and one which provoked comment among Anne's enemies. A later letter from Chapuys noted that 'although I would not kiss or speak to the Concubine, the Princess (Mary) and other good persons have been somewhat jealous at the mutual reverences required by politeness which were done at the church'. Later, after dinner, the king took Chapuys aside to talk. In strong terms, Henry impressed on Chapuys that he would not brook Charles V's meddling in his affairs, specifically referring to the Holy Roman Emperor's demands that Mary be recognized as legitimate (and by implication, Henry's marriage to Katherine sound). Henry also required Charles V to send him a letter asking Henry's forgiveness for his past treatment of the English king, or failing that, a letter that promised to put the past behind them. All such negotiations were designed to persuade Charles V to admit that Henry had been right and that his marriage to Anne Boleyn was entirely valid. While there is clearly a strong element of wilfulness and egoism in Henry's demands, it would have been extraordinarily capricious of Henry to go to these great lengths to have Anne recognized as his wife, if he actually intended to rid himself of her shortly thereafter. This does not preclude the possibility that Anne and Henry were not on the best of terms, but it does make it unlikely that Henry was preparing to abandon the marriage. It also means that it is difficult to sustain an argument based on a characterization of Henry as fickle and uncommitted to his marriage, at least at a political, diplomatic and practical level, or one which posits that Henry deliberately acted to discard and destroy Anne, simply because his eye had strayed elsewhere.[11]

So Why Did Anne Fall?

If Anne's downfall was not the direct result of her miscarriage, nor because Henry planned to make Jane his queen, nor due to a terminal decline in Henry and Anne's relationship, why then did she fall? It seems there are only four or five possible scenarios:

1) That Anne was actually guilty of the charges against her
2) That Cromwell and Jane's relatives, the Seymours, conspired to bring Anne down, and Henry was genuinely deceived, believing Anne to be guilty
3) That Henry was not genuinely deceived and asked Cromwell to bring Anne Boleyn down, even though he knew she was not guilty

4) That Anne's behaviour was risky enough for her to appear guilty, but then 1) or 2) apply
5) That everyone can be exonerated – that neither Cromwell, nor Henry, nor Anne was guilty, but that she appeared so.

The answer is crucial because on it rests our picture of Henry VIII and the effect of this year's events.

Historians such as Eric Ives, David Starkey and G. R. Elton have favoured the second scenario, in which Cromwell and a court faction, including the Seymours, conspired to bring Anne down. Fundamentally, this view rests on an image of Henry as a king who could be manipulated and manoeuvred by the factions of his court, to 'bounce' him into action and tip him 'by a crisis' into rejecting Anne. Faction, and the ability to influence the king, certainly had a role to play in the Henrician court, and there is also some evidence that Anne and Cromwell were on bad terms in April 1536. Anne's influence had also been instrumental in Thomas Wolsey's fall, the king's erstwhile first minister, so Cromwell had reason to be fearful. The problem is that the disagreements posited between Anne and Cromwell – to do with a difference of opinion over the use of funds from the dissolution of the monasteries and matters of foreign policy – seem insufficient as motives to destroy a queen, especially given Cromwell and Anne's long supportive association. The crucial piece of evidence is a remark made by Cromwell to Chapuys after Anne's death in which he claimed to have 'to set himself to devise and conspire the said affair'. One translation (of Chapuys' letter reporting this in French) renders this in a way that suggests Cromwell planned and arranged the plot against Anne, from beginning to end. Yet, although Cromwell clearly arrogates a certain amount of initiative and responsibility for his accomplishment, probably to impress the ambassador with his power, the context of this phrase is that the king had given Cromwell the authority to discover and bring to an end the affair of the 'concubine'. It seems likely that the 'affair' in question was the matter of investigation, trial and execution. This reading suggests the third scenario in which Henry asked Cromwell to take Anne down, knowing she was innocent, but wanting to get rid of her. This is the version adopted by most films that have been made recently about Henry VIII, and therefore, the notion most fixed in the popular imagination. But, as we have already seen, it seems unconvincing that this is the case in terms of Henry's relationships with Anne and Jane prior to the end of April 1536, while neither the interpretation that focuses on Cromwell, nor this theory, sufficiently explore and explain Henry VIII's character in a way that would make such behaviour comprehensible.[12]

The Investigation

In April 1536, something sparked Henry and Cromwell's suspicions that Anne was being unfaithful and prompted an investigation. What this something probably was is suggested by Lancelot de Carles who was secretary to the bishop of Tarbes, the French ambassador in London. In June 1536, de Carles wrote a poetic account in French about Anne Boleyn's fall, which was published in 1545 but circulating in manuscript before this. Although this is a literary account, and written as a tragedy, the date of the poem, written so soon after the events it retells, and the proximity of the writer to one with access to court gossip, makes it credible. De Carles claimed that one of Henry's courtiers, whom G. W. Bernard identifies as Sir Anthony Browne, and his sister, Elizabeth Browne, Lady Worcester, were quarrelling about Lady Worcester's allegedly loose morals. In her defence, she blurted out that her behaviour was nothing compared to that of the queen's, citing Anne's carnal knowledge of 'Marc', Henry Norris and her brother. Browne, considering what to do with such pyrotechnic intelligence, decided to report it to two of the king's favourites, who in turn told Henry. According to the poem, Henry was shocked and his colour changed. Though he remained doubtful of its veracity, he gave permission for the matter to be investigated, with the proviso that should it prove false, those reporting it would pay the penalty. Letters from John Hussey to Lady Lisle in late May substantiate this version of events. They name Lady Worcester as the queen's principal accuser, and in the Tower, Anne 'much lamented my lady of Worcester'. There is even something directing attention to the women of Anne's household in Cromwell's official version of the story, which, assuming that Anne was guilty, described her behaviour as 'so rank and common that the ladies of her privy chamber could not conceal it'.[13]

Another theory floating around Europe was that it was a jealous Mark Smeaton who had started the rumours about Anne's infidelity. It is wise to be cautious as all manner of distorted versions of the facts were circulating on the Continent at the time. These rumours included the belief that Anne was discovered in bed with Smeaton; that Elizabeth was not Anne's daughter but taken from a poor man; that some of the men were arrested as accessories; and that Anne's parents were also arrested. However, that there is something in this theory of Smeaton's garrulousness – representing, I suspect, an additional strand of gossip to Lady Worcester's slip of the tongue – is substantiated by Smeaton's behaviour when arrested.[14]

For, if the source of the intelligence is under any doubt, what happened next is not. Mark Smeaton was arrested by Cromwell on Sunday 30 April, and taken to his house in Stepney for questioning. Smeaton is variously described as an organist or player of the virginals or spinet in the queen's household; as a commoner, he was a relatively easy target. He was interrogated, possibly under torture or under the threat of torture, and confessed to having had sexual intercourse with the queen three times. It was a confession he never retracted. The next day, he was moved to the Tower, and there held in irons.[15]

To understand why he might have done this, it is worth considering the only evidence we have of the nature of Anne and Smeaton's relationship – evidence freely supplied by Anne herself. The greatest insight into Anne's heart and mind at this time is found in the letters written by Sir William Kingston, constable of the Tower, to Cromwell, detailing Anne's remarks and reflections during her imprisonment. Among other things, she anxiously reflected on which conversations between her and the other suspects could be rendered incriminating. She recalled having sent for Smeaton once while at Winchester to play on the virginals, but not speaking to him again until during a strange incident a few days before her imprisonment. On the Saturday before May Day, she had come across him standing in the round window in her presence chamber and asked him why he was so sad. He replied that it was no matter. She reprimanded him with the words, 'You may not look to have me speak to you as I should do a noble man, because you be an inferior person'. Mark replied, 'No, no, madam, a look sufficed me; and thus, fare you well.'

This exchange has been variously interpreted, but perhaps what best illuminates it is the recognition of how improper, ill-mannered and transgressive Smeaton's responses were when addressed to his queen. It was not for a commoner to disregard her question in this way, nor then to dismiss himself from her presence. Anne's tart reminder to him of the nature of hierarchy is a reaction to this and contrasts greatly with her kindly opening question. Nevertheless, there is still something indefinably odd about the encounter. Anne's statement, which one historian has considered to show 'remarkable familiarity', another has deemed 'belittling'. The bizarre nature of the exchange reflects something odd about Smeaton himself. It is he who behaved familiarly with Anne, and the abrupt, inappropriate and slightly disturbing nature of his remarks ('a look sufficed me') suggests the sort of imaginative fantasy one currently associates with the stalkers of celebrities. Perhaps it was this sense that Smeaton was reaching too high that informed Thomas Wyatt's characterization of Smeaton in his poem 'In mourning wise':

Ah, Mark, what moan should I for thee make more
Since that thy death thou hast deserved best,
Save only that mine eye is forced sore
With piteous plaint to moan thee with the rest?
A time thou hadst above thy poor degree,
The fall whereof thy friends may well bemoan.
A rotten twig upon so high a tree
Hath slipped thy hold and thou art dead and gone.

For if Smeaton shared a mentality with modern-day stalkers, then confessing to adultery with the queen might, in his mind, have conferred kudos and associated glory on him. He would have been only too pleased to admit to it, especially if he had been instrumental in circulating rumours to that effect. It was a confession that had devastating effects.[16]

Wyatt was right that Smeaton, of all those accused, best deserved his death, for his confession was absolutely key to everything that followed. It catapulted the investigation into a different order of magnitude. Suddenly rumour became fact; everything was believable. All subsequent evidence was tainted with an irresistible presumption of guilt.[17]

We can hypothesize that Smeaton's confession was reported back to Henry that Sunday afternoon. Henry then made two decisions: to postpone for a week his planned trip to Calais with Anne, which was due to leave on 2 May, and to continue with the May Day jousts as planned. At this stage, Henry did not know what to believe, but he began to suspect that Anne might be guilty. This is evident from a glimpse of a charged encounter between Henry and Anne at Greenwich that day, which was recorded by Scottish theologian Alexander Alesius. He had seen Anne, carrying the little Elizabeth in her arms, piteously entreating Henry as he looked out of an open window down into a courtyard. The king's face and gestures conveyed his fury, and Alesius reported 'it was most obvious to everyone that some deep and difficult question was being discussed'. This was made

79

all the more apparent by the fact that the council had talked long and hard on some matter until it was dark.[18]

Another thing also happened that Sunday, involving Henry Norris, a much more important person at court. The popular Norris was a gentleman of the privy chamber, keeper of the privy purse and groom of the stool. These were positions which allowed him right of entry to the king's privy chambers. Since at least 1515, he had been one of Henry VIII's closest companions, 'the best friend of the king'. On Sunday 30 April 1536, Anne Boleyn had asked Norris to swear before John Skyp, her chaplain, that she 'was a good woman'. Such bizarre behaviour can only be explained as an exercise in damage-limitation after an indiscreet altercation between Anne and Norris, which had occurred at some point over this May Day weekend, the facts of which came spilling out as Anne sat and wondered in the Tower. Anne had asked Norris why he had not yet gone through with his marriage, and he had replied that 'he would tarry a time'. Anne had rashly taunted him with the words, 'you look for dead men's shoes; for if ought came to the king but good, you would look to have me'. Norris' flustered response – that 'if he should have any such thought, he would his head were off' – provoked her further, and she retorted, 'she could undo him if she would'. The nature of this encounter is hard to quantify. As Greg Walker has pointed out, what we do not know is Anne's tone here – 'is she merely flirting, chiding, petulant, angry?' What did Anne mean when she said she could undo him? We also don't know what this represents – the reckless public exposure of an established situation, the voicing of something long tacitly understood or a dreadful and embarrassing misunderstanding on Anne's part. Two things are clear: flirtation had transgressed the boundaries of courtly love, and Anne and Norris had mentioned the possibility of the king's death – something treasonous under the Treason Act of 1534, which held that even words that wished harm to the king were unlawful. What happened next suggests that rumours about this scandalous tiff had reached Henry's ears, and his knowledge of it may even have prompted the angry scene observed by Alesius, and the back-tracking of Norris' oath to Skyp.[19]

The next day, Henry attended the May Day jousts at Greenwich as planned; watched Rochford and Norris leading the challengers and defenders and, according to one source, presented Norris with his own horse when Norris' horse recoiled from the lists. What was striking was that Henry then suddenly left with a small group of six people, at which 'many men mused', and travelled to Whitehall by horseback rather than by royal barge. One of the six travelling in this intimate group with him was Norris. According to George Constantyne, who was Norris' servant at the time, Henry 'had Mr Norris in examination and promised him his pardon in case he would utter the truth'. In the course of this conversation with his close friend, Norris maintained his innocence: 'whatsoever could be said or done, Mr Norris would confess no thing to the King', although Constantyne had heard from Norris' chaplain that Norris later confessed something to Sir William Fitzwilliam, which he retracted again at his arraigning, saying he had been deceived into confessing it. Here we have the fullest flourish of Henry's personal role in the investigation of Anne's offences. Up until this point, he may have ordered Cromwell to question Smeaton and had made decisions about their immediate schedule awaiting the outcome of the inquiry, but at the implication of one so close to him in this affair, Henry now decided to take the process of examination upon himself. Whatever Norris said or didn't say, it was enough to convince Henry of his guilt and to damn him and Anne. The next day, 2 May, Norris, Anne and her brother, Rochford, were arrested and taken to join Smeaton in the Tower. A couple of days later, William Brereton, Sir Francis Weston, Richard Page and Sir Thomas Wyatt were also arrested and put in the Tower. Sir Francis Bryan, a courtier and gentleman of the king's privy chamber, was interrogated by Cromwell and released.[20]

All those arrested for suspected adultery with Anne were members of Henry's privy chamber and part of the intimate circle around the king and queen. The evidence we have for Weston and Rochford suggests that all were judged guilty by association and because of their careless talk with Anne. Just as she had for Norris, while in the Tower Anne recalled her conversations with Weston, and feared their revelation. A year earlier, 'on Whitsun Tuesday last Weston told her that Norris came more unto her chamber for her than for Madge (Shelton)', whom Norris was due to marry: sentiments which if exposed would make her exchange with Norris even more dangerous. Not only this, but Weston had said that he 'loved one in her house' better than either his wife or Madge Shelton. When Anne had fished, 'Who is that?' Weston had replied, 'It is yourself,' at which, Anne said, she 'defied him' – that is, rebuked him. Such talk was a heavily loaded version of the usual banter of courtly love, the convention being that a gentleman would faithfully serve and love a lady of the court, pre-eminently the queen, and woo her with words and gifts. Courtly love demanded that such relationships remained platonic – it was a way of sublimating eroticism and desire – but the beauty of the game lay in its inherent ambiguity. Given Smeaton's confession and Norris' possible slip of admission, the fact that these remarks skirted, and sometimes crossed, the acceptable boundaries of such courtly interchanges, now put them into a very different light. An assumption of the queen's guilt made such flirtation deadly. On 12 May 1536, the commoners were tried before oyer and terminer commissioners (commissions authorized to 'hear and determine' treasons, felonies and other criminal cases at the assizes). Smeaton pleaded guilty to violation and carnal knowledge of the queen; the others pleaded not guilty. The jury returned a verdict of guilty against all four, and the judgment was a traitor's execution – hanging, drawing and quartering.[21]

What of Rochford? Anne and Rochford's trial was held on 15 May, before a crowd of 2,000 in the Tower. They were judged by twenty-six peers of the realm, with Thomas Howard, Duke of Norfolk, the high steward of England, and uncle of the siblings, 'in the King's place and judge'. The indictment detailed the exact carnal nature of Anne's relationship with her brother, but as to the substance of it, Chapuys summarized it as 'by presumption, because he had been once a long while with her, and with certain other little follies'. Both Chapuys and George Constantyne noted that the odds for those betting on it were greatly in favour of Rochford being acquitted. That he was not perhaps suggests that his real crime lay elsewhere. Chapuys noted that Anne and her brother were charged with 'having ridiculed the King, and laughed at his manner of dressing' and his poetry, and for the various other ways in which Anne 'showed... she did not love the King, but was tired of him'. One of the things they had probably laughed about was what Anne was accused of telling her sister-in-law, Rochford's wife, that the king 'was not skilful in copulating with a woman, and he had neither virtue nor potency'. Perhaps it was his knowledge of Anne's judgment on Henry's talents in bed that had led Rochford to doubt openly whether Princess Elizabeth was Henry's child, another accusation levelled at him and one he did not deny. In his trial, these accusations were given to Rochford in written form, with specific instructions not to read them aloud – which Rochford flagrantly disobeyed. It has been suggested that it was this arrogant, ungentlemanly behaviour that sealed his fate, and certainly Constantyne wrote that he had heard, 'he had escaped had it not been for a letter', while Wyatt, in his poem 'In mourning wise', rued Rochford's pride. The pair pleaded not guilty, but when the peers were called on to make their judgment, one by one each and every one of them, from the most junior to the senior, declared Anne, and then Rochford, guilty. Norfolk pronounced the sentence with tears in his eyes: Anne would be beheaded or burned at the king's pleasure; Rochford would be hanged, drawn and quartered.[22]

Two days later, Rochford, Norris, Brereton, Weston and Smeaton were all executed (the sentence was transmuted to beheading) on Tower Hill. The same day, Anne's marriage to

Henry was annulled, probably on account of Henry's previous relationship with Anne's sister. Elizabeth was declared a bastard. That this annulment made something of a mockery of the charges of adultery does not seem to have been considered at the time. On 19 May, Anne herself was brought out to die. The day before her execution she had told Kingston that she had 'heard say that the executioner was very good, and I have a little neck', and putting her hands around it, had laughed heartily. Seeing this, Kingston remarked in his letter to Cromwell that 'this lady hath much joy and pleasure in death'. Anne came to the scaffold with her four attendants, delivered her simple speech of humility and forgiveness, exchanged her ermine mantle and hood for a linen cap, one of her ladies bandaged her eyes, and the French executioner did his office. Wyatt, who sat in the Bell Tower as the executions took place, wrote the following lines:

...These bloody days have broken my heart.
My lust, my youth did them depart,
And blind desire of estate.
Who hastes to climb seeks to revert.
Of truth, *circa Regna tonat.*

The bell tower showed me such sight
That in my head sticks day and night.
There did I learn out of a grate,
For all favour, glory, or might,
That yet *circa Regna tonat.*

By proof, I say, there did I learn:
Wit helpeth not defence too yerne,
Of innocency to plead or prate.
Bear low, therefore, give God the stern,
For sure, *circa Regna tonat.*[23]

Was Anne Guilty?

So, was Anne guilty? This was the view promulgated at the time; it emerges in contemporary comment and has had a recent champion. The official line emerges in Cromwell's letter to Bishop Gardiner, who was on a diplomatic mission to France, on 14 May: 'the Queen's incontinent living was so rank and common that the ladies of her privy chamber could not conceal it'. John Hussey, Lord Lisle's London agent, wrote to Lady Lisle on 13 May, 'if all the books and chronicles were totally revolted, and to the uttermost persecuted and tried, which against women hath been penned... since Adam and Eve, those same were, I think, verily nothing in comparison of that which hath been done and committed by Anne the Queen'. Soon after Henry VIII's death, his first biographer, William Thomas, said that Anne's 'liberal life were too shameful to rehearse'. Others found it hard to believe. Archbishop Cranmer wrote to Henry VIII on 3 May in an attempt to curb the damage that Anne's sudden and apparent disgrace might have on the evangelical cause, a letter that has been described as 'a model of pastoral wisdom and courage'. In it Cranmer wrote:

I am in such a perplexity, that my mind is clearly amazed; for I never had better opinion in woman, than I had in her; which maketh me to think, that she should not be culpable. And again, I think your Highness would not have gone so far, except she had surely been culpable.

His bewilderment and incredulity are palpable. In the end, despite being acquainted with the accusations against her, Cranmer could still not believe her guilt. In the early hours of the morning on the day of her execution, Alexander Alesius found Cranmer walking in the gardens at Lambeth Palace. Cranmer could only manage to say to him, 'Do not you know what is to happen today? ... She who has been the Queen of England upon earth will today become a Queen in heaven', before bursting into tears.[24]

There are, in fact, several pieces of evidence that speak strongly of Anne's innocence. The chronicler Wriothesley claimed that as Anne entered the Tower, she 'fell down on her knees… beseeching God to help her as she was not guilty of her accusement'. The first letter sent by Kingston upon Anne's committal to the Tower reported their first audience and Anne's request for the sacrament in a closet by her chamber, for, she ardently declared, 'I am as clear from the company of man, as for sin… as I am clear from you, and the king's true wedded wife'. Anne reiterated this a few days later. She comforted herself that she would have justice, for 'she said if any man accuse me I can say but nay, & they can bring no witness'. The night before her execution, she also swore 'on peril of her soul's damnation', both before and after receiving the body and blood of Christ, that she was innocent. The significance of this in an age when few doubted the realities of heaven and hell, especially for one who had been a zealous evangelical reformer, is paramount. In addition, she was not the only one professing her innocence. As Sir Edward Baynton put it, 'no man will confess any thing against her, but only Mark [Smeaton] of any actual thing'. While neither Anne nor her co-accused used their scaffold speeches to declare their innocence, as we would perhaps today, on the scaffold it was conventional piety, Eric Ives has argued, for all, as sinners, to express that they deserved to die, to ask forgiveness, and to commend the judicial system that condemned them. Anne demonstrates this precisely in her speech when she said, 'by the law I am judged to die, and therefore I will speak nothing against it', asked God to have mercy on her soul and commended the goodness and gentleness of the king, but her additional comment, 'and as for mine offences, I here accuse no man', suggests there may have been someone to accuse. Finally, even now, three-quarters of the accusations of adulterous liaisons on specific days in specific places made against Anne in her trial can be discredited.[25]

Yet, she was arrested, found guilty and executed. Why? I would argue that the fifth possible scenario (see page 75) describes what actually happened – that neither Henry nor Cromwell malevolently condemned Anne for their own ends, but that Anne's apparent guilt, despite her actual innocence, convinced Henry that she deserved to die.

Let us return to Henry. In all the writing about Anne's fall, Henry's behaviour has never been adequately explained. Eric Ives is the most upfront about this, arguing that 'all discussion of the fall of Anne Boleyn ends in the ultimate unresolvable paradox of Tudor history: Henry VIII's psychology'. We have seen that Henry pushed and pursued the investigation up until the time of his interview with Norris but, persuaded of Anne's guilt, he then changed his behaviour dramatically. Firstly, he became 'morbidly concerned' about the execution plans, including the making of the scaffolds and the ordering of the French executioner from Calais, who used a sword and could behead a person while they knelt. The executioner charged a large fee of £23 6s 8d for his work. Henry wanted to ensure Anne was removed quickly and cleanly and it seems that he channelled his vengeance into practical arrangements for her death. Secondly, he displayed his sense of betrayal in an exaggerated, tragicomedic manner. The evening of the day Anne was taken to the Tower, his (illegitimate) teenage son Henry Fitzroy, the Duke of Richmond, came to say goodnight to his father and Henry wept over him, saying that he and the princess Mary 'were greatly bound to God for having escaped the hands of that accursed whore, who had determined to poison them'. While Anne was in the Tower, Henry was heard saying that he believed that 'upwards of 100 gentlemen' had known her carnally. He also composed a tragedy, that he wrote out in a little book, carried with him and offered for people to read, and, on Ascension Day, he ostentatiously wore white for mourning. This behaviour displays Henry's enormous capacity for hyperbolic self-pity and how quickly his view of Anne had polarized. Finally, he went out of his way to celebrate and step up his relationship with Jane Seymour in a way that seemed flagrant and scandalous to observers. He was reported as 'going about banqueting with ladies, sometimes remaining after midnight and returning by river'. He lodged Jane within a mile of his palace and provided cooks and officers of the royal household to serve her. On 18 May, Chapuys wrote, 'already it sounds ill in the ears of the people, that the King, having received such ignominy, has shown himself more glad than ever since the arrest of the whore' and further 'you never saw a prince or husband show or wear his (cuckold's) horns more patiently and lightly than this one does'. Waiting the two and a half weeks between Anne's arrest and execution apparently grated on Henry: 'I think the King feels the time long that it is not done already'. As soon as Anne was dead, Cranmer, at the king's behest, issued a dispensation for Jane and Henry to marry and they were betrothed on 20 May just one day after Anne's execution and married ten days later. Why such a rush? Charles V's simple statement that 'the king is of an amorous complexion' (or its various reiterations since) will not do as an explanation.[26]

Two contemporary comments provide a clue. Cranmer, in his letter to the king concerning his disbelief at Anne's guilt, wrote that he could not 'deny but your grace hath great causes… of lamentable heaviness; and also, that… your grace's honour of every part is so highly touched', before rushing on to undo these words by disingenuously assuring Henry, 'if the reports of the Queen be true, they are only to her dishonour, not yours'. A similar sentiment was expressed by a European observer, the reformer Philipp Melancthon, when he wrote, 'see how dreadfully this calamity will dishonour the King'. Honour, as we have seen, was chiefly a measure of one's ability to conform to the ideals demanded of one's gender. For a man, it meant exerting masculinity, imposing patriarchy, controlling the women in one's household, maintaining a good reputation and demonstrating physical and sexual prowess. Chiefly, it meant controlling the morality of the women under his care and, specifically, their sexual morality. That Henry had been unable to do this denoted two things: it was evidence of Henry's inability as a man and as a monarch. Contemporary thought made a clear link between a man's sexual potency and his wife's fidelity – men who were cuckolded were those whose 'lack of sexual dominance led their wives to adultery'. 'To be a man', writes Lyndal Roper, 'was to have the power to take a woman.' Anne's very behaviour, if assumed to be true, testified to the king's lack of manliness, and as if this weren't enough, Anne and Rochford's ridicule of the king on this very matter drove the point home. It was not something that went unnoticed in the kingdom. Sir Nicholas Porter, the parson of Freshwater, was reported to have said in 1538, 'Lo, while the King and his Council were busy to put down abbeys and pull away the right of Holy Church, he was made cuckold at home.' There was also a strong connection in the popular mind between impotency and old age – the image of 'Old Adam' whose feeble old body could not satisfy his vigorous young wife was a constant refrain in the ballads found in contemporary broadsides. There were huge repercussions if such a failure were found in a king. Early modern thinking linked the governance of a house with the governance of a realm; as John Dod and Robert Cleaver wrote in 1612, 'it is impossible for a man to understand how to govern the commonwealth, that doth not know how to rule his own house'. Any woman's adultery, but especially that of a queen, upset the social order and gender hierarchy upon which society was based. Cranmer was right the first time – Henry's honour was 'highly touched' by Anne's apparent adultery. This also explains why Henry felt the need to cavort himself with ladies and increase the pace of his relationship with Jane Seymour, marrying her so quickly. It wasn't just, as Alesius later hypothesized, that he was 'openly insulting' Anne: in the light of Anne's devastating assault on his masculinity, Henry did it to restore the patriarchal order and to prove his manhood.[27]

CHAPTER 8

A Dearth of Heirs

$\mathcal{T}$here was a final sub-plot in the events touching Henry VIII's honour in 1536. It is well known that Henry had long sought a legitimate male son and heir. Mary was the only surviving child of his marriage to Katherine of Aragon, who had otherwise suffered five miscarriages, still-births and cot deaths, including the death of a celebrated prince named after his father, who lived for less than eight weeks in 1511. Anne Boleyn had promised him sons – and it had been prophesied that she would have them – but she too had borne him a daughter and miscarried of a son.

Henry did, of course, already have a son. But he was illegitimate. Born to Henry's mistress Elizabeth Blount in June 1519, the boy was named Henry Fitzroy, a name that announced his parentage. He was openly acknowledged by Henry; Thomas Wolsey was even godfather at his christening. In 1525, the boy, aged six, had been ennobled, and made first, Earl of Nottingham and then Duke of Richmond and Somerset. There were only two other dukes in England at this time, and Richmond's double dukedom made him the highest-ranking peer in the country.

His additional Somerset title particularly suggested that Henry VIII was smoothing the path towards legitimating his son, as John Beaufort, a royal bastard who had been legitimated in the late fourteenth century, had been the Earl of Somerset. Being illegitimate did not mean that he lived remote and apart from the king. His recent biographer, Beverley A. Murphy, has argued that a letter from the royal nurse implies Richmond was part of the royal nursery, and he was often at court after 1530. Observers commented on the closeness of the father-son relationship. In 1530, the French ambassador, John Joachim, Seigneur de Vaux, remarked on Richmond's good looks and the fondness of the king for his son, 'a most handsome, urbane and learned young gentleman, very dear to the King on account of his figure, discretion and good manners... he is certainly a wonderful lad for his age'. Arrangements continued to be those appropriate to a king's son: an early marriage was arranged for Richmond with the daughter of the one of the highest-ranking peers, the Duke of Norfolk (uncle to Anne Boleyn). In 1532, Henry presented Richmond to the king of France. Richmond was also deployed on occasion to represent the king, playing host at a feast in November 1534 in honour of a visiting French admiral and attending, in the king's place, the execution of three Carthusian monks who had refused to swear the oath accepting the king's royal supremacy and marriage to Anne Boleyn in May 1535. Richmond's resemblance to the king – he had the same red hair – helped remind onlookers of his line of descent. The Venetian ambassador commented in 1531 on Richmond 'so much does he resemble his father'.[1]

By June 1536, after Elizabeth was bastardized in late May, all Henry's children were illegitimate and unable, therefore, to inherit the throne. Henry was in a worse position than he had ever been and this was compounded in June. At the same time that Cromwell was assuring Chapuys that Henry was thinking of making Mary his heir, Henry insisted that Mary should submit to swearing an oath that acknowledged Henry as 'Supreme Head in Earth, under Christ of the Church of England'. In addition, she was also to swear that the marriage between Henry and Mary's mother had been 'by God's law, and man's law, incestuous and unlawful'. In other words, Mary was required to declare her own bastardy. The document suggests she resisted doing this. Mary had signed her name after declaring the king's position as Supreme Head, as if to write no more, but then was evidently induced to write a further paragraph proclaiming her parents' marriage invalid, under which she signed again. Henry's decision to press for this declaration after years of allowing Mary not to subscribe to this position relates almost certainly to the strength of his conviction about his rightful position as Supreme Head and his desire to assert his pre-eminence anew (as he did in other ways at this time, see chapter 11), in light of the humiliating betrayal and bruising damage he had just suffered. This accords with Henry's behaviour when Mary initially refused to sign – he grew 'desperate with anger' and swore 'in a great passion' that if she did not, she and several others would suffer for it. One other, and not mutually exclusive, possibility is that Henry had started to reconsider his options. Chapuys reported in early June that there had been a provocative suggestion made by Robert Radcliffe, Earl of Sussex, who had 'stated the other day in the Privy Council in the King's presence, that, considering the Princess was a bastard, as well as the Duke of Richmond, it was advisable to prefer the male to the female for the succession to the Crown.' Chapuys worried that 'this opinion of the Earl not having been contradicted by the King might hereafter gain ground and have adherents'. Chapuys certainly interpreted the timing of Henry's insistence as evidence that Henry was gearing up to legitimate Richmond and wanted Mary's status to be indisputable. In mid-June, threatened with legal proceedings against her if she didn't conform, Mary signed.[2]

Until such time as Jane bore children, the next-in-line to the throne was now James V of Scotland. His sister (and therefore, second in line to the throne) was Henry's niece, Margaret

Douglas, daughter of Henry's elder sister, also called Margaret. In June 1536, it was discovered that Margaret Douglas had secretly married the Duke of Norfolk's younger brother, Lord Thomas Howard. For one so close to the throne to marry without consulting the king was sheer folly, possibly even high treason. It suggested, as the act of parliament concerning the attainder of Lord Thomas stated, that 'the said Lord Thomas falsely, craftily and traitorously hath imagined and compassed, that in case our said Sovereign Lord should die without heirs of his body, which God defend, that then the said Lord Thomas by reason of marriage in so high a blood... should aspire... to the Dignity of the said Imperial Crown of this Realm'. Henry 'was very much annoyed at his niece's marriage' and in July, both Margaret and Thomas Howard were sent to the Tower. Lord Thomas was sentenced to execution (he, in fact, died in the Tower on 31 October 1537), but Margaret was excused death, largely, Chapuys thought, as the marriage had not been consummated, but also perhaps because her mother pleaded with her brother, the king, for mercy.[3]

With three illegitimate children and a future possible heir in the Tower, the situation seemed hardly able to get any worse. But it did. In early July, Richmond fell ill, and on 23 July 1536, Henry's beloved and only son died of tuberculosis. At this point, Jane Seymour was not even pregnant, and a month later, Henry would indicate his doubt whether she would conceive. The timing could not have been worse – earlier in July, parliament had passed an act which, for the first time, did not confine the succession to the legitimate line but allowed Henry to designate whomever he liked as his successor. The act had not named a successor, for fear that if 'such person... should be so named, (they) might happen to take great heart and courage, and by presumption fall into inobedience and rebellion', a clause that spoke of Henry's growing fear of betrayal. It is possible that this new act had deliberately opened up the succession and with it the possibility that Richmond could one day inherit the throne. If it had, the king's hopes and intentions would only have intensified his grief at his son's death.[4]

Henry reacted strangely to the news. He initially ordered the Duke of Norfolk, Richmond's father-in-law, to arrange a secret funeral. This was done at Thetford Priory in Norfolk according to the king's instructions, as Chapuys observed: 'Richmond, whom the King had certainly intended to succeed to the Crown, after being dead eight days, has been secretly carried in a wagon, covered with straw, without any company except two persons clothed in green, who followed at a distance.' The two persons were George and Richard Cotton, who had been governor and comptroller of Richmond's household. Only three other people attended the funeral: Norfolk, Richmond's brother-in-law, the Earl of Surrey and his widow. Such a quiet, guarded affair was a hardly a fitting funeral for a duke of this rank, let alone the son of a king. It was as if Henry wanted 'to sweep the whole thing under the carpet'. Within days though, Henry had written to Norfolk reproaching him for not having buried Richmond honourably. Such contradictory behaviour suggests that Henry was experiencing a mixture of denial, confusion and deep grief.[5]

CHAPTER 9

Masculinity and Image

*I*n 1536, Hans Holbein the younger painted a new portrait of Henry VIII. This painting, conserved in the Thyssen-Bornemisza Collection in Madrid, is the only surviving picture of Henry VIII universally agreed to be by Holbein himself. It marked a departure from previous representations of the king. This was partly simply a result of Holbein's extraordinary talent and his astonishing and innovative technique of representing his sitters with almost photographic realism. Yet, the painting is also remarkable because of the characteristics that it appears to give Henry VIII: strong, ultra-masculine qualities that were even more forcefully deployed in a full-length portrait of Henry VIII painted by Holbein a year later. Although the Holbein original of this full-length representation – a wall mural at Whitehall Palace – was destroyed in the late seventeenth century, multiple copies of it mean that it now is the primary image through which we imagine and identify Henry VIII. As a result, the qualities with which it imbues Henry are ones that we now associate with him. The process of creating a picture is a complex thing – how much the finished result depends on the painter, or, in this case, the sitter and patron cannot be known – but it is probable that Henry VIII had something to say about how he was depicted. The production of these pictures, which conveyed strength and virility so hot on the heels of the events of early 1536, and the attribution of qualities so far from those being associated with Henry VIII at that moment, suggest that the themes of these portraits were influenced by the events of 1536. Perhaps they can be seen as a reaction to the challenge that 1536 had presented to Henry VIII's sense of his own masculinity.

The Thyssen Portrait

Holbein had first visited England between 1526 and 1528 and in this period produced several portraits for Thomas More and his family. He returned in 1532 and at some point between 1532 and 1537 was employed by Henry VIII. In September 1536, Holbein's friend, Nicolas Bourbon, described him in a letter as the 'royal painter' and, although the royal account books for May 1531 to January 1538 are lost, we can see that from 1538, Holbein received a salary of £30 a year, which was paid quarterly.[1]

The Thyssen portrait was probably painted after the execution of Anne Boleyn on 19 May 1536 and Henry's engagement to Jane Seymour the next day. It is small: 28 by 20 cm, but its size belies its power. It shows Henry VIII almost looming out of the small frame. Against a vibrant blue background, the king is pictured with his face turned to a three-quarter angle and his eyes looking back to the viewer. His chest appears vast, so much so that his shoulders do not even fit in the picture, and the image is made more overpowering by the opulence and finery of his clothing and jewellery. Such magnificent clothing contrasts with the smooth and realistic structure of Henry's broad face: the high cheekbones, the strong jaw emphasized by his clipped beard, the small, piercing eyes with their heavy lids, his long nose and tight, pursed lips. It is not a wholly flattering depiction. But, rather than showing a handsome, softened image as in, for example, Joos van Cleve's imagined portrait of Henry VIII in 1535, Holbein's image imbues Henry with a certain severity, steeliness and power. This forceful sense of mastery and potency was undoubtedly Holbein's goal. One commentator epitomized the picture when he wrote that 'the unbridled vitality of this ruler can be tangibly felt'.[2]

It is a striking image in a way few earlier pictures of Henry were. In the portrait of Henry painted in the 1520s, he is shown as a round-shouldered insipid youth. In Lucas Horenbout's miniatures, Henry is wan, anemic and insubstantial. In sharp contrast, the Henry of Holbein's 1536 portrait has been transformed into a force to be reckoned with. Here, he appears magnificent, powerful, potent, strong, fierce and calmly terrifying. It was a remarkable new image of the king. It also is not too great a stretch of the imagination to conclude that as far as portraits were concerned, after this point, this representation became the 'officially sanctioned image' of Henry VIII. This new image wasn't intended for propaganda in the modern sense of the word – it was not designed to be seen by vast numbers of people – but it was to be seen by those people who mattered, and it was intended to communicate certain ideas about the king's character. Holbein's ability to attribute character through his paintings can be seen by comparing the Thyssen with Holbein's portrait of Jane Seymour, also painted in 1536. While Henry's shoulders and upper arms do not make it into the picture, in order to emphasize his grandeur, practically all of Jane's voluminous sleeves do. She might also be ornately bejewelled but her positioning, stance and expression mean that, in comparison to Henry's steely power, she looks petite, demure and submissive.[3]

This portrait was an image painted by Holbein but it is unlikely to have been solely of Holbein's making in inspiration and message. The production of portraits was a process of negotiation. Images of Henry produced as a result of a royal commission needed, above all, to satisfy the monarch's conception of himself. They were given in anticipation of what would make them pleasing to the sitter. So while Henry must have been recognizable in Holbein's portrait, it is likely that the picture was also acceptable because it depicted a vision of the king's character of which Henry VIII approved. It is clear that Holbein responded to the needs and expectations of his monarch, and it is also inconceivable that he would not have been aware of the events at court in the early part of 1536 and the resulting political climate. Whatever the process of creation, his final product was evidently a great success, for it formed the basis of all the later images of the king.[4]

The Whitehall Mural

One of the images strongly influenced by Holbein's portrait of 1536 was his full-length portrait of Henry painted the following year. This familiar image was part of a wall mural painted in the king's chambers at Whitehall Palace. As such, because the palace burned down in 1698 (only the Banqueting House remains standing), the original painting was destroyed, and only the original sketch (cartoon) of Henry and two later seventeenth-century copies of the whole mural remain. There are also a large number of sixteenth-century copies, some dating from within Henry's lifetime, of the portion of the mural that comprises Henry VIII's portrait. This extraordinary image was the first full-length life-size portrait of a monarch in England, and one of the first in Europe.[5]

This powerful image is how we know Henry VIII. The historian G. R. Elton once famously suggested that Henry VIII is the only English monarch identifiable from his silhouette alone. The silhouette of Henry in our mind's eye is a man standing with legs astride, with extraordinarily wide shoulders bulked out by padded clothing and with arms bent at the elbow. This silhouette was the one given to Henry in Holbein's full-length portrait, and this, together with the image of Henry's face in Holbein's Thyssen portrait, have ingrained themselves in our collective consciousness. When we think of Henry VIII, we visualize the stance, bulk, clothing and countenance of these images. But even more than this, Henry VIII's image makes us all think we know him. David Starkey has argued that Holbein's full-length portrait is not just the most memorable image of an English monarch, 'it *is* Henry... the reason why he fascinates us... the beginning of his biography and the key to his mind'.[6]

The full-length portrait of Henry VIII is part of the Whitehall mural, which also showed Henry VII and his wife Elizabeth of York and Henry VIII's third wife Jane Seymour, grouped around a stone plinth or altar. They stand on a richly draped carpet against a background of ornate architectural features, including cartouches supported by mermen and mermaids and a large scalloped shell. They are all dressed in rich fabrics – Henry VII and Elizabeth of York wear gold, lined with ermine. He leans an arm on the top of the altar, while she folds one arm over the other and gathers her skirts in one hand. Jane Seymour stands with her hands clasped in front of her, as demurely as she had in the portrait of 1536, and a small dog is curled up on her train. All three avert their gaze from the viewer – the wives are particularly submissive, with closed body language. To the left of the altar, Henry VIII stands squarely but at a slightly defiant angle, his feet planted wide apart and his arms bent at the elbow, and with one hand he carries his gloves while the other rests on the cords of his dagger. He looks, arrestingly, straight out at the viewer. The mural measures roughly nine by twelve feet and, judging from the cartoon, the impact of the vast mural must have been tremendous. Henry VIII, in particular, at over six feet tall and extraordinarily broad, must have been hugely intimidating.[7]

For, it is the representation of Henry VIII's body that makes this image so spectacular. His wide stance has been described as a 'fantastic amalgam of the static and the swaggering'. It derives from depictions of chivalric and spiritual heroes in the fifteenth century – Donatello's St George, Andrea del Castagno's Pippo Spano and Perugino's St Michael – and thus was a stance that embodied knightly triumph. In addition, it alludes to the posture of a man in battle, as it mimics the stance of a man standing in full armour or mounted on horseback. Without any symbols of military equipment then, this pose sparked instinctive associations of Henry VIII with martial glory. In fact, Holbein's decision here is very telling, as it seems that straddled legs were considered 'improper' except in the case of legendary heroes – the representation of Henry VIII in this way thus makes a claim for his status and is also at the very edge of the acceptable, bordering on lewd. To emphasize the power of the pose, Holbein also elongated Henry's legs – much like the legs of female fashion models are stretched and airbrushed today. We know this from comparing the life-size cartoon with a model of armour made for the king in 1540 from which his actual legs appear to be considerably shorter. This strong pose, together with Henry's tautly held arms and fists, means that he appears to brim with latent energy.[8]

Henry's shoulders are, as in the Thyssen, fantastically broad, a fact that is exaggerated by the puffed sleeves of his gown and the angle of his arms – they 'metaphorically bear weight, and assume burdens'. Interestingly, a comparison of the cartoon with later copies suggests that in the original mural Henry's shoulders were particularly wide, indicating that this was an important element of the composition. It has been noted that Holbein had used the wide-shouldered, feet-apart posture in some of his previous portraits, notably of Charles de Solier (who was the French ambassador in England at the time it was painted), Sir Henry Guildford and Jean de Dinteville, in his *Ambassadors*. The former is a particularly impressive image but shows only three-quarters of Solier's figure, while Guildford is shown looking away from the viewer. In Henry's portrait, the successful elements of all these pictures have been combined by Holbein to produce a stance and figure of striking power. As a result, it has been described as showing Henry as a 'human fortress of imperial strength' and depicting the 'anatomy of a ruthless tyrant'. These are recent descriptions, but contemporaries also felt its force. Karel van Mander, in the early seventeenth century, described his reaction to the painting: Henry 'stood there, majestic in his splendour... so lifelike that the spectator felt abashed, annihilated in his presence'. This was precisely its purpose. The picture was designed to induce awe and to intimidate the beholder.[9]

Holbein also made one crucial last-minute change in his depiction of Henry VIII that further emphasized Henry VIII's confident dominance. In the draft cartoon or sketch of the mural, Henry's face is identical to the 1536 rendering, but in the final version, Holbein made a masterly alteration: he changed the angle of Henry's face so that the king looks out at the spectator face-on, confrontationally catching the eye and holding the gaze. While Henry's face is characterized by the same strong structure and squareness with which Holbein had painted him the previous year, it is clear that this face-on Henry was chosen because it more closely reflected the other messages of the painting. It could be that this compositional change may have been Henry's suggestion after Holbein had showed him the cartoon. Either way, the final position of Henry's head displays Henry's will and power in an even more concentrated and forceful way than in previous representations.

Everything about the way Henry's body has been depicted by Holbein is intended to convey masculinity and virility. The taut limbs, brimming with latent energy, are the very model of that epitome of masculinity, the 'man of excess'. Art historian Tatiana String recently examined the evident motifs of masculine prowess in this picture. After drawing attention to Henry's military stance and broad shoulders, she highlighted his 'thrusting elbow, which works as a ready sign of assertion, power and masculinity', and his beard – which, as we saw in chapter 6, was a clear signifier of manhood. (Henry VII's lack of a beard in this mural is a further way in which Henry VIII claims his pre-eminence as a king and as a man.) String also highlights the way in which Henry's figure has been arranged as two triangles with one going across the shoulders and down the arms, and one going between Henry's straddled feet and up his legs. The triangles converge and direct the gaze at Henry's codpiece. Using measurements of the cartoon and copies, we can tell that in the cartoon, and possibly the original mural, the spread of Henry's legs was wider, the shoulders broader and the height of the figure greater, exaggerating this focal point even more. A codpiece was a padded box in which the genitals could rest, and contemporary portraits often show men sporting particularly large, often upright, codpieces, which were very suggestive. String notes though that by comparison with other portraits, the elaborately decorated and contrastingly coloured codpiece worn by Henry in the mural is even more overt and bulging than normal. A knotted bow directly above it further directs attention to Henry's potency. A large codpiece obviously indicated virility and fertility – there is every likelihood that this detail in the mural reflects the news of Jane Seymour's pregnancy – but there is more to it than that. Although we cannot delve into Henry VIII's thoughts, nor know how Holbein was instructed, it's not absurd to suggest that there may well have been some link between this showy display of masculinity and the emasculating events of the previous year. The man whose potency had been so publicly ridiculed and whose sense of his own male power had suffered such a devastating blow in 1536 appears here to be reasserting his masculinity in an astonishingly striking way. One further indication that this might be the case is the situation of the mural, which meant that this message of virility and strength was conveyed to those who mattered. The mural covered a wall in the king's privy chamber at Whitehall Palace, a room accessible only to the elite of the elite – the very same courtiers, councillors and ambassadors who would have been present to witness Henry's disgrace and dishonour at the hands of Anne Boleyn. It appears likely that Holbein had drawn on every device imaginable to produce an 'unusually intensive concentration of masculinity', to appease the badly-bruised ego of his king.[10]

If it were the case, it was a successful strategy because it has determined that posterity, at least, has remembered Henry VIII as the epitome of manhood. The Whitehall image was the basis for all later paintings of Henry VIII and even guided the representations of later monarchs. Since then, the pose and costume of Henry VIII have been affectionately parodied, and it has been this image of Henry that has guided all portrayals of the king since, on stage and film. It is an image that has subsequently formed the basis of all other attempts to personify Henry VIII, from Richard Burton to Ray Winstone, until, in fact, the recent series, *The Tudors,* as Brett Dolman, Curator of Collections at Historic Royal Palaces, commented in an article in *The Sunday Times*: 'It's the first time anyone has been brave enough to do a Henry VIII programme that hasn't started with the Holbein image!' In April 1989, it was this image of Henry VIII that was blown up to six metres high to represent England at Coquelles near Calais to celebrate the breakthrough of the Eurotunnel (Francis I, Henry's rival, represented France). It has become 'the default image of royal power', and the epitome of masculinity. It is also, of course, the stance adopted by the superheroes of popular culture: Superman and Batman project their masculinity because they fashion themselves after Holbein's image of Henry VIII – an image whose composition may have been guided by the need to compensate for the events of 1536.[11]

The shocks of 1536 had been very great. Time and time again, Henry's trust and certainties had been shown to be misplaced. In a play written in 1569 called *The Longer You Livest, the More Fool Thou Art* by William Wager, the protagonist Moros enters his fourth and final age and is stripped of his health, children, possessions and honour. It seems that almost the same had happened to Henry. In August 1536, Chapuys reported that 'the King had lately told... [Cromwell] that he felt himself already growing old, and doubted whether he should have any child by the Queen'. The blow of all his successive losses – his lost sons by miscarriage and death, two once-loved wives now dead, his health and youth severely impaired, his masculinity and honour completely discredited – hit him very hard. The impact of these events was to make Henry, at the turn of his forty-fifth year, truly an old man. Aristotle defined a key characteristic of the aged as that if they are taken in and betrayed, they become cynical and suspicious. This is precisely what happened to Henry. He became jaundiced and disillusioned by the events of 1536. Mistrust and paranoia were not characteristics associated with Henry VIII before 1536; they were afterwards. There were later flashes, bursts of renewed youth – at the birth of Edward, at the marriage to Catherine Howard, even in his 'merry countenance' in his wedding to Kateryn Parr – but these were repeatedly dashed by successive events. After Edward was born, Jane Seymour contracted puerperal or childbirth fever, and her death plunged the king into mourning for over two years. Catherine Howard betrayed him and Henry was devastated – raging and weeping before his Council, he was described that year as being 'very old and grey'. After 1536, Henry VIII, even as he grew larger physically, was diminished, and in his succeeding years, his behaviour was a continual reaction to the challenge the year 1536 had posed to his potency.[12]

PART THREE
The King's Religion

Henry, the page, wants to be God
and to do as he pleases.

Martin Luther[1]

$\mathcal{W}$hen we think of Henry VIII and religion, our first thought is of the break with Rome and the creation of the Anglican Church. The break with Rome happened in piecemeal fashion over the early 1530s but, contrary to our expectations, the new Church of England was not automatically a Protestant one. In fact, until, 1536, all Henry had done was 'in effect, to create an English Catholic Church'. The Reformation, in its true sense of trying to reform the beliefs and practices of the church, did not actually commence at state level until 1536. This was the year in which Henry promulgated his new vision of church doctrine and began the work of reformation. This is not to say that crucial changes had not occurred before this point – chiefly that Henry had declared himself Supreme Head of the Church of England, with responsibilities encompassing the right to determine orthodox belief and the cure (or care) of souls. But in 1536, he actually started to implement these powers to shape the new Anglican Church. As a result of his idiosyncratic religious views, even after 1536, the theological framework of the church that Henry and his advisers and bishops created was neither thoroughly Protestant nor thoroughly Catholic.[2]

The decision to exercise the rights of his royal supremacy to decide theological doctrine and practice, despite Anne Boleyn's fall and Henry's remarriage to Jane Seymour (who was rumoured to be conservative in religion) came as a surprise to some European commentators, who had hoped for Henry's return to the Catholic fold once Anne was safely out of the way. Instead, Henry's decision to use the occasion to insist on the illegitimacy of his daughter Mary, to set his first minister, a layman, permanently up as his vicar-general, and to put forth his own definition of right theology, were defiant gestures. The religious rulings of this year indicated the king's commitment to shaping his church in line with his own character and conscience. This was the year in which Henry set out the defining values of Anglicanism – values that would shape Henry's decisions on religious policy until his death, and which can even be seen to have fundamentally shaped the church established by his daughter Elizabeth and, therefore, the Church of England today. This isn't to suggest that Henry's theology remained static over the succeeding years of his life – the events of 1536 themselves, especially Henry VIII's reaction to the disobedience shown by his subjects, led to unforeseen consequences. Yet, by examining the central values of the Henrician church established in 1536 and the effect of the events of 1536 in shaping Henry's attitudes so that these values were further entrenched, the following chapters argue for the importance and impact of Henry VIII on the Church of England, not just in its creation but in its very shaping.

CHAPTER 10

The Reformation in England

The story of the Reformation in England is far from straightforward. Histories of it have been confused by an assumption that the later polarized categories of 'Catholic' and 'Protestant' had meaning in Henry VIII's England; they didn't. This was a period of exploration and fluidity – when these later polarized categories were just being created. In recent years, there has been vigorous debate among historians about the progress of reform, stemming in large part from reactions to the classic Protestant history of the Reformation, as symbolized by John Foxe's *Acts and Monuments*. Popularly known as Foxe's *Book of Martyrs*, it was published in 1563 and ever since has been hugely influential in telling the story of the English church. The essential story Foxe told was of the inexorable rise of Protestantism: that the Reformation was necessary and wanted. Historians following Foxe, like A. G. Dickens, pointed to substantial evidence of decadence and moral decay in the Roman Catholic Church, with a flourishing industry of unscriptural practices, including the selling of indulgences and forged relics, and among the clergy, who ranged from ill-educated parish priests to sickeningly wealthy bishops, widespread practices of simony or the sale of offices, pluralism or the holding of more than one benefice at a time, clerical absenteeism and the keeping of concubines. At the time, even those who ultimately resisted Protestantism, such as Erasmus and Thomas More, recognized the need for reform.[1]

But recent revisionist historians like Eamon Duffy and Christopher Haigh have done a good job of reminding us that, in fact, the English pre-Reformation Catholic Church was far from unpopular. There is strong evidence of piety in the 1520s and, rather than being in terminal decline, the strength and rigour of the late medieval church suggests that not all people would have happily accepted the Reformation. In contrast with the colour, pageantry, sights, sounds and smells of traditional religion, the Reformation brought a religion which stripped away the externals in favour of an interior intimate experience which relied on the printed scriptural word. Haigh has concluded that Protestantism could not have been an attractive religion for the masses because of the high levels of illiteracy, and that reformation was, by many, neither expected nor welcomed. There is evidence of opposition to implementing the changes of the Reformation at parish level. Thomas Wylley, vicar of Yoxford, wrote a letter to Thomas Cromwell saying that in his parish loyalty to traditional religion ran deep. Haigh also found a reluctance to erase the Pope's name from service books as ordered in April 1535, with reports of disobedience in Warwickshire, Rutland, Suffolk, Essex, Croydon, Kent and Somerset. The evidence of people's wills showed that even in the 1540s a majority of people making wills in London still sought the intercession of the Virgin and saints in heaven at their deaths. This revisionary research is important because it has helped us recognize that the church before the Reformation was strong and rich but it leaves an unanswered question: if the church was so vital and dynamic, why did it shatter so easily?[2]

For the Reformation in England did happen and, apart from

the rebels in the Pilgrimage of Grace (explored in chapter 15), enthusiasm for the old church was not sufficient in Henry's reign to produce the sort of civil war and violence seen on the continent in response to reform. Although Duffy and Haigh's evidence makes clear that there was loyalty and affection for the old church, it masks the fact that some of this loyalty was born of indifferent traditionalism, as well as sincere conviction. In addition, in the early sixteenth century, a number of people were searching for a new depth of religious experience and were dissatisfied by the old ways. So, in Henry VIII's England, there were important pockets of evangelical belief. These believers were disproportionately important, wealthy and powerful, and geographically concentrated so as to magnify their influence – mainly in urban areas like London, Cambridge and Norwich. These evangelical reformers believed that the church needed to be reformed in accordance with the scriptural text of the Gospels. They believed a new depth of intimacy with God was possible and that they were justified by faith alone. This meant that humans could be made right with God by simply believing in the sufficiency of Christ's death on the cross to pardon sins and that this belief would be formed by reading and hearing the scriptures in the vernacular. They considered monasteries, images, shrines, vows, masses, pilgrimages, the veneration of saints and confession to priests to be unhelpful distractions, and worship of the Virgin Mary and a belief in purgatory to be erroneous. In other words, their beliefs turned old ways of relating to the church, God, life and death on their heads. A key text for evangelicals was William Tyndale's English translation of the New Testament. It had been banned in England since its publication in 1526 because it controversially reinterpreted key words. The Greek word *metanoeite*, for instance, was retranslated as 'repent' instead of 'do penance', as in the traditional Latin version. Doing penance required confession to priests and meant good works needed to be done to compensate for sin, so the retranslation of this one word had huge implications for the power of the church and for beliefs about salvation. Other evangelical books decried the abuses of the Catholic Church. Simon Fish's *A Supplication for the Beggars* said that purgatory was a 'thing invented by the covetousness' of the church. A work by Cambridge graduate John Frith, *Disputacion of Purgatory* went even further and he was captured and burned at the stake as a heretic at Smithfield in July 1533. The extent to which these evangelical beliefs would be adopted by the new Anglican Church remained to be seen.

CHAPTER 11

1536: The Church Established

*M*any contemporaries expected that Anne Boleyn's downfall would lead to a reversal of the royal supremacy and the break with Rome. It had been, in fact, a constant hope across Catholic Europe ever since Henry and Anne's marriage in 1533. After Henry fell from his horse in January 1536 the papal nuncio in France, Bishop de Faenza, had raised the possibility of Henry's return to Rome, together with his conviction that 'if the Pope gave the sentence against the king of England and acted with strictness, he [Henry VIII] would probably give in, seeing that the Pope and the Emperor were his enemies, and that he could hope for nothing [from the French]'. The nuncio was referring to the ever-present threat posed by the as yet unpublished papal bull, which would deprive Henry VIII of his kingdom and make insurgence against his rule entirely legitimate. Writing in March 1536, Charles V offered advice to his ambassador at the English court, Eustace Chapuys, on how to influence the king to return to the church of Rome and suggested that he stress the division, confusion and manifest danger that would result from the bull's publication.[1]

After May 1536, with now both Katherine and Anne out of the way, the obstacles preventing Henry's return to Rome seemed few. It seemed as if there were now many good reasons for Henry to mend the breach and restore himself to the open, welcoming arms of the Roman church. On 24 May, Faenza reflected that 'it would be easy to bring back the King if it were not for his avarice', adding 'there was not a better opportunity of wiping out the stains on his character and making himself the most glorious King in the world'. Another European correspondent gossiped about the news of Anne's death and the possibility of a change of religion by linking her execution to the fact that 'images have been restored and purgatory is declared again'. Not only conservatives hoped for this, evangelicals feared it – if Cranmer's letter to Henry on discovering the news of Anne's apparent adultery is representative. He entreated Henry, perhaps a little disingenuously, 'I trust… you will bear no less zeal to the Gospel than you did before, as your favour to the Gospel was not led by affection to her'. Marrying Jane also gave Rome further cause for hope. Reginald Pole, Henry's cousin, a high-ranking noble of royal blood, who was studying abroad, would write in August that year, I 'had trusted that that woman [Anne] has been the cause of all these dishonours had taken away all dishonour with her, especially hearing what a good lady the king hath now taken'. In June 1536, it was rumoured that Jane had 'five times thrown herself publicly at the King's feet, requesting him to send for his daughter and declare her Princess'. Later, another story that she 'threw herself on her knees before the King and begged him to restore the abbeys', suggests her loyalties were firmly with traditional religion and that she was the ideal woman to lead the king back home. Observers convinced themselves that this process would start with legitimating Mary as his heir, and putting her back in the line of succession. Chapuys expressed his hope of this on the day of Anne Boleyn's execution and Cromwell seems to have fuelled this belief. Faenza hoped Mary would be declared princess in the parliament of June 1536, because 'the King was much softened', and 'after this would follow the King's return to the Church'. In other words, there was a very real possibility, in the minds of European contemporaries, that Henry would drop all his pretensions to the royal supremacy and reunite his country with Rome. They had reason to suspect this would happen in 1536 – and how different history would have been if it had.[2]

They were, however, mistaken. They calculated without realizing the depth of Henry's investment in the royal supremacy, or the vehemence with which, after the ego-bruising episodes of the fall and Anne's perceived treachery, he would assert his right to exercise in practice the pre-eminent directorial role in the church that he had previously claimed only in law. Henry's self-esteem had also recently suffered another blow, aimed directly at his position as Supreme Head. His own cousin, Reginald Pole, had in March 1536 written a treatise in the form of a letter to Henry VIII, ostensibly for the king's eyes only. This treatise, which became known as *De Unitate* (On the Unity of the Church), attacked Henry's assumption of the title of Supreme Head, sided with the men who had defied him – Fisher and More exhorted Charles V and Francis I to invade and referred to 'whole legions' of a fifth column lurking in England. Pole warned Henry he would never get away with disinheriting Mary and urged the king to repent and do penance. Finally, he compared Henry to past tyrants and the Great Turk, and called him a wild beast, incestuous, a robber, a murderer and an enemy of Christianity. Perhaps it was supposed to shock Henry into submission. Instead, it riled him and further inflamed his sense of outrage and betrayal, which flared out into reaction.[3]

An outline of events suggests how profound this reaction was. Firstly, in March 1536, parliament passed the crucially important Act for the Dissolution of the Lesser Monasteries. In June, after the arrest and death of Anne Boleyn, and Henry's remarriage, Henry signalled he had no intention to resubmit to the authority of the pope. This was illustrated by his requirement that Mary should swear the oath that declared her father's royal supremacy, the invalidity of his marriage to her mother and, therefore, her own illegitimacy. This insistence on Mary's submission was echoed by significant developments in the doctrine and theology of the Anglican Church that suggested the king was starting to exercise his expanded role in the theological leadership of the church (one that had previously been claimed in word but not implemented in deed). Thomas Cromwell, the king's chief minister and, crucially, a layman, had previously exercised authority over the visitation of the English church in the run-up to the act suppressing the lesser monasteries. Now, after being made keeper of the privy seal, Baron Cromwell and a knight, Cromwell was appointed vicegerent in spirituals and vicar-general for the whole church and over *all* ecclesiastical affairs. The king was centralizing religious control. This centralized power was mobilized in July 1536 when Henry VIII published his 'Ten Articles'. This consisted of ten points of doctrine which represented the first doctrinal statement of the Anglican Church and defined acceptable religious belief in England. At the same time, an act was passed in parliament 'extinguishing' papal authority and incurring penalties for all who upheld the rights of the Pope. The act referred to the manner in which the Pope had 'rob[bed] the King's Majesty, being only the supreme head of this his Realm of England immediately under God, of his honour, right and pre-eminence due unto him by the law of God'. The act, therefore, sought to bolster such honour and pre-eminence. These innovations were followed in August 1536 by Cromwell's publication of royal injunctions or orders to enforce the doctrine set out in the Ten Articles.[4]

The overall intention of all these developments was clearly and adamantly to assert Henry VIII's position and rights as Supreme Head of the Church of England. The specific timing of these manoeuvres and their defiant quality in the light of European opinion and the threat of the papal bull seems likely to have been linked to the challenge that recent humiliations had posed to the king's self-esteem and power. By both demanding Mary's submission and demonstrating that as Supreme Head he could dictate doctrine, Henry reasserted the superiority of his status. It was the perfect antidote to a scenario in which Henry VIII's ability to govern had been implicitly questioned. In addition, the theology revealed in these dictates, as in later theological outputs, was particularly focused on the ideas of kingship and obedience, rule and submission, orders and compliance – a set of binaries, that Henry would, as the events of the year unfolded, enshrine even more vehemently. From this point on, we can chart the efforts made to shape English subjects into religious conformity and obedience, and the destruction of the institutions, observances and spectacle of the piety of the late middle ages.[5]

The Dissolution of the Monasteries

The first religious innovation of 1536 was the Act for the Dissolution of the Lesser Monasteries. In 1535, Thomas Cromwell had directed and ordered royal commissioners to examine under oath all monks, nuns, clergy and ecclesiastical officials, in order to produce a catalogue of the annual income of every ecclesiastical benefice and monastic house in the country. These detailed investigations were collected together as the *Valor Ecclesiasticus*. Before they were finished, in late 1535, Cromwell ordered a second visitation of monastic houses, which sought to identify vice, laxity and the practice of 'superstitions' and 'abuses', such as the reverence of suspect relics, shrines, pilgrimages and sexual corruption among the monks. It is no surprise that they found what they were looking for. The private questioning of individual monks and nuns about the leadership of the abbots, the adherence to their Rule and the sincerity of their vocation and their chastity by determined, worldly-wise lawyers inevitably produced the scandal and rumour that the commissioners expected to find. Very few were given the glowing references of Catesby Nunnery, where the commissioners reported that they had found 'the house in very perfect order, the prioress a wise, discreet and religious woman, with nine devout nuns under her, as good as we have ever seen… If any religious house is to stand, none is more meet for the King's charity and pity than Catesby'. The apparent offences and superstitions of other nuns and monks were listed remorselessly in a document called the *Compendium Compertorum*, alongside the name of their founder and annual rent:

…Lichfield Cathedral. – Here a pilgrimage is held to St Chad. Annual rent, 400l. Founder, the King.

Monastery of Repyngdon, alias *Repton.* – Thomas Rede, sub-prior and three others named as sodomites *per voluntaries polluciones.* Superstition: a pilgrimage is made to St Guthlac and his bell, which they put upon people's heads to alleviate headache…

Garadon. – 5 names noted as sodomites, one with 10 boys. 3 of the monks seek release from religion. Foundress, the Countess of Oxford…

Grace Dieu Monialium. – 2 nuns charged with incontinence, with note "*pepererunt*". Superstition: they hold in reverence the girdle and part of the tunic of St Francis, which are supposed to help lying-in women.

Nuns of St. Mary Derby. – Superstition: they have part of the shirt of St Thomas, which is reverenced among pregnant women…

Shelford. – 3 sodomites, 3 guilty of incontinence, 3 desire

release from religion. They venerate the girdle and milk
of St Mary and part of a candle which it is believed she
carried at the time of her purification...

Kaldham Monialium. – Here they have part of Holy Cross
and a finger of St Stephen, which is lent to lying-in
women...

The extraordinary scepticism of these notes, which treats
monastic devotion to relics as subjects fit for mockery, is only
surpassed by the prurient focus on sexual misconduct. The
category 'sodomites' may have been designed, intentionally, to
blacken the reputation of the monks, as to the vast majority was
added the appellation *per voluntaries polluciones* ('by voluntary
pollutions' or self-abuse), which implies masturbation, not
homosexuality. The commissioners also left each monastery
with a strict list of injunctions on how to conduct themselves
in future.[6]

These commissioners worked up until February 1536, but even
before their work was completed, their accumulating evidence
was sufficient basis for the king and Cromwell to present a bill to
parliament requiring all religious houses with an annual income
of less than £200 to be dissolved. The bill, which became law
in March 1536, focused its attack on the 'manifest sin, vicious,
carnal and abominable living [that] is daily used and committed
among the little and small abbeys, priories and other religious
houses of monks, canon and nuns' and how their 'vicious living
shamelessly increases'. The lands, goods and property of the
suppressed monasteries would pass directly to the crown, via
a newly created government department called the Court of
Augmentations. Chapuys commented on 1 April,

the King and Council are busy setting officers for the
provision and exaction of the revenues of the churches
which are to be suppressed; which, it is said, will be

in number above 300, and are expected to bring in a revenue of 120,000 ducats. The silver plate, chalices and reliquaries, the church ornaments, bells, lead from the roofs, cattle and furniture belonging to them, which will come to the King, will be of inestimable amount.

Chapuys was right in that the 'lesser' religious houses totalled nearly 300 – 191 monasteries and 103 nunneries. It is sobering to read the pleas written to Cromwell by abbots asking for clemency or politely declining the opportunity to resign their offices. One John Shepey, abbot of Faversham, to Cromwell's suggestion he resign his charge because of his age and debility, responded that he 'trusts he is not yet so far enfeebled but he can govern as well as ever' and explained that while it might be to his comfort, his resignation and the consequent taxes would put his house into ruin and 'Christ forbid that I should so heinously offend against God and the King as to further the ruin of so godly and ancient a foundation'. Chapuys commented in 1537 that it was a

lamentable thing to see a legion of monks and nuns who have been chased from their monasteries wandering miserably hither and thither seeking means to live, and several honest men have told me that what with monks, nuns and persons dependent on the monasteries suppressed, there were over 20,000 who knew not how to live.

Other letters to Cromwell came from those coveting monastic lands and hoping to get a share of the spoils.[7]

The real question is why the monasteries were attacked in this way. It is certainly true that their great wealth made them an obvious target for a revenue-hungry king. It is hardly laudable that Henry installed the church windows of Rewley Abbey outside Oxford in his bowling alley at Hampton Court. The monasteries were also suspected of treasonous tendencies, being tainted by their allegiance to a foreign ruler, the Pope. Equivocation towards the monasteries perhaps also represented Henry VIII's ambiguity towards the idea of purgatory. One of the primary roles of monasteries was to pray for the souls of the dead in purgatory but Henry VIII's official statements from 1536 would start to cast doubt on this belief. Until late 1536, though, there are reasons to believe that the dissolution of the smaller monasteries was also positively intended to bring about religious reform. The act of 1536 specifically refers to monks and nuns moving from the smaller monastic houses into 'such honourable great monasteries in this realm wherein good religion is observed', suggesting that a wholesale destruction of monasticism was not intended and that morally upright monasteries were thought to exist. The act was the first deployment of the power of the supremacy to change the religious landscape of England by reforming abuses and rectifying vice.[8]

The Ten Articles and Royal Injunctions

In July 1536, the Ten Articles were agreed and published. These Articles were a quickly composed yet authoritative statement of doctrine for the new Anglican Church. According to a letter Henry sent to his bishops in November 1536, the Articles were largely conceived by the king himself. Like many of Henry's later proclamations, they show a preoccupation with bringing unity and concord to his kingdom. They were entitled 'articles devised by the King's Highness Majesty, to establish Christian quietness and unity among us, and to avoid contentious opinions'. The preamble explained that they were written because 'of late, to our great regret, [we are] credibly advertized of such diversity in opinions, as have grown and sprung in this realm'. In order to avoid 'the danger of souls' and 'outward inquietness', after much pain, study, labour and travail, the king and his clergy had agreed which matters are 'commanded of God and are necessary to our salvation'. It was a striking new implementation of the king's prerogative as Supreme Head to assert his competence with his clergy to determine precisely what beliefs and practices were necessary for the salvation of souls.⁹

The doctrine was an odd mix of conservative and evangelical. The first noticeable feature of this doctrinal statement was the recognition of only three sacraments: baptism, Eucharist and penance. This was in contrast to the Roman Catholic Church, which recognized seven sacraments. On the other hand, the articles stated, in line with traditional belief, that baptism was necessary for attaining everlasting life, because infants were born in original sin. Penance, that is, confession and absolution by priests and the performance of good works, was 'necessary for man's salvation'. For 'although Christ and his death be the sufficient oblation, sacrifice, satisfaction and recompense... yet all men truly penitent, contrite and confessed must needs also bring forth the fruits of penance... and also must do all other good works of mercy and charity... or else they shall never be saved'. This, taken with the fifth article that declared sinners attain 'justification by contrition and faith *joined with charity*', was a clear rejection of the evangelical conviction that man was made righteous in the sight of God by faith alone, and not by the performance of good works. The articles added that Christ's body and blood were 'verily, substantially and really' present in the Eucharist, though the emotive term 'transubstantiation', associated with Catholicism, was absent.¹⁰

The Articles also modified certain traditionally integral religious practices. One article praised the honouring of saints, but 'not with that confidence and honour which are only due unto God', nor in the 'vain superstition' that prayer to a saint would be more readily answered than that to God. Another proclaimed that while it was right to have images in church, people should not cense them, kneel before them, offer things to them or 'other like worshippings'. Finally, the last article ambiguously concluded that, while it was a good and charitable deed to pray for souls departed, it was admitted that 'the place where they be, the name thereof and kinds of pain there' were uncertain and unknown, and that the abuses committed by the Roman church under the name of 'purgatory' should 'be clearly put away'. One could pray for the dead, but what such prayers would do was unclear.

In other words, the Ten Articles, as a doctrinal statement of a reformed church, actually set out an ambiguous programme of a little reform mixed in with substantial amounts of conservatism, especially because salvation depended on good works as much as faith, a tenet that Henry held to until his death. This was perhaps partly because it was not a full and comprehensive statement of doctrine but a limited one only dealing with the controversial issues of the day. But as we shall see, it also seems to have reflected Henry VIII's key concerns and convictions. The most significant innovation was to reduce the number of sacraments from seven to three (which was bumped up to four in 1543, when marriage was reinstated, an unsurprising addition for a king who obviously esteemed it greatly). In one fell swoop, this downgraded the sacraments which boosted clerical power and status: confirmation, extreme unction and priestly ordination. By reducing the power of the clergy, Henry boosted his own sacred status. It was crucial, in this year, for Henry to defend the supremacy that he had created.[11]

The theme of Henry's Supreme Headship was also dominant in a set of royal injunctions issued to the clergy in August 1536. These were essentially designed to enforce the Ten Articles at parish level and suggest that the impact of the Articles in practice may have been more than mildly reformist. The crux of them was to ensure that the clergy continued to preach against papal supremacy while expounding the content of the Ten Articles, so people would know 'which of them be necessary to be believed and observed for their salvation, and which be not necessary'. The clergy were reminded that for the

abolishing and extirpation of the Bishop of Rome's pretended and usurped power and jurisdiction... and for

123

the establishment and confirmation of the king's authority and jurisdiction within the same, as of the supreme head of the Church of England, [they] shall to the uttermost of their wit, knowledge and learning, purely, sincerely, and without any colour or dissimulation declare, manifest, and open for the space of one quarter of a year now next ensuing, once every Sunday, and after that at the leastwise twice every quarter, in their sermons and other collations, that the Bishop of Rome's usurped power... was of most just causes taken away and abolished...

This was not the first time that the clergy had been ordered to preach on royal supremacy – in June 1535, they had similarly been instructed to preach on the subject every Sunday – but this reiteration suggested that the issue remained – or had again become – deeply topical and important. In July 1536, Henry also revoked a number of licences to preach, citing the number of 'indiscreet persons, with neither learning nor judgment, who... blow abroad their folly', and instructing Cranmer to ensure that 'our people may be fed with wholesome food, neither savouring the corruption of the bishop of Rome nor led into doubt by novelties'. The corruption meant was repeated in the injunctions, which repeated the command that noone should extol images, relics, miracles or go on pilgrimages for any saint, 'to the intent that all superstition and hypocrisy, crept into divers man's hearts, may vanish away'. This was in keeping with the Ten Articles but a radical departure from traditional religion. For the vast majority of illiterate people in early Tudor England, their faith was something forged in the visual and kinaesthetic – it was a religion of the eye and not the written word. These alterations to their relationship with objects they could see and touch, while stopping far short of the iconoclasm of Edward VI's reign, was to make that relationship fraught and uncertain; it was to rob their faith of some of its colour and confidence. In addition, the rhythm of their faith was also to change. A proclamation, issued between the Articles and injunctions, decreed that saints' feast days were to be kept on the first Sunday in October and not on the traditional saints' days, when work would continue as usual. 'At one stroke,' says one commentator, 'the Crown decimated the ritual year'. The church had been shaken up, while still maintaining conservative perspectives that would have disappointed those hoping for the sort of reform seen on the Continent. It was a peculiarly Henrician settlement.[12]

CHAPTER 12

The Role of Henry VIII in Later Reformation

The promulgations of 1536 suggest that Henry VIII intended to shape the Church of England in line with his own personal religious beliefs. Yet the progress of the Reformation in England after 1536 has produced two debates in recent scholarship – one questioning the personal involvement of Henry VIII in the shaping of religious policy, and the other asking whether reform was halted and reversed in the late 1530s and 1540s.[1]

Historians have been divided over Henry VIII's role in the Reformation and his influence on religious policy, which really comes down to a difference of opinion about Henry VIII's character. One set of historians has described the divorce and break from Rome as a politically expedient act to satisfy the king's desire for an heir, and every attendant or subsequent act of religious reformation as incidental and unintended by the king. These historians paint Henry as a king easily manipulated by his close associates. The king was a puppet, whose suspicious, fickle and callous personality meant that he could be controlled by the dominant group or faction at court. These historians attribute bursts of religious reform, for instance in the 1530s, wholly to the influence of evangelicals at court, such as Thomas Cromwell and Thomas Cranmer, Henry's archbishop of Canterbury from 1533. Similarly, they hold the new power of conservatives at court responsible for the apparent retreats from reform in the 1540s. In this reading, evangelicals at court could tempt and confound the king into religious reform that Henry never intended nor foresaw.[2]

But a recent theory has rejected this view of Henry as a vacillating pawn of his ministers and stressed instead the evidence of the king's firm direction of the Reformation. For some, this had an erratic and unpredictable quality. Diarmaid MacCulloch describes Henry's beliefs as a 'ragbag of emotional preferences'. Others stress its controlled coherence along a *via media* or middle way. 'The Henrician Reformation was,' says Greg Walker, 'just that, a Reformation begotten, nurtured and finally almost smothered in its infancy, by its creator; Henry VIII himself.' It was Henry's undertaking, and not Cromwell's, though the latter was undoubtedly important and influential. Henry may have been ruthless, but he was also deliberate and rational, choosing to do what he considered to be in the best interests of his country and church. The impetus of the Reformation was the conscience of the king, and his conscience defined the religious system of a whole kingdom.[3]

If this is true, Henry's own devotion and religious fervour are very important. We know Henry was devout. In his early years, he went on pilgrimage to Walsingham and he heard several Masses a day. He also defended the Pope, battling both by sword against Louis XII of France and by pen, in writing the *Assertio Septum Sacramentorum* [*Defence of the Seven Sacraments*] in 1521, a diatribe refuting Luther's criticisms of the papacy. Throughout his life, Henry cherished his beautiful rosary and maintained the Latin Mass in all its splendour. His break from Katherine and Rome, and his marriage to Anne only played out as it did because Henry 'refused to see the question as anything other than theological'. He also took time off from hunting and fighting wars to read and write theology. In the great crises of his life – after Jane Seymour's death and Catherine Howard's infidelity – Henry patiently and eagerly corrected theological drafts. In November 1536, he scolded his bishops for their contemptuous words against the articles he had set forth. The king who said it pained him to write penned around 100 corrections and annotations to the text of the Bishops' Book, a statement of doctrine prepared by his bishops in 1537. This is a testament to his zeal. Finally, some of his meditative annotations to his personal psalter, which was given to him in 1542, are touching. In response to the first few verses of the modern Psalm 28, 'To you I will cry, O Lord my rock: Do not be silent to me', Henry has added in the margin, '*extollatione manuum*', 'with hands raised'. To his reading of the modern Psalm 102:9–11

> For I have eaten ashes like bread,
> And mingled my drink with weeping,
> Because of Your indignation and Your wrath:
> For You have lifted me up, and cast me away.
> My days are like a shadow that lengthens;
> And I wither away like grass.

he adds, '*non in perpetuum irascetur*', 'he will not be angry for ever'. Such heartfelt engagement with the psalms of David, with whom he identified, suggests true religious feeling. He also left money in his will to ensure that prayers were said for his soul (although the amount he left suggests that this may have been him hedging his bets).[4]

Others have concluded, though, that Henry's faith was dutiful and ritualistic. J. J. Scarisbrick described it as 'a formal, habitual thing, devoid of much interiority'. Henry's elevation of the authority figure of the Pope in his *Assertio* and his original

Bust portrait of Henry VIII, Hans Holbein, c.1536–37

Henry VIII by an unknown artist c.1520

Remigius van Leemput, copy after Holbein's
Whitehall mural, 1667

iii

Cartoon Showing Henry VIII and
Henry VII, Hans Holbein, 1537

The Walker – Henry VIII, artist unknown,
painted between 1537 and 1562?

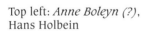

Top left: *Anne Boleyn (?)*, Hans Holbein

Top right: *Jane Seymour*

Bottom left: Portrait miniature of *Henry Fitzroy*, Lucas Horenbout, 1534–35

Bottom right: *Archbishop Thomas Cranmer*, 1546

Thomas Cromwell, after Hans Holbein, 1533–34,

Title page of the Great Bible, published 1539

deference to the Pope and to the law over the divorce issue (it was undoubtedly to Clement VII's surprise that Henry insisted on marrying Anne rather than taking her as a mistress) illustrates a tendency to inflated conceptions of authority and to legalism. In adopting the title of Supreme Head, his elevated sense of authority was being transferred from the Pope to a recognition of his own responsibility and authority as king to govern the church in his kingdom.[5]

The second question historians have asked is whether steps towards Protestantism were halted in the later part of Henry VIII's reign. Many have argued that by 1539 Henry VIII felt too much reform had occurred and so he inaugurated a period of reaction and increased conservatism. In fact, the evidence strongly suggests that Henry stayed true to the legacy of 1536. In only one major idea – Henry VIII's attitude towards monasticism – was there significant change. Otherwise, every important principle of doctrine that Henry set out in 1536 was retained throughout his reign. The religious developments after 1536 show that it was decisive in the formation of the Anglican Church.

Firstly, after 1536, Henry VIII's perspective towards the monasteries changed. In October–December 1536, a huge rebellion in the north of the country against the king in reaction to, among other things, the suppression of the monasteries (explored in detail in chapter 15), fanned into flame Henry's ire towards monasticism and cemented his association between monks and treason. His responses to his commanders dealing with the rebellion constantly reveal his belief in the monks' scandalous behaviour, hypocrisy, vice and 'traitorous conspiracies', and his commanders were instructed to deal with them most severely. From 1537, the erstwhile 'honourable great monasteries' also came under attack. They suffered fresh pressures, harassments and taxes. Further investigations were made into their behaviour, and one by one, abbots were persuaded into surrendering their houses 'voluntarily' to the king's commissioners. Some resisted – the abbot of Glastonbury, Richard Whiting, was one of a handful who never conceded. In September 1539, commissioners were sent to interview him and, although his answers did not give them the proof they needed, a search of his study produced treasonable and papist literature. This evidence of 'his cankered and traitorous heart and mind against the King's majesty and his succession' were grounds enough for his imprisonment in the Tower and trial two months later in Wells. The justice of this trial can perhaps be judged by the fact that the execution had already been arranged for the following day on Glastonbury Tor, overlooking the deserted shell of his former abbey. Once he had been hanged and quartered, his head was left to rot above the abbey gate.[6]

What had started in 1536 as a reformation became, as a result of the events of late 1536, nothing less than a determined destruction of monasticism, culminating in the Act for the Dissolution of the Abbeys in 1539. In total, some 800 religious houses were dissolved between 1536 and 1540. The monks and nuns within them were pensioned off and put back into the community, while the lands and income of the foundations were absorbed by the Crown or sold to nobility as the Crown saw fit. This was a decisive and dramatic change, considerably more dramatic than the Reformation in many princely Lutheran states. Across the country, people had witnessed the dissolution and destruction of the monasteries, and it permanently altered the religious and physical landscape of England.[7]

Aside from the dissolution of the monasteries, there were two royal decisions after 1536 that clearly continued the path towards reform. In September 1538, the order was given for English Bibles to be put in every parish church in the land, and extracts from the New Testament to be read out every Sunday and holy day. This decision was, in comparison to Henry's early beliefs, an extraordinary volte-face, and it has a haunting link to 1536. William Tyndale had been condemned for heresy by Henry VIII (despite Henry's fondness for the doctrines of his book,

The Obedience of a Christian Man); he fled and was eventually arrested in Flanders in 1535. After a long imprisonment, Tyndale was strangled and burned at the stake in October 1536; his dying words were a prayer, 'Lord, open the king of England's eyes!' His prayer was answered. In 1538, Cromwell commissioned Miles Coverdale to produce a Bible in English, which was printed from late 1538 and distributed in 1539. The magnificent title-page of Coverdale's Great Bible shows Henry, in the full regalia of a sacred king and under a rather squashed God, munificently handing out the Word of God to the people. The title-page was a visual reinforcement of Henry VIII's royal supremacy, making it clear that papal authority had been replaced in England by a direct relationship between God and the king. The illustration showed how Henry's position as Supreme Head gave him Henry temporal power, symbolized by Cromwell, and spiritual authority, symbolized by Cranmer. The fact that this powerful image would have been present in every parish church means that it truly can be called a 'consciously planned act of mass propaganda'. The title-page also contained another crucial message, which deliberately responded to king's promulgation of doctrine in 1536 and the rebellion of later that year: it reaffirmed the role of the king in guiding the spirituality of his people and reasserted that this guidance would happen through the established social and political hierarchy. The role of the lowest ranks in society is depicted as one of simple obedience – they cry 'God save the King!' Also, in 1538, Henry VIII issued a new set of injunctions, which expressed the 1536 concern to avoid the worship of images, but which were more strongly worded, stating the need to avoid 'the most detestable sin of idolatry'.[8]

There are four developments which are thought to chart the king's reaction to reform and repudiation of his earlier religious decisions. Firstly, in November 1538, Henry presided over the trial of John Lambert. Dressed ostentatiously in white, the colour of theological purity, Henry personally disputed theology with Lambert, who had been denounced as a heretic for being a sacramentarian (sacramentarians were radical evangelical Protestants who believed that the bread and wine of the Eucharist did not become the actual body and blood of Jesus Christ). It is a salutary thought that this difference of opinion was sufficient for Lambert to be classified as an extremist and a heretic – matters of theology were life and death issues in the sixteenth century. After five hours of hearing authorities speak on the Eucharist, Henry asked Lambert whether he would accept the arguments for the real presence of Christ in the sacrament of communion that had been put before him. Lambert's answer hedged his bets: 'I commend my soul into the hands of God, but my body I wholly yield and submit unto your clemency.' But it seems that on this issue, Henry was not inclined to be merciful. He replied, 'In that case you must die, for I will not be a patron unto heretics' and Lambert was condemned to be burned as a heretic at Smithfield. But this wasn't so much reaction against reform as a way – admittedly a rather hideous one – for Henry to delineate the boundaries of his reformation. It was a powerful enactment of the definition of the Eucharist as the 'real presence' of Christ that had featured in the Ten Articles of 1536.[9]

Secondly, a key piece of evidence cited by those who say the reformation ended in 1539 is the Act of Six Articles. This act, designed to abolish 'diversity in opinions', affirmed six points of doctrine and had a conservative flavour. It reiterated the real presence of the Christ in the bread and the wine and stated that communion of both kinds (that is, both bread and wine) was unnecessary for the laity. More controversially, it decreed that priests were not to marry and that vows of chastity and widowhood were to be kept. Finally, it concluded that private Masses were to continue (though it conceded they were not necessary) and again insisted on the obligatory nature of auricular confession. Terrible penalties were threatened for those who failed to keep these articles. Many historians have considered this act a retrograde step into conservative reaction, following the chronicler Edward Hall who described it as the 'whip with six strings... the bloody statute'. In reality though, the articles did not actually undo any of the reforms of the 1530s. The purpose of the Six Articles was to proclaim the Henrician orthodoxy of 1536 and to signal that some areas were off-limits for Henry's reformation. Having said that, the clause forbidding the marriage of clergy was an area in which English evangelicals had seriously hoped for further reformation. Expecting imminent change on this issue, Cranmer himself had secretly married the niece of the reformer Andreas Osiander when on a diplomatic mission to Nuremberg in 1532, and had had to send her into hiding before banishing her completely.[10]

The third event that is seen as evidence of reaction against reform is the publication of Henry VIII's reworking of a theological text put together by his bishops in 1543. This was called 'A Necessary Doctrine and Erudition for any Christian Man, set forth by the King's Majesty of England', but became known as the King's Book. It was Henry's final and definitive statement of doctrine. The King's Book differed from the Ten Articles in that it reinstated the sacrament of matrimony. It once again rejected the view that had been put forward by his bishops – that justification was by faith alone. Instead, it confirmed Henry's conviction that justification resulted from a combination of God's work and man's own deeds – but this was not new: it had been announced in 1536! In addition, the King's Book reiterated Henry's unchanging stance on the Eucharist as the 'very body and blood of Christ in its very substance'. Even on the subject of purgatory, the tone was very similar to the articles of 1536, again concluding that, while praying for the souls of the departed was a good thing, the place and condition of such souls was uncertain. The papist abuses of purgatory were again distained, but this time it was explicitly stated 'we therefore abstain from the name of purgatory, and no more dispute or reason thereof'. This final clause suggests that above all what Henry wanted to avoid was undue dispute on the subject. The reason for this new statement of doctrine is explained in its preamble. It praised the initial progress of Henry's reformation, stating that 'in the time of darkness and ignorance, finding our people seduced and drawn from the truth by hypocrisy and superstition' the king had powerfully 'travailed to purge and cleanse our realm'. But people's hearts had become inclined to 'sinister understandings of scripture, presumption, arrogancy, carnal liberty and contention', so the King's Book was intended – just as the Ten Articles and the Six Articles had been – to eradicate 'diversity in opinions' by setting forth a clear, uniform doctrine for everyone to follow. It was not new – just a necessary repeat.[11]

The final piece of evidence used to suggest reform had ended in 1539 is the 1543 'Act for the Advancement of True Religion'. This Act put restrictions on who could read the new English Bible, limiting access to nobles, gentry and merchants, and barring all 'women, artificers, apprentices, journeymen, serving men… husbandmen and labourers' from reading the scriptures. Was this reactionary? It does seem to be, but not to the idea of an English Bible – instead the restriction suggests that the step of handing out the Bible to the masses was now perceived to have caused more contention than clarity. The goal had been to remove ignorance – the result appeared to be yet greater disputes and divisions. In 1545, Henry complained at 'how unreverently that most precious jewel the word of God is disputed, rimed, sung and jangled in every alehouse and tavern' and explained that the scriptures had been translated into English 'only to inform your own conference, and to instruct your children and family, and not to dispute'. This is in keeping with Henry's depiction of the proper ordering of society on the frontispiece of the Great Bible: he had only ever intended the Word of God to be taught by superiors to those under their care. No doubt in his mind, this was not a deviation from his earlier pronouncements – just a change of method to achieve the same result.[12]

A change of method is also, I suggest, why historians have intimated that the last years of Henry VIII's reign saw a reaction and return to conservatism. While Henry's theology might have remained relatively unchanged, his methods of dealing with dissidents did change. After 1536, he became vastly more repressive and harsh towards those who disagreed with his religious views. This increased despotism became a marked feature of his character and stemmed from an inflamed response towards betrayal, treason and rebellion – which Henry VIII had started to conflate – as a result of the events of this year (see chapter 18 for more on this subject). Perhaps as Luther later mockingly commented, Henry 'want[ed] to be God and to do as he please[d]'.[13]

CHAPTER 13

Henry VIII's Theology

$\mathcal{H}$enry VIII's theology seems to have situated itself somewhere between the later identities of Protestant and Catholic, and even somewhere between the contemporary beliefs of evangelicals and conservatives.

There appear to have been six key characteristics of Henry VIII's theology, which were all present in the statements of doctrine produced in 1536. This is not to suggest nothing changed in Henry's thinking – as we've clearly seen, his reaction to the rebellion of 1536 significantly altered his approach to monasticism, while his thinking on access to the vernacular scriptures fluctuated in response to the priority he gave to knowledge or unity. The people around him mattered too. Henry did not make policy in isolation and was in fact always quick to highlight the role played by his bishops and nobility in the creation of religious statutes and proclamations. Yet key values and themes emerge which do appear to be roughly consistent.[1]

The first was that for Henry VIII, the royal supremacy and his divine-right kingship under God, with responsibility for the cure of souls and the righting of religious abuses in the church, had become an article of faith. Henry had grown convinced of his unique position as God's anointed deputy on earth, believing that the Supreme Headship was his birthright, and expected others to believe it too. This was contrasted in his mind with excessive clerical power and status. This was evident in the message clergy were told to preach in 1536, the king's promulgation of doctrine, the stunning visual depiction of the supremacy on the title-page of the Great Bible and even in his questioning of John Lambert. His self-identification with leaders of the Old Testament, such as Abraham and David, is seen in such acts as his commissioning of the vastly expensive Abraham tapestries in 1540 to hang in his Great Hall at Hampton Court. It is also seen in the representation of David on the frontispiece of the Great Bible (suggesting Henry had picked up where David left off) and his approval of his depiction as David in the illustrations of his personal psalter which was presented to him in 1542 by Jean Mallard. Henry, like Abraham and David, was a leader who had a close relationship with God, modelled theocratic kingship and had a mandate to lead his people out of error into truth. In return for his royal care, he expected obedience from his subjects, in conscience as well as action.[2]

Secondly, Henry was preoccupied with preserving unity and concord in his kingdom. The Ten Articles had been entitled 'articles devised... to establish Christian quietness and unity... and to avoid contentious opinions', and the Six Articles and King's Book reiterated this theme. So did an English primer, or prayer book, that Henry VIII issued in 1545. Designed to set forward one uniform manner of praying 'for the avoiding of strife and contention', it included a five-page-long prayer for the peace of the church, which vividly expresses Henry VIII's horror of the 'chaos' of 'evil wavering opinions'. A particularly striking example of this concern was Henry's Christmas speech of 1545 to parliament (what Diarmaid MacCulloch has called the 'pioneer Christmas broadcast'). Henry took the unusual step of speaking for himself (rather than via the Lord Chancellor) for he alone could 'open and set forth my mind and meaning, and the secrets of my heart'. It was an impassioned and eloquent speech; one of those who heard him remarked how Henry's kingly, fatherly speech 'was such a joy and marvellous comfort' that the listener reckoned the day one of the happiest of his life. In it, Henry lamented the religious divisions in his kingdom, pleading with his subjects about the lack of charity and concord amongst them and the presence of much discord and dissension in their place. Henry brought himself to tears as he beseeched his people to live in unity and, according to William Petre, few of his audience could refrain from weeping too.[3]

Henry's third article of faith was the real presence of Christ's body and blood in the Eucharist. He asserted this in the Ten Articles in 1536 and in all later statements of doctrine, always avoiding the contentious and papist term 'transubstantiation' but, similarly, rejecting the sacramentarian view of the Eucharist as a mere memorial. This is why he presided over Lambert's trial and maintained the Mass in his own private chapel until his death. Error in this also seems to have caused greatest offence – of twenty-eight people burned as heretics in 1540–46, twenty of them were sacramentarians.[4]

A fourth doctrine of great importance to Henry was his conviction that Christian belief should manifest itself in good and lawful behaviour, and that anything discouraging this was erroneous. This meant Henry refused to follow Luther and consistently rejected the evangelical notion of 'justification by faith alone', stalwartly arguing that justification was by faith and grace 'joined with charity'. This conviction informed the changes he made to the Bishop's Book to produce his definitive statement of theology, the King's Book. It was on this basis that William Jerome, the vicar of Stepney, was sent to the Tower on the king's command after he had preached at St Paul's Cross on 7 March 1540. There, Jerome had said that 'the promise of justification is without condition, for he that putteth a condition on it doth exclude grace'. It was a thesis that Henry could not accept. The king's antipathy towards it was probably rooted in his concern that without the restraining power of a doctrine of justification by good works, wicked, immoral and rebellious behaviour would be unleashed among his subjects. One can only speculate on the personal and psychological reasons for his aversion to free grace.[5]

Henry was also convinced of the duty incumbent upon him to preside over the reform of religious abuses in the church. 1536 saw the beginning of this process with the dissolution of the lesser vice-ridden monasteries, a reduction in the number of saints' days and reform in attitudes towards images, shrines and pilgrimages. In a letter of 1537 to his bishops, Henry urged them to eliminate 'all manner of idolatry, superstition, [and] hypocrisy'. It was a theme that recurred in the injunctions of 1538, the King's Book and in Henry's primer of 1545 in which, unusually, the saints were not individually mentioned by name. Perhaps it is most obvious in the way Henry, in his annotations to his psalter, associated himself, not only with David, but also Josiah and Phineas, king and judge of the Old Testament, ordained by God to reform religious abuses, rescue Israel from idolatry and destroy superstitious images and shrines. The role that Henry had conceived for himself was one that showed a commitment to reform and renewal in the church, while insisting on unity and the essential truths of the faith.[6]

Finally, Henry appears to have believed that he was establishing a workable reformed way between the religious extremes of heresy and papistry. His purpose was, as he declared in January 1536, that his flock should be

fed and nourished with wholesome and godly doctrine and not seduced with the filthy and corrupt abominations of the bishop of Rome or his disciples and adherents, nor yet by the setting forth of novelties and the continual inculcation of things not necessary, brought and led to unquietness of mind and doubt of conscience.

In his 1545 speech to parliament, the king complained about those 'too stiff in their old mumpsimus' and others 'too busy and curious in their new sumpsimus'. 'Mumpsimus' was a common evangelical jibe at the Latin mutterings of the conservatives; 'sumpsimus' is derived from the Latin *sumere*, to take up. His impartiality was brutally enacted at Smithfield in July 1540 when three papists, Richard Fetherston, Edward Powell and Thomas Abel were hanged at the same time that Robert Barnes, Thomas Garrett and William Jerome were burned for heresy. The parallel execution of three religious radicals and three papists was a dramatic, striking event. The French ambassador at the time, Charles de Marillac, commented, 'it was a strange spectacle to see the adherents of two opposite parties die thus on the same day and at the same hour… the scene was as painful as it was monstrous'. The historian Christopher Haigh has described the deaths of the six martyrs as a 'gruesome symmetry'.[7]

There were other strands of thought in Henry's theology – the abhorrence of clerical marriage, for instance, and the insistence on social hierarchy and order in spirituality (quite unlike the Protestant commitment to a 'priesthood of all believers'), but these six values were constants – and all had been articulated (if not in all fullness) in 1536, when Henry, as Supreme Head, started to prescribe the theology of the nation. His conclusions derived from his own studies of scripture, together with the judgments of his advisers, but there was a strong sense that some of his judgments were also influenced by his reactionary approach to circumstances, chiefly, the 1536 threat of rebellion and disobedience.

CHAPTER 14

The Aftermath of the Reformation

*I*n his role as Supreme Head of the Church of England, Henry VIII's reformation brought great upheaval and uncertainty to many and altered traditional religious practices. The dissolution of the monasteries and sale of monastic lands changed the religious, social, architectural and topographical face of Britain. The destruction of monastic buildings was of huge architectural consequence, even while it preserved important buildings through the setting up of secular cathedrals. The sale of monastic lands created a land market in England, enriching a new British aristocracy and redefining where the nobility lived. It could be argued that the buying and selling of land and the building of new houses for the nobility on the outskirts of London in fact created the Home Counties and the ideal of the English country house.

Henry VIII was also the first English king to authorize the translation and publication of the Bible in English. Ordering that an English Bible be put in every parish church in the land, allowed, for the first time, the access of all English people to this crucial religious text in the vernacular – even despite the act of 1543, for this was a very difficult act to enforce. As many recent commentators have noted, the English language was decisively shaped by translations of the Bible into English in Henry VIII's reign. The translation by William Tyndale and the adoption of many of his turns of phrase into the officially sanctioned Great Bible of 1539 gave us classic formulations such as 'the powers that be', 'signs of the times', 'all things to all men', 'let there be light', 'a law unto themselves', 'my brother's keeper', 'a man after his own heart', 'scapegoat', 'give up the ghost', 'the salt of the earth' and 'blessed are the peacemakers'. The irony is that while Henry insisted on his right to tell people what to believe, his actions allowed ordinary people to engage with scripture and God directly, and the legacy of this tenet of evangelicalism has fundamentally fashioned our ideas about the personal nature of religion and spirituality.

While there is a horror in the twenty-eight people burned as heretics after 1540, and the fourteen executed for papistry, Henry's accommodation with Protestantism meant that England did not see the bloody inter-Nicene wars of the continent. In Holland, in 1539–45, 105 people died, while the later Wars of Religion in France were bloody affairs – 2,000 people died in Paris alone on 24 August 1572 in the St Bartholomew's Day Massacre. Yet it is ironic that Henry's desperate anxiety about religious unity could not prevent the religious extremes and reverses the reigns of his son, Edward, and his daughter, Mary. The tutors that Henry VIII chose for his son – Richard Cox and John Cheke – were reformist, evangelically inclined scholars from Cambridge, and Edward, together with his Lord Protector (the brother of Jane Seymour), presided over a thorough reformation during his reign. Had Henry VIII known or guessed this would be the case? Mary's accession to the throne turned the tide the other way, and 300 were executed for heresy in her five-year reign, including the former archbishop, Thomas Cranmer, in Oxford on 25 March 1556. It was the idiosyncrasy of Henry's religious beliefs that made the division likely.[1]

Perhaps the real successor to Henry's reformation was Elizabeth I. It may be easy to contrast the policies of the queen who famously had no desire 'to make windows into men's hearts' with the king who published an act 'abolishing diversity in opinions'. Yet in reality the substance of the Elizabethan religious settlement reflected, in large part, the priorities and values of Elizabeth's father, Henry VIII. The Acts of Supremacy and Uniformity of 1559 powerfully echoed Henry's commitment to the English Crown as Supreme Head (although Elizabeth became Supreme Governor, partly in deference to her gender), and to Henry's preoccupation with unity. They illustrated Elizabeth I's intention to keep religion under the control of the Crown, as her father had done. The Spanish ambassador to her court, Count de Feria, reported that she 'resolved to restore religion as her father left it'. Under her archbishop, Matthew Parker, who had been Henry VIII's chaplain, Elizabeth mediated a course between the extremes of Edward and Mary as if determined to adhere to Henry VIII's middle way between the 'abominations of the bishop of Rome' and 'novelties and... things not necessary'. In addition, following Henry VIII, the Elizabethan Royal Injunctions of 1559, and later, in 1563, the Thirty-nine Articles, showed a resolve to continue the eradication of idolatry and superstitious practices, such as pilgrimages, invocation of saints and the worship of images and relics, while avoiding the intense iconoclasm of Edward VI's reign. The wording of the Act of Uniformity, in contrast to the original Reformation bill, allowed for a continued understanding of the Eucharist as the real presence of Christ, a view that Henry VIII had insisted upon. Elizabeth told Feria that 'she differed very little from [Roman Catholics], as she believed that God was in the sacrament of the Eucharist and only dissented from two or three things in the Mass', even though the Thirty-nine Articles of 1563 explicitly rejected 'transubstantiation'. Henry and Elizabeth may well also have shared opinions on purgatory and the sufficiency of scripture and, although clerical marriage was permitted in Elizabeth's reign, she herself appears to have abhorred it, and never received the wives of clerics at court.[2]

Only in one crucial aspect did Henry's daughter substantially alter her religious inheritance. The Thirty-nine Articles adopted that most Protestant of doctrines, that the justification of man came by faith and not by works. As a result, only two sacraments (baptism and the Eucharist) were to be recognized by the Anglican Church – not the three of Henry's Ten Articles (or the four of the King's Book). The third, penance, had no place in this new Protestant understanding of justification. Yet even here, the change appears to be simply one that was a logical result of the passing of time and changing attitudes towards what were the extremities of faith in the 1530s. Few mainstream evangelicals during Henry's reign held to this Lutheran doctrine. In addition, the Thirty-nine Articles were keen to stress, immediately after the assertion of *solafidenism*, the need for good works that 'spring necessarily of a true and lively faith', suggesting a continued deference to the faith of her father, in spirit if not in letter.

Henry VIII was a more pious and devout man than is currently touted in popular history. His personal beliefs came to define the religion of a kingdom. From 1536 until Henry's death in 1547, there was, between Catholicism and Protestantism, 'Henricianism', and while it was unable to protect England from the confessional divisions of Edward and Mary's reigns, it greatly influenced the Elizabethan religious settlement, which has shaped and defined Anglicanism to this day.[3]

PART FOUR
Henry the Tyrant

I saw a royal throne
Where Justice should have sit,
But in her stead was one
Of moody cruel wit.

Anne Askew, from *The Ballad which
Anne Askew Made and Sang
when She was in Newgate*[1]

*I*n 1521, Cardinal Wolsey commissioned the master craftsman Giovanni del Maiano to make him eight terracotta roundels to adorn his palace at Hampton Court. These painted and gilded roundels were busts of Roman emperors, and in this age of humanism, they symbolized the qualities of a good ruler, which Wolsey, in commissioning them, was celebrating in his king. When Henry VIII took over Hampton Court a few years later, the roundels remained. Yet the paragons of good rule either side of the Great Gatehouse at Hampton Court were – and still are – busts of the emperors Tiberius and Nero. One was not afraid to be hated and famously bestowed severe punishments on traitors and the other known for persecuting Christians and pursuing his lusts; both, in other words, renowned tyrants. Although in 1521, Henry was regarded as England's golden prince, in 1536, observers may have had good reason to link these unfortunate examples of oppression more closely to the kingdom's crown. For such injudicious choices inadvertently prefigured an opinion that was gaining ground in England in the 1530s, culminating in 1536 – that Henry VIII was, in fact, a tyrant.

This is the image of Henry VIII that has descended to posterity. It is the one that fills films and popular literature today. Even mere decades after Henry VIII's death, Sir Walter Raleigh wrote, in the preface to his *History of the World*, the infamous lines:

Now for King Henry the Eighth; if all the pictures and patterns of a merciless prince were lost in the world, they might all again be painted to the life, out of the story of this king. For how many servants did he advance in haste (but for what virtue no man could suspect) and with the change of his fancy ruined again, no man knowing for what offence? To how many others of more desert gave he abundant flowers, from whence to gather honey and in the end of harvest burned them in the hive? How many wives did he cut off, and cast off, as his fancy and affection changed? How many princes of the blood (whereof some

147

of them for age could hardly crawl towards the block) with a world of others of all degrees (of whom our common chronicles have kept the account) did he execute?

Yet, for those who lived during Henry's reign, it was a perilous thing to call one's king a tyrant. From 1535, it could even be fatal. A remarkable act passed in 1534, which came into effect in February 1535, stated that 'if any person or persons... do maliciously wish, will or desire by words or writings, or by craft imagine, invent, practise or attempt any bodily harm to be done or committed to the King's most royal person' or to 'slanderously and maliciously publish and pronounce... that the King our sovereign lord should be heretic, schismatic, tyrant, infidel or usurper of the crown', they would be guilty of high treason. The charge was often not directly spoken in England, for walls had ears. But it was the talk of foreigners, was alluded to in English court poetry and was whispered among commons; for 1536 saw the largest ever single popular uprising against a reigning English monarch. This uprising was a series of linked rebellions in Lincolnshire and Yorkshire of up to 50,000 rebels from the north who called themselves Pilgrims of Grace, and whom Henry did not have sufficient troops to face, let alone defeat, in battle. It was whispered among these Pilgrims that perhaps the king was the 'mouldwarp' or mole, an evil and tyrannous king prophesied by Merlin, who would bring down the kingdom. Why had the country, which had rejoiced at Henry's accession, broken faith with him? Opposition stemmed, in part, from the dubious legality and shocking treatment of Thomas More and Bishop John Fisher in 1535, but this further disloyalty, in a year of challenge and betrayal, only entrenched Henry's position such that the events of 1536 and afterwards were to make More and Fisher's deaths look like harbingers of worse to come. By these latter years of his reign, Henry VIII had become intransigent, volatile, reactionary and dangerous to know.[2]

CHAPTER 15

The Pilgrimage of Grace

The events of early 1536 had exposed Henry VIII to betrayal, ill health and his own mortality, all of which had made him both disillusioned and mistrustful. But the accompanying challenge and ridicule of his virility, which carried with it the question of his ability to rule a household (and thus a kingdom), helped produce in the king a reaction that cemented his pride and obduracy. These elements were all present in his response to those who rebelled against him between October and December 1536, and the cycle of perceived treachery and reaction was to be repeated again and again, with important and long-lasting consequences.

The rebellion, which was actually a series of linked local revolts, started with an uprising in Louth in Lincolnshire. Two days after Michaelmas, on Sunday 1 October, Thomas Foster, a yeoman with land worth £10, had warned the congregation assembled to process around the church after Mass that they 'be like to follow [the crosses] no more'. He was referring to the valuable silver processional crosses belonging to the church. His outburst ignited the currents of fear that were sweeping through

149

the area as a result of the religious changes of the last few years, namely the break with Rome, the royal supremacy, the new doctrine recently set out in the Ten Articles, the treatment of the clergy and the act commanding the dissolution of the lesser monasteries. In October 1536, three sets of government commissioners were working simultaneously in Lincolnshire: one to evaluate the resources of the smaller monasteries; one assessing and collecting a government subsidy; and another investigating the morals and competence of the clergy. The presence of these commissioners had sparked anxious rumours about the pace of religious change and the future intentions of the government towards those things which the commons regarded as their own and central to the spiritual well-being of the kingdom: the parish churches, the monasteries and the jewels and plate used in processions and Masses, of which the silver crosses at Louth were fine examples.[1]

The rumours suggested that the king planned to charge a tax on all cattle, prevent the commons eating white bread, pig, goose or capon without paying a gratuity, exact taxes for weddings, christenings and funerals, and, most importantly, confiscate the goods of the parish churches and pull down churches so there would be only one in each five-mile radius. For people who had seen the number of holy days (read 'holidays') reduced and monasteries being suppressed, such fears were far from irrational. As John Hallom recalled under examination in 1537, 'because the people saw many abbeys pulled down in deed, they believed the rest to be true'.[2]

Against this background, Thomas Foster's comment stirred up the crowd led by Nicholas Melton, nicknamed 'Captain Cobbler', which that very evening, demanded the keys to the church treasure house from the churchwarden in order to protect the parish plate and jewels from the commissioners. When the bishop of Lincoln's registrar arrived the next day to carry out the assessment of the clergy, he was seized by the ever-increasing crowd, who burned his papers before marching him to Legbourne nunnery, where they captured the king's commissioners at work there. At the news that the subsidy commissioners would be working in nearby Caistor the next day, the commons of Louth, now numbering 3,000, marched to Caistor, and the commissioners fled at the sight of this great multitude advancing upon them. Caistor and Horncastle joined the uprising and by 4 October, the gentry had taken leading roles. On the same day, Dr John Raynes, the despised Chancellor of the bishop of Lincoln, was dragged before the commons in Horncastle and beaten to death with their staves.[3]

A few days later, 10,000 men marched to Lincoln, where they produced a set of articles or list of demands, which was sent to the king. These contained five complaints: the first was against the suppression of religious houses; the second and third dealt with issues of taxation: the Act of Uses enacted in 1536 – a statute that had rectified a loophole in land-ownership which had prevented royal dues being paid, and a direct tax called the 'fifteenth and the tenth', which was felt unreasonable in the economic climate. The final two complaints concerned those people advising the king. The commons complained that the king's council was made up of 'persons of low birth and small reputation', who had 'procured these things [above all, the dissolution] for their own advantage, whom we suspect to be Lord Cromwell and Sir Richard Rich, Chancellor of the Augmentations'. Finally, they named seven bishops whom they felt had 'subverted the faith of Christ'. Henry's damning response, to which we shall return below, rebuked the commons in no uncertain terms and threatened severe retribution unless the rebellion was quelled instantly. The gentry, fearing for their lives, refused to proceed, and this rising foundered.[4]

The rising at Lincolnshire was, however, only the beginning. On 8 October, there was a rising in Beverley in Yorkshire, also in response to the rumours, and now prompted by the catalyst of the Lincolnshire revolt. One Robert Aske emerged as leader. He was a lawyer who became known as the 'Chief Captain'; by the end of

October, there were nine armies totalling 50,000 men, each army led by a captain under Aske's leadership. The rebels started to march towards York and were joined on their way by other groups from East Riding and Marshland. By the time they reached York, on 16 October, the force had snowballed to 10,000 men and the city yielded to them. Aske had started to talk of the revolt as a pilgrimage, a 'pilgrimage of grace for the commonwealth', in that they sought the king's grace for the health of the kingdom. In York, Aske spelled this out, proclaiming,

> **this pilgrimage… is for the preservation of Christ's Church, of the realm of England, the King our Sovereign Lord, the nobility and commons of the same, and to the intent to make petition to the King's Highness for the reformation of that which is amiss, within this his realm and for the punishment of heretics and subverters of the laws.**

That same week, there were risings in the North Riding, and troops assembled at Richmond and swore in their local gentry as their leaders: Lord Latimer of Snape (who was married to Kateryn Parr, later Henry VIII's wife), Sir Christopher Danby of Masham and, chiefly, Sir Robert Bowes, another lawyer. They sent forces to join Aske in York on 18 October. There were also risings in Westmorland and Lancashire. The amassed troops marched to Pontefract Castle, where Lord Darcy, Edward Lee, the archbishop of York and other gentlemen had congregated for safety. Darcy had been writing desperate letters to Henry asking for support: 'the insurrection has so increased all over the North that we are in great danger of our lives and see no way it can be repressed', but amazingly the government appeared unaware of the scale of the revolt – thinking it had all quietened down after Lincolnshire – and Darcy was forced to surrender the castle on 21 October. Before long, however, Darcy and even Sir Robert Constable, who had helped Henry VII defeat the Cornish Rebellion in 1497, had joined the rebel leadership.[5]

Henry sent Lancaster Herald to Pontefract on 21 October to read a proclamation to the rebels, but Aske refused to let the proclamation be read, for its contents were incendiary. Lancaster Herald's report back, however, provided insight into the Pilgrims' intentions. Aske said he intended

> **to go with his company to London on pilgrimage to the King to have all vile blood put from his Council and noble blood set up again; to have the faith of Christ and God's laws kept, and restitution for the wrongs done to the Church, and the commonalty used as they should be...**

In addition to sending Lancaster Herald, Henry had also deployed the Earl of Shrewsbury and the Duke of Norfolk to lead the royal troops against the rebels. Aware of the vast discrepancies between the sizes of the two armies – the royal army was a maximum of 9,000 men – Norfolk arranged a meeting between the two sides at Doncaster Bridge. Here it was agreed, on 27 October, that two representatives of the Pilgrims, Sir Ralph Ellerker and Sir Robert Bowes, would take a copy of the Pilgrims' petition to the king, and a truce would be observed until their return.[6]

When the king read their petition on 2 November, he dashed off a self-righteous and condemnatory reply (see below). Norfolk persuaded him not send this (although in fact it was leaked), and instead a 'kind and mild' message was sent back with Ellerker and Bowes that did not respond to the complaints made by the rebels (except to call them 'general, dark and obscure'), but offered the prospect of further negotiations between the Pilgrims and Norfolk. The Pilgrim representatives arrived on 18 November and gave a detailed account of their visit to Windsor before the Pilgrims' council in York on 21 November. A second meeting with Norfolk at Doncaster was fixed for 6 December and meanwhile a council was arranged for 2–4 December to clarify and encapsulate the rebel concerns. This council, aping the form of a parliament, drew up a manifesto of 24 articles, which were also agreed by convocation of clergy gathered in Pontefract Priory. Finally, 40 Pilgrim representatives met Norfolk on 6 December.[7]

Norfolk had strict instructions from Henry on how to act and what to offer, but what Norfolk actually agreed was rather different. He promised a free pardon to all and that a parliament should be held at York to re-examine (and it was implied, redress) the concerns raised by the rebels. Crucially, there are no proper records of what else was agreed, a fact that was to become a matter of contention over the following months. It was later unclear, for instance, whether Norfolk had agreed that the abbeys that had been restored during the Pilgrimage should remain standing until the parliament met, and whether in the same period, the disputed taxes should remain unpaid. Even Norfolk's promise about the parliament may have simply been that he would be a suitor to the king for the parliament – not quite the same thing at all. Nevertheless, the Pilgrims accepted the terms as a clear-cut victory, which was announced by Aske on 7 December; and on 8 December, Lancaster Herald read the king's pardon to the assembled crowds and they dispersed homeward. It was, for the king, a serendipitous turn of events. If the Pilgrims had continued to march on London, the royal troops would have been powerless to stand against them. As J. J. Scarisbrick wrote of Henry and the Pilgrimage, 'the truth is that, if it had wanted, it might have swamped him'.[8]

Reasons to Rebel

Historians writing about the Pilgrimage of Grace have chiefly disagreed over the motives and aspirations of the rebels and whether economic or religious preoccupations were uppermost. The truth is probably that different groups of rebels had slightly different priorities, although there are some clear themes.[9]

Certainly, there was concern that taxes were being levied in unconventional ways. It was normal at this time for the population to be taxed only to support wars, and there was usually a rebate for the poor, but the subsidy, the fifteenth and the tenth did not conform to these standards. Henry VIII pointed out to the rebels that the subsidy was only levied on men possessing goods worth £20 – so did not affect the vast majority of the rebels – and even then, was only 6d in the pound, 'so,' he complained, 'a man worth £40 is a very traitor for that 20s'.[10]

Henry was missing the point though – it was the unprecedented circumstances of the tax that was the chief sticking point and , with it, the fear that this would open the door to other impositions – such as those taxes rumoured on cattle and weddings. The taxes were linked, in the popular mind, to the king's intentions regarding the jewels and plate of the parish churches and the riches of the monasteries. This also stuck in Henry's throat, as he wrote on 19 October, 'we know also that ye our commons have much complained in time past that most of the goods and lands of the realm were in the spiritual men's hands; yet, now pretending to be loyal subjects, you cannot endure that your prince should have part thereof'. This concern with the material culture of religion should also be recognized as an important part of popular spirituality and a sense of things being rightly ordered and conducted. Behind the rebellion 'was a set of fundamental and almost universal notions about the failures and inadequacies of the Henrician regime: the government was avaricious, sacrilegious and led by evil counsellors'. And avarice and impiety were believed to go hand in hand.[11]

Religious motives were, however, paramount. From the beginning of the rebellion, Aske had proclaimed that 'evil disposed persons, being of the king's council, hath... incensed his grace with many and sundry new inventions, which be contrary to the faith of God... and thereby intendeth to destroy the Church of England and ministers of the same'. Therefore, the pilgrimage was 'undertaken for the preservation of Christ's Church'. Representing themselves as pilgrims was in itself controversial as recent government injunctions had denounced pilgrimages as 'superstition and hypocrisy'. The rebels also adopted badges and carried banners bearing the five wounds of Christ – vestiges of a crusade led by Lord Darcy in 1511 against the Moors – which symbolically asserted their claim for the moral high ground, pronounced the essentially religious nature of their venture and situated their religiosity within a strong medieval tradition of devotion to the wounds of Christ. Their religious worries were that only three of the seven sacraments and 'no purgatory' had been included in the Ten Articles, and that heresies and heretics were infiltrating the country, chiefly through certain bishops and counsellors, such as Cromwell. They were also disturbed about Henry's adoption of the title of Supreme Head 'touching *cure animarum* (the care of souls)' because the rebels felt that this should 'be reserved unto the see of Rome as before it was accustomed to be'. The importance of this has been debated: one commentator has recently suggested that the qualification 'touching cure animarum' meant it was not a total condemnation of the king's new position. Yet Aske also said that 'all men much murmured' about the supremacy and said 'it could not stand with God's law', while its qualification probably stems from the fact that it was actually treasonous to deny the king's supremacy. Nor did the qualification count for much: Henry clearly envisaged that his role as Supreme Head encompassed the care of souls.[12]

But the central theme in the rebels' rhetoric was the suppression of the monasteries. Later, Aske was to cite the importance of the dissolution in sparking off the revolt, stating 'in all parts of the realm men's hearts much grudged the suppression of the abbeys and the fruits by reason the same would be the destruction of the whole religion in England'. He posited it as the dominant issue in the uprising: 'those bruits [rumours] were one of the greatest causes, but the suppression of the abbeys was the greatest cause of the said insurrection, which the hearts of the commons most grudged at'. This was why Richard Rich as chancellor of the Court of Augmentations – the organization responsible for administrating the dissolution – had been included in both the Lincolnshire articles and the Pilgrims' Pontefract articles. As they went along, the Pilgrims restored sixteen monasteries out of a total fifty-five that had been suppressed by the king's commissioners.[13]

Henry VIII's Reaction

On hearing of the outbreak of rebellion, Henry's initial response was one of alarm. Chapuys recorded on 7 October in a letter to Charles V that 'the King is all the more dejected, and as Cromwell's nephew said today in secret to an honest man, he [the king] was in great fear'. Just as he had with Anne Boleyn's apparent infidelity, Henry quelled his panic at the rebels' deceit with the pride and stubbornness that were characteristic of him. His letters, proclamations and instructions to the rebels and his commanders from this point on all focus on the maintenance of his honour, and are filled with hectoring, bombast and intransigence.[14]

From the outset, he saw the uprising as unequivocally treasonous. The rebels were 'false traitors and rebels' of 'wretched and devilish intents', concerned with perpetrating the 'malice and iniquity of this rebellion'. He also believed their fears were wholly unfounded and lambasted them for rebelling on the basis of 'light tales… and such light causes'. At one point in his answer to the Lincolnshire rebels, he exclaimed contemptuously, 'we marvel what madness is in your brain!' He believed that the rebels acted with 'great unkindness' and 'much unnaturalness'. Above all, he was affronted that his subjects should tell him how to rule:

> Concerning choosing of counsellors, I never have read, heard or known, that princes' councillors and prelates should be appointed by rude and ignorant common people; nor that they were persons meet or of ability, to discern and choose meet and sufficient councillors for a prince: how presumptuous then are ye the rude commons of

one shire, and that one of the most brute and beastly of
the whole realm... to find fault with your prince for the
electing of his councillors and prelates, and to take upon
you, contrary to God's law, and man's law, to rule your
prince, whom you are bound by all laws to obey...

He rebuked them for their interference and advised them to:

show yourself as bounden and obedient subjects, and
no more... intermeddle yourselves from henceforth with
the weighty affairs of the realm, the direction whereof
only appertains to us your king and such noble men and
councillors, as we list to elect and choose.

Henry also stressed that consent by these noble men, knights
and gentlemen gave legitimacy to his policies in these 'weighty
affairs'. He pointed out that all had been agreed and 'granted
to us by Parliament and not set forth by the mere will of any
councillor' and that, in religious matters, he had 'done nothing
but what the whole clergy of the province of York, as well as that
of Canterbury, have found to be conformable to God's word'.
To Henry's mind (a classic example of the aforementioned
dissonance theory, perhaps? See page 72), it was clear that
everything he had done had been lawful and with the consent
of others, which therefore made the actions of the northerners
wholly inappropriate and illegitimate.[15]

Such unprovoked treason would be dealt with severely. In his
first letter of early October to the commissioners of the subsidy,
he recommended that the commissioners send '100 of the
ringleaders, with halters about their necks, to our lieutenant',
or else threatened his army of '100,000 men, horse and foot,
in harness, with munitions and artillery, which they cannot
resist', adding savagely that this army would 'burn, spoil and
destroy their goods, wives and children with all extremity'.
Later in October, having heard of a rising at Sawley Abbey, he

commanded the Earl of Derby to act ruthlessly towards the monks, instructing: 'You are to take the said abbot and monks forth with violence and have them hanged without delay in their monks' apparel.' This was summary justice, to be delivered without trial or process of law. Despite all evidence to the contrary, right up until the December pardon, Henry continued to believe in a military solution and ordered the continued muster of troops and construction of fortifications. He continued to boast of his overstated army. He also adamantly held out for the execution of a number of ringleaders and for the rebels' official submission before opening negotiations. Crucially, he believed his 'honour would be touched' if circumstances were otherwise. They were, and, as we shall see, it was.[16]

The Question of Obedience and Tyranny

It might be helpful to put Henry's response in some context. All mainstream thinkers in the sixteenth century believed that subjects were commanded to be obedient and active rebellion was forbidden, no matter how abominably a king had behaved. Archbishop Cranmer, for example, wrote, 'though the magistrates be evil and very tyrants against the commonwealth, yet the subjects must obey in all worldly things'. Even radicals such as Robert Barnes, who was executed as a heretic in 1540, concurred: he wrote 'the Scripture commands us to obey wicked Princes'. This was also clearly Henry VIII's point of view. Henry had wholeheartedly approved of Anne Boleyn's gift of a copy of William Tyndale's *The Obedience of a Christian Man*. In it, Tyndale argued that, 'He that judges the king judges God; and he that resists the king resists God and damns God's law and ordinance... The king is, in this world, without law, and may at his lust do right or wrong and shall give accounts but to God only.' It was an objection that Henry raised with the Pilgrims. In a circular sent to his bishops in November 1536, Henry commanded them to go from place to place within their dioceses declaring 'the obedience due by God's law to the Sovereign, whose commandments they have no right to resist even though they were unjust'. He raised this point directly with the rebel representatives Sir Ralph Ellerker and Sir Robert Bowes on 27 November, reminding them that 'God commanded them to obey their prince whatever he be, yea though he should not direct them justly'. Henry knew his political theory.[17]

The corollary to this doctrine of obedience was that kings were to act for the common good. In 1517, Erasmus had sent Henry a copy of his book *The Education of a Christian Prince* in which he set forth his vision of how to prepare princes to rule justly and virtuously. According to Erasmus, a good king knows that he is dependent on the consent and will of his subjects, and that it is only such consent that entitles him to exercise authority. In addition, to be good a king ought to take advice and seek wisdom, for Erasmus warned, 'power without goodness is unmitigated tyranny', so 'make it your business to acquire for yourself the greatest store of wisdom so that you alone of all men may best be able to see what should be striven for and what should be avoided'. A tyrant would, by contrast, surround himself with flatterers who would not speak frankly to him. A monarch served by good, strong counsellors preserved the kingdom from tyranny and held evil at bay. It was a duty incumbent on courtiers to counsel their king, and it was the king's responsibility to listen to his counsellors. 'The 'uncounselled king' was, almost by definition, a tyrant'.[18]

This left the Pilgrims in something of a tricky situation. Most responded by trying to square the circle by blaming, at least in their rhetoric, evil laws on the king's counsellors rather than the king himself. Most of the rebels, mindful of the 1534 Act of Treason, did not go as far as the abbot of Colchester, who openly and angrily spoke out against the king, saying 'what a world is this: I hear say that all the abbeys shall go down: these tyrants and bloodsuckers doth thrust out of their houses these good religious fathers against all right and law'. Nor did they go as far as another man, who told a royal servant, William Breyar, 'thy master is a thief, for he pulls down all the churches in the country'. The response of the crowd around Breyar was to protest angrily, 'it is not the king's deed but the deed of Crumwell, and if we had him here we would crum him and crum him so that he was never so crummed' (a play on words of Cromwell's name), 'and if thy master were here we would new crown him'! The Lincolnshire rebels declared that Cromwell, Richard Rich, Thomas Audley, Sir Christopher Hales (Master of the Rolls) and the 'new bishops' were 'the devisers of all the false laws' and 'the doers of all mischief'. Aske similarly denounced certain 'evil disposed persons, being of the king's council', while the Pontefract articles and other demands specifically identified Cromwell and the others as heretics and subverters of the laws. In fact, the rebels believed they 'had not offended the King', as their complaint was against 'the gentlemen [who] caused the proclamations to be made in his name'. With no trace of irony, the rebels proclaimed themselves the king's 'true and faithful subjects'.[19]

It was ostensibly a safe route. In 1525, Henry had sought to raise money to invade France and had asked his subjects for voluntary donations, which became known as the Amicable Grant. When his commissioners had met widespread resistance, Henry had made it known that he was appalled that his subjects had – without his knowledge – been imposed upon so unreasonably. He had shifted the blame to his chief councillor, Thomas Wolsey, who had publicly admitted that the enterprise was his own, and Henry had been able to play the role of the benevolent and just prince (in practice, Henry had had a central role in levying the tax).[20]

Yet, in 1536, Henry took the rebellion personally. This time round, he did not take the easy way out of allowing the rebels to blame his counsellors and leave him in the clear. Instead, by volubly objecting to their attempts to dictate his choice of counsellors, chastising them for their presumption in finding fault with his choice and insisting on his right to appoint whom he wished, Henry neatly snookered himself. Had he forgotten the words of Erasmus? If a sixteenth-century tyrant was one who only listened to flatterers and didn't remove evil counsellors, it looked as if Henry had appointed himself to this role. Erasmus, who died on 12 July 1536, was probably fortunate not to see the king on whom his hope had rested brought so low.

The Post-Pardon Revolts

Events in early 1537 have influenced history's view of the rebellion and pardon, but two historians, Michael Bush and David Bownes, have argued that by examining the situation in December 1536 without the benefit of hindsight, one realizes that the pardon offered to the rebels would have been greatly humiliating for the king. Despite bluster and boasts about the vast army he would bring to bear on the rebels, no such large army was forthcoming for Henry: the rebels outnumbered the royal troops by a large margin (50,000 to 9,000). Failing a military option, Henry always intended that a pardon should be offered on the basis of a prior oath of submission to him, with the exception of a certain number of ringleaders (as had been the case in Lincolnshire), and without any concession to the rebel demands, conditions which Norfolk had, in the face of the rebels' superior might and resolve, been forced to relinquish. Adhering to the terms agreed with the rebels would have meant holding a parliament that would probably have overturned many of the religious changes of the previous years. Bush and Bownes suggest 'what is certain is that the Anglican Church would have returned to Roman Catholicism; the dissolution of the monasteries would not have occurred... most of what Thomas Cromwell stood for would have been rejected...' This is not, however, what happened, and why it did not has much to do with the course of events in early 1537 and, above all, with Henry's intention that once the government was in a position to do so, those who had humiliated Henry in the past would be made to pay.[21]

At first glance, Henry's actions immediately following the pardon appear quite curious. In late November, in a letter to

Norfolk, Henry had described that 'villain... Aske' as 'having neither wit nor experience... a common pedlar of the law'. Yet in mid-December, he wrote inviting the 'trusty and well-beloved' Aske to come to court secretly, claiming a great desire to speak with him and 'to hear, of your mouth, the whole circumstances and beginning of that matter'. When Aske arrived, Henry 'received him into his favour and gave unto him apparel and great rewards', and soon after he left, Aske wrote to Darcy that the king had been a 'gracious sovereign lord to me' and extended 'mercy from the heart'. Other rebel leaders had also been invited to join him at court, and when they returned home in January, all were confident of the king's 'liberal pardon', and his intentions to hold a parliament and crown Queen Jane at York.[22]

This shift from wanting to execute the ringleaders to wanting to have them round for tea is intriguing. Some historians, considering the December pardon to be a spectacularly devious bluff by Norfolk (who, it is suggested, knew his master's true character would lead inevitably to reprisals), have characterized Henry's subsequent show of charm and mercy towards Aske and the other rebel leaders as unmitigated deceit and guile. Others have interpreted Henry's actions as evidence of a genuine commitment to the terms reached in Doncaster. Even if we accept that the December pardon reflected a necessary and unwished-for compromise by Norfolk on Henry's behalf, rather than a calculated scheme of great contrivance, it is undeniable that Henry's attitude, as seen either side of Aske's visit through his letters to his commanders in December and January, appears to be consistently one of great antipathy and obduracy towards the rebels. So how can we explain the way Henry humoured and charmed the man he would later call 'the grand worker of that insurrection'?[23]

In December, the king met with his council to discuss ways and means 'for the maintenance of perfect quiet in the future', because although the insurrection was 'now appeased... there remain persons who desire, either by Parliament or else by another rebellion, to compass a change from their present state'. Crucially, in terms of how he was to behave with Aske, this document noted that the 'King should allure the nobles and gentry of those parts to obedience by his affability, assuring them that he has passed there [*sic*] crimes wholly to oblivion', for 'by this mean [*sic*] his Grace shall also by little and little find out the root of this matter'. Here we have the key to the approach Henry took with Aske – it was charm designed to win him over to obedience. In January, Aske's attempts to assure people of the king's adherence to his pardon suggests it had worked and, in fact, Aske believed Henry had kept the pardon even at his death a few months later. Henry also hoped his treatment of Aske would help him discover the true culprits and causes of the rebellion for, as we have seen, Henry was not persuaded of the sufficiency of the motives stated by the rebels. In other words, it is right to consider Henry's treatment of Aske a form of artifice, appropriate to the underdog position of the government in December 1536 but designed as a means to reverse that.[24]

As the play-acting with Aske suggests, the impact on Henry's honour meant that Henry and his councillors were desperately looking at a range of ways to redeem the situation. For the time being – and these strategies showed how powerless the government really was at this time – the council's plans included sending a lieutenant to the north, dispatching 'learned personages to preach and teach the word of God that the people may better know their duties… the ignorance whereof brought to them to their late trouble', and making arrangements to contain the southern counties 'if the king will in person proceed to the North to hold his Parliament'. In addition, the council planned to make preparations in case of a renewed military threat, having garrisons planted and provisions made of arms. These were schemes that demonstrate that the king understood the necessity of implementing the agreements made in the pardon but also hoped and prepared to turn things his way. The king was about to have a bit of luck.[25]

Meanwhile, the absence of any tangible realization of the terms agreed at Doncaster was worrying for the rebels. By mid-January, no official message from the king was forthcoming and Aske wrote to the king on 18 January to chivvy this along, saying 'the commons, as I brought no writing, begin to suspect me'. Was this deliberate? It seems probable that the government and the commons had wildly different expectations for the schedule of change – Henry talked of having a parliament at Michaelmas 1537 but these ambitions were not shared with the people of the north, who would have wanted it far sooner. For the erstwhile rebels, the lack of an agreed date for the parliament was accompanied by a growing suspicion that the leaders and gentry had betrayed the commons, and these fears fuelled a new series of revolts in early 1537. The first, in the East Riding, broke out in mid-January and was led by Sir Francis Bigod and John Hallom. Bigod was captured on 10 February, but this did not stop further outbreaks in West Riding, Lancashire, Cumberland and Westmorland. These revolts were on a much smaller scale than the Pilgrimage for many refused to fight, trusting in the king's pardon, but they were sufficient to provide Henry with an opportunity to claim that the rebels had broken their side of the bargain, leaving him free to break his.[26]

Norfolk, Sussex and Derby had been dispatched to the north to administer the oath of loyalty required by the pardon. The king's instructions to them show his continuing conviction that the rebellion had been treasonous and that redress should be made before the news of the post-pardon revolts was even known. The duke and two earls were briefed to find the instigators of the insurrection and to make all men swear an oath confessing their 'untrue demeanour' to the king and vowing henceforth to be true subjects and maintain all acts of parliaments made during the king's reign. This would have been a difficult oath for the rebels to swear, especially as the clause about the acts of parliament suggested the curtailment of opportunities for future change anticipated in the northern parliament. Henry's three envoys were instructed to treat those who refused the oath 'as the King's rebel' (that is, to execute them as traitors) unless force of opinion in the crowd meant such behaviour made the lieutenant's position dangerous. The instructions also explicitly ordered them to suppress again those monasteries recently restored, and although it is just about possible that one reading of the pardon permitted this, Henry's tone showed little willingness to compromise. This reflected Henry's conviction that the monks were hypocrites devoted to the 'nourishing of vice and abominable living', whose 'traitorous conspiracies' he held largely responsible for 'all these troubles'.[27]

The outbreak of renewed rebellion, then, simply played into Henry's hands and permitted treatment of the rebels as the traitors Henry had always considered them to be. In February alone, Norfolk presided over trials of those involved in the Bigod/Hallom revolt, where eight rebels were convicted of treason and condemned to death. He then declared martial law in Carlisle, stringing up a further seventy-four rebels. Henry wrote in approval and brutally commanded 'before you close it [the banner] up again (that is, end the period of martial law), you must cause such dreadful execution upon a good number of inhabitants, hanging them on trees, quartering them and setting their heads and quarters in every town, as shall be a fearful warning'. Further trials took place in March and in April, Aske, Darcy and Constable were arrested and taken to the Tower. Between May and July, they and other leading rebels and clerics were publicly executed. Henry took pleasure in ordering Sir Robert Constable be hanged in chains in Hull, where he had led the revolt, while Aske was to suffer the same treatment in York, 'where he was in his greatest and most frantic glory'. The indignity of the body left hanging in gibbet irons until it rotted away (Norfolk wrote to Cromwell of Constable's corpse in July, 'I think his bones will hang there this hundred year') was immense, for the prevention of proper burial was thought of with great horror. It demonstrates Henry's great desire for retribution. In total, between 144 and

153 people were executed for their involvement in the revolts. Ostensibly, all were executed on the basis of their post-pardon crimes: Norfolk was instructed to spread the word that 'nothing is done to them for their offences before the pardon, but for those treasons they had committed since'. This apparent adherence to the terms of the pardon displays Henry's usual legalistic relish for appearing to do things by the book (note his earlier enthusiasm for making the most of the period of martial law). Yet it didn't tie his hands too much. Dubious evidence was gathered to 'prove' post-pardon treason even when there had been none. Nevertheless, the political and pragmatic reasons – the need to appear merciful and lawful, in order to sustain the goodwill and cooperation of his subjects – undoubtedly constrained his ability to take vengeance and there were also many acquittals.[28]

The promised parliament never transpired, nor did Henry have his queen crowned in York. While some of the rebels' fears were groundless, many of the things they had opposed – the taxes, treatment of the clergy, injunctions against images and pilgrimages – remained in place. England remained outside the Roman Catholic Church and the 'heretical' bishops and councillors retained their positions of power (excepting Cromwell's execution in 1540, of which more below). Although the Bishops' Book (a statement of doctrine prepared by the bishops and not ratified by the king) of 1537 discussed all seven sacraments, crucially, the king retained his royal supremacy, including for the 'care of souls' which reserved him the right to continue to make doctrinal changes in line with his conscience. His use of the supremacy to condemn those who did not agree with him was, in fact, considerably more pronounced after this point; the rebels' opposition only entrenched his position.

This was especially the case with that central issue of the rebellion: the suppression of the monasteries. On 8 December, just days after the pardon had been agreed, Henry had written to Sir William Fitzwilliam and John, Lord Russell 'in that point touching the abbeys, we shall never consent to their desires'.

In early 1537, Norfolk and others dissolved those monasteries that the rebels had restored, but other houses that had not been part of the earlier campaign were also suppressed, notably Furness, Jervaulx, Bridlington and Whalley. There is little to suggest that in 1536 Henry VIII had intended to dissolve all the monasteries, but the king's conviction that the monks had been leading figures in the Pilgrimage changed the focus and scope of the suppression. From this point on, the dissolution of the monasteries accelerated, though the means had changed. No longer did Henry intend only to suppress those worth less than £200 or to introduce a blanket suppression by statute that might produce further revolt. Instead, abbot after abbot was persuaded 'voluntarily' to 'confess' his vice, denounce his way of life and surrender his abbey; those who refused, like the abbots of Reading, Glastonbury and Colchester, found themselves imprisoned and executed for denying the royal supremacy by opposing the king's will.[29]

The Pilgrimage of Grace and the King's Image

At the same time that the ringleaders of the Pilgrimage of Grace were finally dispatched in mid-1537, we can deduce that Holbein started painting the Whitehall Privy Chamber mural, including his great full-body, life-size portrait of Henry VIII. The exact dates of commission and completion are unknown, but it was certainly painted after Anne Boleyn's death and Henry's marriage to Jane Seymour in May 1536, because of the latter's inclusion in the mural. There was also an inscription of '1537' in the final version of the mural (according to the Leemput copy), replacing the earlier use of Henry and Jane's initials tied by a lover's knot. Some have suggested it was Jane's death that prompted Henry to commission the picture, while others have highlighted the lack of allusion in the mural to the birth – actual or anticipated – of Henry VIII's son and heir, Prince Edward, which might suggest that the picture pre-dates knowledge of Jane's pregnancy. David Starkey has argued the opposite:

that Jane was included precisely because she was pregnant. He therefore dates the commissioning of the picture from the announcement of Jane's pregnancy on 23 May 1537. While it is perfectly possible that Jane Seymour might have been included purely on the basis of being, in Henry's opinion, his only true wife (his marriages to Katherine of Aragon and Anne Boleyn had both been annulled), the spring-summer of 1537 seems a likely date for the commissioning for another reason. The message of the picture strongly suggests that it was produced in the aftermath of Henry's reaction to the Pilgrims of Grace.[30]

We have already established that this mural was designed to impress and intimidate, with its splendour, magnificence and power (see chapter 9). Holbein's depiction of Henry VIII made the king into a symbol of strength and virility. Yet there is a further layer of meaning to the picture. Although Henry dominates the composition, it is the stone altar that is at the centre of the painting. Its Latin inscription succinctly gives the viewer the message against which the painting should be read. It reads:

If it rejoice thee to behold the glorious likenesses of heroes, look on these, for greater no tablet ever bore. Great the contest and the rivalry, great the debate whether the father or the son were victor. Each was the victor, the father over his foes, for he quenched the fires of civil strife and to his people granted lasting peace. The son, born to yet greater destiny, from the altars banished the undeserving and in their place set men of worth. To his outstanding virtue the presumption of popes yielded, and as long as Henry VIII wields the sceptre in his hand, true religion is restored, and in his reign the precepts of God have begun to be held in his honour.

This panegyric legend explicitly boasts of Henry VIII's superiority over his father (Henry VII's restoration of peace after the Wars of the Roses is dealt with swiftly) and focuses the attention squarely on Henry VIII's religious policies. It is now even clearer why Henry VIII's broad-shouldered, powerful stance contrasts so powerfully with the languid, round-shouldered posture of his father: because Henry was asserting his superiority over his father as a man and a monarch.[31] Henry VIII was also making a claim for his iconic status: he is the king who has restored true religion and reformed abuses; it is he who has conquered over the pope, rooted out unworthy priests, and returned the country to the obedience of God's laws. Such an inscription provides a powerful insight into Henry's perspective on the religious changes he had instituted – it is a clear statement of his pride in the royal supremacy and in the return to proper religious practice that his reign had engendered.[32]

This inscription, if taken together with the timing of the picture and the virile strength of Henry VIII in it, suggests one reason why the mural may have been commissioned. The mural is, above all, an enduring testimony to Henry's reaction to the events of 1536. As we have seen, it was probably an attempt to compensate for the emasculation of early 1536 – it was also a hugely powerful assertion of the royal supremacy, just as the creation of Cromwell as vicegerent, Mary's submission and the 1536 promulgation of doctrine had been. The reason to assert the royal supremacy at this time was, surely, to reinforce Henry's religious position and the entrenched nature of religious reform after the challenge posed by the Pilgrimage of Grace to these very ideas. It seems to have been a defiant, triumphant reaction to the Pilgrimage of Grace and its aftermath. This could explain both the aggressive tone of the inscription and Henry's commanding and authoritative full-frontal glare. It was a statement of victory and strength, directed at those courtiers and councillors nearest the Crown and also probably intended to bolster Henry's sense of his own superiority. If this reasoning is correct, the mural was probably, then, commissioned after the Crown's reaction against the erstwhile Pilgrims when the royal victory seemed complete, probably after Aske was arrested in

April 1537. It is a clear declaration of the unassailable position of the king.[33]

When years later, in 1541, Henry finally visited York, he came from a powerful position of victorious triumph, not negotiating defeat. He was met by 200 gentlemen and 4,000 yeomen who knelt before him, while Sir Robert Bowes, the erstwhile rebel leader, made a speech confessing their 'unnatural, most odious and detestable offences of outrageous disobedience and traitorous rebellion'. The king had won.[34]

CHAPTER 16

The Mouldwarp Prophecy

A fascinating aspect of the Pilgrimage of Grace is the proliferation of rumours and prophecies among the rebels. Quasi-historical, cryptic and mystical, political prophecies claimed a centuries-old heritage and consequently carried great authority and power. The inclusion of recognizable historical events in the prophecies gave credence to what followed. As the originators of the stories were quite hard to trace, these myths and riddles could easily be deployed as a form of resistance against the powerful in society. They were classic examples of what has been called 'a social space in which offstage dissent to the official transcript of power may be voiced'.[1]

There were many prophecies doing the rounds in the 1530s and they shared both a tone and a sort of coded vocabulary. The tone was pseudo-biblical or allegorical; prophecies were often inspired by the book of Revelations or the apocryphal book of Esdras. Other prophecies were said to date back to Myrddin or Merlin, and featured in Geoffrey of Monmouth's twelfth-century book *Prophetiae Merlini* or the seventh book of his *Historia Regum Britanniae*. People were alluded to in the prophecies by their initials, plays on words or references to beasts, often those depicted in their heraldry: the eagle was, for instance, a symbol of the Holy Roman Emperor, Charles V, because it appeared in the Hapsburg badge. Both of these elements are used by Shakespeare, in *Henry IV Part One*, who puts a complaint about the currency of these prophetic animal symbols in the mouth of Hotspur:

...sometimes he angers me
With telling me of the moldwarp [*sic*] and the ant,
Of the dreamer Merlin and his prophecies,
And of a dragon and a finless-fish,
A clip-wing'd griffin and a moulten raven,
A couching lion and a ramping cat,
And such a deal of skimble-skamble stuff
As puts me from my faith.

The deployment of these motifs suggests that Shakespeare was confident of his audience's familiarity with these old tales and knew their value: the playwright signals that by dismissing them and Glendower who speaks them, Hotspur is exhibiting his weaknesses of rash judgment and hot-headedness.[2]

The first prophecy mentioned by Shakespeare was one that, in particular, caught the imagination of the Pilgrims. Probably dating from the early fourteenth century, the Mouldwarp prophecy, or to give it its proper name, 'The Prophecy of the Six Kings to Follow King John' was thought to be a prophecy of Merlin's devising. It portrayed the six kings after King John as animals: a Lamb (Henry III), a Dragon (Edward I), a Goat (Edward II), a Lion or a Boar (Edward III), an Ass (Richard II) and an evil Mole or, using the ancient English word for a mole, 'Mouldwarp' (Henry IV). The Mouldwarp, a representative of the devil, was said to be cursed of God's own mouth, proud, caitiff (a villain) and cowardly, with a rough, hairy hide like a goat. He would at first be greatly praised by his people, then would be 'cast down

173

with sin and with pride'. After losing a battle for his kingdom, he would be driven from the land by a dragon from the north, a wolf from the west and a lion out of Ireland. England would be divided into three parts and the Mouldwarp would be forced to give up two parts of his land to his enemies, in order to rule one third of it in peace. Although the chronology was incorrect for Henry, the identification of Henry VIII as the Mouldwarp seems to have spread extensively by word of mouth in the mid-1530s. It was particularly popular among the clergy, was championed by the Pilgrim rebels, and Catholic sympathizers spread the word that Henry, as the Mouldwarp, would have to flee the realm.[3]

The first records of this prophecy being used against Henry VIII date from 1535. John Hale, the vicar of Isleworth, was cross-questioned in April 1535, having been accused of calling the king 'the Molywarppe that Merlin prophesised of', and adding that 'the King was accursed of God's own mouth and that the marriage between the King and Queen [Anne] was unlawful'. The grounds Hale gave for this assertion are an extraordinarily colourful condemnation of the king, a 'robber and pillager' of the commonwealth who,

boasteth himself to be above and to excel all other Christian king and princes, thereby being puffed with vain glory and pride, where, of a truth, he is the most cruellest, capital heretic, defacer, and treader under foot of Christ and his Church... he doth impoverish, destroy, and kill, for none other intent but that he may enjoy and use his foul pleasures, and increased to himself great treasure and riches... And if thou wilt look deeply upon his life, thou shalt find it more foul and more stinking that a sow, wallowing and defiling herself in any filthy place; for how great so ever he is, he is fully given to his foul pleasure of the flesh and other voluptuousness. And look how many matrons be in the court, or given to marriage; these almost all he hath violated, so often neglecting his duty to his

wife and offending the holy sacrament of matrimony; and he hath taken to his wife of fornication this matron Anne, not only to the highest shame and undoing of himself, but also of all this realm.

Hale admitted hearing prophecies of Merlin from a man called Laynam and confessed to having repeated them but pleaded that he was 'aged and oblivious', had been very sick and 'troubled in his wits' and asked the forgiveness of God and the king and queen. The unfortunate Hale was sentenced to a traitor's death at Tyburn. William Saunderson of Lounsburgh was also cross-examined in 1535 for having said that the king would be 'destroyed by the most vile people in the world' and flee the realm, which sounds like a fragment of the Mouldwarp prophecy.[4]

It was from 1536 and the Pilgrimage of Grace, however, that the prophecy really got wings. The evidence for most of these rumours stems from Cromwell's attempt to start collecting prophecies and hunting down those who offended against the 1534 Act of Treason by citing them. In 1536–37, three people sent Cromwell books or texts of prophecies to add to his collection – Norfolk, Lord Hungerford of Windsor and Bishop Latimer. Others found themselves under investigation for reciting prophecies. One of those charged in 1536 was Thomas Syson, the abbot of Garendon. He had declared 'that in the year of Our Lord a thousand and 500 and 35... the church by my book will have a great fall and by the 39... it will rise again and be as high as it ever was', adding that 'the eagle shall rise with such a number that the King shall go forth of the realm' and be slain on his return. He described Henry as 'the mole... curst of God's own mouth, for he rooteth up the churches as the mole rooteth up the hills'. Such talk clearly fell into the category of imagining bodily harm to be done to the king and came very close to calling Henry a heretic, schismatic or infidel. Themes of the prophecy also emerge in the examination of William Todd, the prior of Malton, who was charged with inciting the rebels of Sir Francis Bigod and John Hallom's revolt with prophecies in early 1537. He had said that the king 'should be fain to fly out his realm' and, returning, would give up two thirds of the land, to settle on one third of it. Richard Bishop's version described Henry as a mole who would be 'subdued and put down', leaving the land to be fought over by three kings. Finally, in late 1537, John Dobson, the vicar of Muston, was tried for repeating certain prophecies against the king. The theme of the king being driven from the land and returning to a third part of it was reiterated here, with the addition, like Thomas Syson, that the eagle (the Emperor) 'should spread his wings over all this realm' and the dun cow, a symbol for the Pope, 'should jingle his keys and come into this realm and set it in the right faith again'. For saying these things, Dobson became yet another victim for the executioner in 1538.[5]

Cromwell's investigations convey how seriously the establishment took these prophecies. It was believed, with good reason, that they encouraged English subjects to rebellion. One document which attests to both their power and to government attempts to diminish them is a poetic account of the Pilgrimage of Grace called 'The Fall and Evil Success of Rebellion', which was written by an evangelical Yorkshire schoolmaster called Wilfred Holme in 1537. Holme devoted the final section to tackling one of the Pilgrims' beliefs by attempting to prove that Henry VIII was not the Mouldwarp, because he was not the sixth king after John nor cowardly, caitiff or hairy:

> The prophecy of the Mouldwarp, declareth he shall be
> A Caitiff, a Coward, with an elderly skin:
> But is he a Caitiff, when plainly we may see
> His portraiture and vigour a very Herculine?
> And is he a coward the truth to define,
> When in France and in Scotland his noble chivalry,
> And in many mo[re] so gloriously doth shine,
> That he is accounted a gem in activity?

However, Holme's reasoning does not seem, in the years after the Pilgrimage of Grace, to have stopped people continuing to apply the appellation of Mouldwarp to Henry. By 1542, the government was so concerned about the identification of Henry VIII with the Mouldwarp that a law was passed against the communication of such prophecies, under threat of death and forfeiture of goods. Crucially, given the identities of the prophesiers, there would be no benefit of clergy or sanctuary. All the way up until Henry's death, the authorities continued to try to scotch the rumours by confiscating books of prophecy and imprisoning offenders.[6]

The resurgence of this ancient prophecy and its levelling against Henry VIII suggests an important shift in perspective: from the splendid young king of 1509, Henry was now, for the first time, seen as an evil king, cursed by God, who should be driven from his land. From 1536, clerics and, increasingly, laymen, like many of the Pilgrims, were calling Henry 'Mouldwarp'. Hale's 1535 denunciation focused on Henry's pride, greed and lust and reacted to Henry's marriage to Anne Boleyn and the Act of Supremacy. From 1536, the new emphasis was, above all, on the 'rooting up' and despoliation of the church, seen in the suppression of the monasteries. By claiming as a prophecy the 'great fall' of the church in 1535, a barely veiled reference to Henry's Act of Supremacy, the prophesiers brought weight to their auguries that the church would rise again by 1539, and the Pope would put England back 'in the right faith again'. They also foretold an invasion by the emperor, who would defeat the king and drive him from the realm. From this point on, the government would have to battle the resurgence of this prophecy, and others similar, until Henry's death. In some ways, the Mouldwarp prophecy marked a 'before' and 'after' for Henry: it signified the transition from Henry VIII being thought of as a splendid young king, to conjecture that he had become a tyrant.

CHAPTER 17

Courtly Dissent

The Pilgrims of Grace were not the only ones covertly expressing their reservations about the king's behaviour in 1536. At much higher levels of society, there were those who, with even more caution and circumspection, voiced their concerns. Chief among them was the poet Sir Thomas Wyatt. He had been one of the group of courtiers arrested in May 1536 as part of Queen Anne's entourage. His verse of the 1520s suggests an early flirtation, courtship or even relationship with Anne Boleyn, but in 1536 he escaped execution because there was little evidence of any recent indiscretions and, perhaps more importantly, because Cromwell may have acted on his behalf, at the behest of Wyatt's father. So instead of dying with the others, Wyatt had probably watched the executions on Tower Hill from his cell and subsequently wrote two poems, 'Who list his wealth and ease retain' and 'In mourning wise'. After his release from the Tower, Wyatt, on the king's orders, went into exile from the court at his family estate in Allington, and in the poetry he wrote there and subsequently, Wyatt criticizes Henry VIII's seemingly tyrannical behaviour.

One of course needs to tread carefully when hunting for the real world of the court in courtly poetry; else, to quote Wyatt himself, 'sithens in a net I seek to hold the wind'. There was no freedom of speech in this court where words could be treason, and poets' self-revelation needed to be obscured in esoteric verse never intended for publication. Wyatt, whom the poet Henry Howard, Earl of Surrey, would later describe as 'A heart, where dread was never so impressed,/To hide the thought, that might the truth advance', was aware of the danger of speaking candidly and perceptive enough to realize that Castiglione had underestimated the difficulty of honest service to dishonest princes. Yet it is possible to see, in both Wyatt and Surrey's poetry, glimpses of a sixteenth-century tyrant king.[1]

Like many of Wyatt's poems, his satire 'Mine Own John Poyntz', composed at Allington in the summer of 1536, was a translation and paraphrase. All translations are to some extent also interpretations, and it is Wyatt's specific additions to or alterations of the text of his original that are particularly important. 'Mine Own John Poyntz' was based on a political satire by Luigi Alamanni which had been published in Lyons in 1532–3. It expresses an aversion to the court – the poet flees it 'rather than to live thrall under the awe / Of lordly looks'. Such anti-court rhetoric was a common humanist trope and Wyatt had previously written of the 'brackish joys' and 'slipper top / Of court's estates', but there is evidence in this poem that Wyatt was reacting to a specific court and, even more so, a specific king.

The speaker in the poem makes it clear that his antipathy is not because he rejects hierarchy or the rule of kings in general:

It is not because I scorn or mock
The power of them to whom Fortune hath lent
Charge over us, ...

but in doing so, he signals precisely how that rule is presently enforced –

... of right to strike the stroke

– with a sword. It seems probable that Wyatt's vision from the Bell Tower on 17 May – the 'bloody days' that had broken his heart – came to mind as he wrote these words. Wyatt makes another reference to the executioner's death in another poem, 'Stand whoso list', whose dating is uncertain, concluding that it is preferable to die 'aged after the common trace' than 'dazed, with dreadful face', words he adds to his Latin source, Seneca. The trouble for the speaker in 'Mine Own John Poyntz' is that he finds himself unable to give counsel to one who ignores it –

I cannot frame my tune to feign
To cloak the truth for praise, without desert,
Of them that list all vice for to retain

nor fawn and flatter with the rest: 'Grin when he laugheth that beareth all the sway, / Frown when he frowneth and groan when he is pale'. That Wyatt uses a singular 'he' here is a deliberate alteration from Alamanni's many 'masters' and focuses the attention on a single oppressive ruler. The identity of this ruler becomes clear as the speaker protests that he –

...cannot crouch nor kneel to do such wrong
To worship them like God on earth alone
That are like wolves these silly lambs among.

Even in the context of standard anti-court satire, this was strong stuff because 'on earth alone' and the picture of the ravenous wolf among the lambs are both additions to the text by Wyatt and strikingly conspicuous imagery. The first echoes Henry's adoption of the title of Supreme Head of the Church and is unwittingly similar to Bishop Gardiner's description of Henry VIII as the image of God upon earth. The second is reminiscent of one of Thomas More's epithets on tyranny: 'What is the good king? He is the watchdog, the guardian of his flock, who by barking keeps the wolves from the sheep. What is the bad king? He is the wolf.' This reference to savagery is matched by the speaker's insistence that he 'cannot wrest the law to fill the coffer / With innocent blood to feed myself fat...', which in the context of the deaths of Anne Boleyn and the gentlemen of the privy chamber seems remarkably close to the bone. Finally, at the climax of the poem, the speaker's most devastating blow is in his refusal to call 'The lecher a lover, a tyranny / To be the right of a prince's reign.' Wyatt had come perilously close to committing high treason by calling his king a tyrant.[2]

Surrey, whose eulogy of Wyatt indicates his admiration for the older poet, was to follow suit, though within the confines of biblical and classical allusion. In 1541, Wyatt, back at Allington, wrote a version of King David's penitential psalms, which Surrey subsequently circulated in holograph manuscript prefaced by one of his own sonnets, 'The Great Macedon'. The similarities between Henry VIII and David – as wise rulers, close to God had been emphasized by Henry in his depiction in the miniatures of his private psalter as David. Wyatt had, in his psalms, been circumspect about those less imitable aspects of David's character – his adultery and tyrannical abuse of royal power – but Surrey's preface was far less cautious. Here, Surrey explicitly directed the reader's attention to the example David gave of lustfulness:

> Of just David by perfect penitence,
> Where Rulers may see in a mirror clear
> The bitter fruit of false concupiscence...

The indiscretion of this allusion, and the implications for Henry's version of himself, were immense. It also puts the opening lines of Surrey's later poem, 'Th' Assyrian king' into a different light. Was Surrey making reference to his own king when he wrote 'Th' Assyrian king, in peace, with foul desire / And filthy lusts that stain'd his regal heart'? Although this poem ostensibly focused on the Assyrian king Sardanapalus, a character conventionally used to symbolise intemperate behaviour, the link between his lusts and the 'false concupiscence' of David drew parallels that were dangerous to draw. Cloaked in literary precedent, the poets of Henry VIII's court were also quietly, but powerfully expressing their disapproval of the king's increasing despotism.[3]

CHAPTER 18

Did Henry VIII Become a Tyrant?

*W*hy did it matter that Henry VIII's subjects had started to call him a tyrant? It mattered because in the sixteenth century, it was one of the worst insults one could use against a king. It was also a statement about Henry VIII's character and how he had changed. It mattered, perhaps above all, because these mutterings of tyranny among his subjects were not without substance. The actions of Henry in 1536 were not those of a man who was 'affable and gracious [and] harmed no one', as he had once been described. From around this time, Henry VIII appears to have become more suspicious, and the government that he commanded more repressive and brutal. He increasingly condemned his enemies to die without due process of law. This was partly a rational response to changed circumstances: after the divorce from Katherine, the break with Rome and Fisher and More's deaths, Henry VIII did have more enemies. There were plots and traitors, and those continuing their allegiance to Rome could be seen as a dreaded fifth column. There were also external threats: it must have seemed that Francis I and Charles V were poised for invasion and, although the threat of the papal bull was not realized in 1536, it was an ever-present threat that was eventually published in 1538. Nevertheless, Henry's new enthusiasm for revenge still seems disproportionate, and there was a palpable shift in his personal response to perceived threats. The origin of some of this was pain and age – over time, ill-health combined with age to make him more anxious and insecure, and the constant pain in his leg produced by his ulcer made him increasingly irascible. It is after this stage that the records start to speak of the king's displays of bad temper. More serious, as we shall explore below, was the way Henry now reacted to alleged betrayal or treason. While it is impossible to prove, the timing and nature of this change in his behaviour makes it seem likely to be the result of an aggrieved, overblown and readily mobilized sense of betrayal in the light of Anne Boleyn's apparent adultery and later, the Pilgrimage of Grace. Henry had become markedly more distrustful and despotic – in short, a tyrant.[1]

Being a Tyrant

Calling Henry VIII a tyrant has, over the intervening years, raised all sorts of issues – and hackles. The doyen of Tudor political history, G. R. Elton, argues tirelessly that Henry VIII's rule was constitutional and limited, maintaining the exclusive legislative authority of parliament and preserving the principle of the superiority of the king-in-parliament over the king alone. In addition, Elton and others have pointed out how dependent the king was on the cooperation of the nation, as the Pilgrimage of Grace tellingly shows. Steven G. Ellis, analyzing the reprisals that Henry took against a rebellion in Ireland in 1534, says they were necessarily limited in order not to alienate the local community and argues that this means 'Henry VIII was so far from establishing a despotism that he could not even be sure of enforcing undoubted rights'. Both historians have pointed to how Henry's actions conformed to the rule of law, although both also admit that there were a few 'notorious examples' of 'acts of doubtful legality'. It is absolutely true that Henry VIII was often painstaking in his adherence to the letter of the law. But as several scholars have pointed out, that is not necessarily incompatible with tyranny. Even Elton concludes that in the sixteenth century, the rule of law permitted horrors.[2]

In the sixteenth century, being a tyrant was less a question of what a king did than who he was. The crux of tyranny was the spirit or character that gave rise to tyrannical behaviour. William Thomas, Henry VIII's first biographer, quoted an unnamed Italian, who after Henry VIII's death in 1547, called him 'the greatest tyrant that ever was in England' before going on to describe a tyrant in the following terms:

> The principal token of a tyrant is the immoderate satisfaction of an unlawful appetite, when the person, whether by right or wrong, hath power to achieve his sensual will, and that person, also, who by force draws unto him that which of right is not his, in the unlawful usurping commits express tyranny.

A tyrant could principally be identified by his character with its inclination to unbridled greed and avarice, having unrestrained lusts and appetites for things not belonging to him. When he possessed and used his power unlawfully to usurp such things, his tyranny was expressed – but was it always latent in his flawed character?[3]

By a modern definition (though framing the question within the standard of the period in which the subject lived), a tyrant is

> a ruler who exercises arbitrary power beyond the scope permitted by the laws, customs and standards of his time and society and who does so with a view to maintaining or increasing that power.

If we wanted to test Henry VIII against this definition, we could examine vast amounts of evidence to see where arbitrary power was exercised with a view to enhancing that power. In fact, there is so much evidence that a study of the indices of tyranny in Henry VIII's reign could produce a complete book in and of itself. Yet even a cursory survey suggests that the evidence of tyranny emerges primarily from the 1530s and later, reaching increasing pace towards 1536 and maintaining this until the end of Henry VIII's reign.[4]

One of the characteristics frequently associated with tyranny is the creation of a totalitarian state and the suppression of dissent. This is hard to measure in the sixteenth century, because while contemporary thought extolled the virtues of freedom, it was not a freedom with which the modern mind would be familiar. The Henrician state was undeniably extremely intrusive into the lives of its subjects and curtailed a vast range of personal freedoms. It introduced a large number of new laws to control the behaviour of English subjects, including the Beggars Act of 1531. This legislated that vagrants, beggars and vagabonds should be half-stripped and whipped through the town or set in the stocks for three days and nights on bread and water. Other new statutes included the introduction of the penalty of death by hanging for those found guilty of buggery in 1534 (first enacted in 1540) and the first law against witchcraft in 1542. Other acts created new felonies – fishing in private ponds after dark or selling horses to the Scots both became capital offences! There was also never freedom to believe what one wanted: it was perfectly accepted that some religious beliefs were heretical, and even Thomas More, who is often championed as a defender of free speech, had as Lord Chancellor been a great persecutor of heretics. It was usual to wish to control men's thoughts to some extent. Yet, even set in this context of the customs and standards of his time, Henry VIII's ambitions to govern men's minds were unusual. The manner in which Henry attempted to command men's thoughts in order to suppress all opposition to his rule are the actions of a tyrant. The Acts of Succession and Supremacy of 1534 required that subjects swear oaths subscribing to their terms, which 'they shall truly, firmly and constantly without fraud or guile observe, fulfil, maintain, defend and keep to their cunning, wit and uttermost of their powers'. Here was an attempt to coerce all subjects into committing themselves to Henry's controversial policies in mind and spirit, as well as deed. As C. S. L. Davies wrote, 'a regime which demands a show of unanimous consent is more coercive than one which merely imposes its will from above'. It effectively forbade dissent, as the chronicler Edward Hall illustrated by his comment on the Catholic Friar Forest, 'how could he say the King was not supreme head of the church, when he himself had sworn to the contrary'. Henry believed that as Supreme Head his role encompassed the direction of theology, and his initiatives, such as the Ten Articles of 1536 designed to 'establish Christian quietness and unity among us, and to avoid contentious opinions' or the 1539 act 'abolishing diversity in opinions', were intended to conform all men to a uniform belief.[5]

Other evidence of the onset of tyranny is perhaps more tangible. There were convictions obtained on the basis of flimsy evidence, such as that of Edward Stafford, Duke of Buckingham, condemned as a traitor in 1521 (it was alleged that Buckingham had listened to prophecies saying he would become king when Henry died), or on the evidence of minimal witnesses, as shown by Cromwell's note of November 1539 concerning Giles Heron, and 'what shall be done with him, for as much as there is but one witness'. Heron was executed in 1540. The incidence of rigged trials is worthy of investigation, as is the passing of new laws to permit execution. Thomas More was, for example, originally imprisoned for refusing to swear the Oath of Succession in April 1534. He was, however, executed on 6 July 1535 on the grounds that he had rejected the king's new title of Supreme Head, following the passing of the Act of Supremacy of November 1534 and the Treasons Act, which came into force in February

1535 and made words treasonous. One could also examine grey areas in the law, including the treatment and use of torture in the period between arrest and trial. In 1535, three Carthusian monks were chained by their necks and arms, and had their legs fettered with locks and chains in the Tower for thirteen days before their hanging and quartering, and even gentlefolk such as Anne Askew were illegally tortured: Anne was racked to make her confess to heresy and to implicate others, including Queen Kateryn Parr, in 1546. The new punishments that were introduced during Henry's reign, including the horrific capital sentence of boiling in cases of poisoning, meted out to Richard Roose in 1531, might also be judged as evidence of tyranny. The treatment of the church and the manner in which the monasteries were dissolved could be considered, as could the issue of consent to new laws. Further evidence could be supplied by the work of other historians who have explored the king's judicious and unpredictable use of pardons – there was a tendency for general pardons to remit fewer and fewer crimes of importance as the reign wore on – and Henry's dangerous and manipulative role in the attempted coups against Archbishop Cranmer, Bishop Gardiner and Kateryn Parr in the 1540s. Another key discussion has been about the 1539 act which decreed that proclamations made by the king should be obeyed; historians have questioned the extent to which this was a despotic measure that sought to give royal proclamations the same status and power as acts of parliament. This could be compared with the 1536 Minorities Act, which gave Henry's heir, on reaching the age of twenty-four, 'full power and authority' to revoke by letters patent any act of parliament made before that point, and the extent to which Henry VIII's use of parliament made it an unchecked instrument of the royal will. To what extent did Tudor statutes add to the personal power of the king? Maurice Latey believes that tyrants often become convinced of their own divinity, and Henry VIII's assumption of the title of Supreme Head of the Church of England suggests a version of this.[6]

In all these areas, I am persuaded that symptoms of tyranny were rare until the 1530s (Buckingham's execution in 1521 is a notable, but singular, exception), when gradually the incidence of questionable and inhumane practices accelerated, reaching its apogee in 1535–6: after this point, as we shall see, the evidence of tyranny became compelling.

Henry VIII's Revenge

We can chart change in Henry VIII's character from the differing reports that observers made of him in these later years, compared with those made when the king was a young man, which primarily stressed his ease of companionship and gentle graciousness. In the guarded, diplomatic and understated language of ambassadors, comments were now made about Henry's increasingly irascible temper – that the 'King was irritated and that his ministers were at a loss to account for it' and capricious unpredictability – 'people worth credit say he is often of a different opinion in the morning than after dinner'. Other remarks were made about the pig-headedness that made him 'very stern and opinionate', or how he mistreated his counsellors – he would, for example, 'beknave' Thomas Cromwell twice a week, hitting 'him well about the pate'. After Cromwell's death, Henry turned his fury on his other counsellors, reproaching them for forcing his hand and blaming them that 'upon light pretexts, by false accusations, they made him put to death the most faithful servant he ever had'. In March 1541, when his leg was particularly bad, Henry was said to have a '*mal d'esprit*', and he responded angrily to tales that his subjects were murmuring at the charges imposed upon them and their ill-treatment over religious matters, by complaining that 'he had an unhappy people to govern whom he would shortly make so poor that they would not have the boldness nor the power to oppose him'. It was reported that Henry had also 'conceived a sinister opinion of some of his chief men' and railed against them 'that most of his Privy Council, under pretence of serving him, were only temporising for their own profit, but he knew the good servants from the flatterers, and ...would take care their projects should not succeed'. While those at Henry's court could hope for glory, wealth and position, the dangers and trials of being in close proximity to this mercurial and volatile king were great.[7]

Charles de Marillac, the French ambassador, provided a damning analysis of Henry VIII in August 1540, which is worth quoting at some length:

> This Prince seems tainted, among other vices, with three which in a King may be called plagues. The first is that he is so covetous that all the riches in the world would not satisfy him... Everything is good prize, and he does not reflect that to make himself rich he has impoverished his people, and does not gain in goods what he loses in renown.... Thence proceeds the second plague, distrust and fear. This King, knowing how many changes he has made, and what tragedies and scandals he has created, would fain keep in favour with everybody, but does not trust a single man, expecting to see them all offended, and he will not cease to dip his hand in blood as long as he doubts his people. Hence every day edicts are published so sanguinary that with a thousand guards one would scarce be safe... The third plague, lightness and inconstancy, proceeds partly from the other two... and has perverted the rights of religion, marriage, faith and promise...

Taken with evidence of Henry's spiteful interest in the manner of Anne Boleyn's death and the viciousness of his letters on how to deal with the Pilgrims, this all adds considerably to the body of evidence that suggests Henry VIII had become tyrannical. This is not to suggest that temper, egoism, pride and obstinacy sprang suddenly from a character who had always previously shown peace and light. According to the sixteenth-century's notion of tyranny, tyranny would always have been latent in his character. We know that although Henry was kind, affable and generous in his younger years, he was also wilful and egotistic. Nevertheless, this wilfulness and egoism had now reached a new level: something had catalyzed this latent tyranny into reality.[8]

The necessarily muted and circumspect language of diplomats at Henry's court means, though, that our best evidence for the king's changing character is his actions; specifically, as Marillac described it, the way he dipped his hand in blood. A classical story gives a hint about how tyranny manifests itself. Periander, a tyrant who ruled Corinth in seventh century BC, was once asked for advice on how to rule by Thrasybulus of Miletus. Periander took the messenger out into the fields and, without saying a word, lopped off the tallest ears of corn with his stick. In his book, *In the Lion's Court,* Derek Wilson argues that Henry did just that after 1536: 'most of the reign's acts of sanguinary statecraft occurred during the last decade... It was in 1536 that bloodletting of those close to the Crown became frequent...[and] in his later years the lion's claws were out more often'. For a striking difference between Henry's early reign and his last decade is the way that Henry treated those he knew personally whom he thought had wronged him. The incidence and circumstances of such executions before and after 1536, and, especially, the increasing tendency not to pursue conviction through due process and common law trial but through parliamentary attainder and a widening definition of treason, provides compelling evidence of Henry VIII's increasingly savage temper and misanthropic character.[9]

Prior to 1536, there had been a handful of executions of high-status victims following conviction of treason by common law. Sir Richard Empson and Edmund Dudley, who had been councillors to Henry VII, were executed in August 1510. This was probably either because they were held to blame for the injustices and oppressions of Henry VII's reign, and because the young king, who had come to the throne only a year before, needed to prove his justice, or as the result of a court coup. The charge of treason came from the fact that on 22 April 1509, both had, allegedly, conspired 'to hold, guide and govern the King and his Council' by summoning a force of men to come to London as Henry VII lay dying – the suggestion being that they had intended to stage a coup d'état and destroy the new king, Henry VIII. Having been imprisoned in the Tower since 1506, Edmund de la Pole was finally executed (despite Henry VII's earlier promise that he would not be) in May 1513 on a charge of treason. This was because of his previous association with a recently re-emerged Yorkist conspiracy led by his brother, Richard. The Duke of Buckingham was, as we have seen, executed in 1521, having been found guilty of treason before a jury of peers. Like Edmund de la Pole, his royal blood (by descent from Edward III) made him dangerous and, while his conviction for treason was on the basis of allegation, hearsay and speculation, it is likely that his ambitions for the throne were plausible. At a time when Henry VIII was starting to worry about his succession, Buckingham was perceived as a threat to the crown. Finally, More and Fisher's deaths, along with the Carthusian monks in 1535, more than a year after they went to the Tower and on the basis of laws enacted during their incarceration, were particularly notable as evidence of Henry's steadily growing despotism.[10]

It all came to a head in 1536, when Anne Boleyn, Rochford, Henry Norris and the others were tried by common law and found guilty of high treason. The actual charge of treason was conspiracy to procure the king's death (referring presumably to Anne's conversations with Norris) but this was dressed up with a charge of adultery, even though adultery by or with a queen was actually not an act of treason by law. The charges of adultery were prefaced by the repetition of the words 'treasonably violated the queen', but if the intercourse had been consensual, no crime remained. This is highlighted by the fact that adultery with the queen was created a treason in later legislation to deal with Catherine Howard's infidelity.[11]

Other significant figures indicted and tried after this point include the rebels of 1536 – Aske, Darcy and Constable etc., on the basis of evidence constructed to prove treason after the December pardon – and a group of alleged conspirators in 1538, including Henry's cousins, Henry Courtenay, Marquess of Exeter and Henry Pole, Lord Montague (Reginald Pole's brother). The alleged conspirators were charged with two counts under the 1534 Act of Treason: desiring the king's death and denying him his title of Supreme Head. Of their supposed armed rebellion there is little evidence. They were followed a few months later by Henry VIII's close companion and childhood friend, Nicholas Carew, after he had responded angrily to an insult made by the king, for his part in 'abetting' Exeter's conspiracy. All three deaths provide a striking example of Henry's willingness, by this point in his life, to send those near him to the block in cases of perceived threat or personal betrayal. As examined in chapter 7, the king had suffered great humiliation in Anne and Rochford's trial. Perhaps the hope of avoiding a repeat of this incident helps explain why after this point, of all the influential and high-status people executed at the king's behest, only the Pilgrims' leaders and the Exeter conspirators were tried and executed by judicial process. Everyone else of high status accused of high treason was convicted and executed on the basis of parliamentary attainder – a route that was just about legal but one which entirely circumvented the due process of trial and defence, and which thus removed any possibility of the accused being found innocent and released. It is not simply that the number of people close to the king who were executed increased after 1536 – something which could, in part, be justified on the basis of increased threats to the throne – it was also that the method of dealing with these miscreants became more savage; for Henry had changed.[12]

Parliamentary attainder had traditionally been used to convict fugitives in exile or to extend the terms of convictions already passed through common law, generally to ensure that the estates of those who had been convicted and executed through common law were forfeited to the Crown. In the first twenty years of his reign, Henry VIII used them in this traditional and infrequent manner. But studies by scholars Stanford Lehmberg and William Stacy show that the use of the attainder dramatically increased in the 1530s – in fact, this decade saw the heaviest use of parliamentary attainder in English history – and, moreover, the attainder was being used in an entirely new manner. Now, an act passed through parliament could in itself declare the accused guilty and condemn them to death – even when defendants were available for trial by common law – without needing to cite specific evidence or name precise crimes.[13]

The first attainder of this ilk was in February 1531, when Richard Roose, a cook in Bishop John Fisher's household, was attainted of high treason by parliament after mixing poison into the porridge. Fisher hadn't eaten it but both a guest and one of the charitable poor fed at the bishop's gate had died, and presumably the grave crime of attempting to kill a bishop (an irony perhaps not lost on others four years later) had prompted an attainder for high treason for what was not a treasonous act, without indictment or trial. Roose was the poor soul ordered to be boiled alive. Three years later, the same procedure – attainder without indictment or trial – was directed at Elizabeth Barton and her associates. Barton, also known as the Holy Nun of Kent, was charged with having preached that Henry was not the rightful king and that if he married again, he would soon die. There was no judicial process, but, in contrast to later attainders, her offences (which prefigured the Treason Act of 1534) were described in great detail and she and her followers were convicted and sentenced to death on the basis of alleged confessions. John Bellamy has suggested that attainder was used in her case because the crimes with which she was charged were not treasonous and judges refused to declare them as such; Cromwell and Henry used the attainder to demonstrate that they would get their way, nonetheless.[14]

These were important cases, but it remains undeniable that the use of attainder snowballed from 1536, especially for those towards whom the king was likely to have felt personal antipathy. In July 1536, Thomas Fitzgerald, the Earl of Kildare, was attainted anew for his involvement in the Irish Kildare rebellion of 1534, along with five of his uncles (at least two of whom had previously been scheduled to receive a pardon). All of them were executed in February 1537. None were given common law trials. For attempting to marry the king's niece, Lady Margaret Douglas, without royal consent, Lord Thomas Howard was also attainted that year. His offence was his indirect claim to the throne but the 'high treason' for which he was convicted only became a crime in the text of the bill that attainted him, a rather circular and not wholly legal process that evinces Henry's paranoia. Lord Thomas was sentenced to be executed as a traitor, but in fact died in the Tower in October 1537 before his sentence was carried out. In 1536, Sir Thomas More was also posthumously attainted for treason, and the attainder was applied to two suspected common murderers, John Lewes and John Wolf (the latter had fled making his attainder more traditional, though he had only been charged with felony).[15]

What is important is that after this point a number of astonishingly high-profile and high-status individuals, in other words, people the king knew, were attainted and executed without trial. In 1539, fifty-three people were condemned by attainder – more than a third of all those condemned in this way over the course of the whole century! Twenty-seven had faced trial, including the Pilgrim leaders, Exeter, Montague and Carew, who were all attainted after their trials in the conventional way. Five others had been indicted but not tried, because they had fled abroad. The rest, however, were convicted of high treason and sentenced to death without any indictment or trial at all. These included Gertrude Courtenay, marchioness of Exeter, and Margaret Pole, Countess of Salisbury, accused of conspiring with Exeter and Carew. The marchioness had the fortune to remain in the Tower (if such a statement can be made) until Mary's accession in 1554, when she was freed. The Countess was, however, executed in 1541, and Greg Walker has remarked that 'the death of the septuagenarian Countess, so infirm and weakened by interrogation that she had to be carried to the scaffold in a chair... marked the nadir of royal vindictiveness'. It was a chilling example of Henry's capacity for despicable and unnecessary cruelty. The Countess might have had royal blood but she was evidently no threat to Henry. Sir Adrian Fortescue was also attainted on the basis of unnamed 'divers and sundry detestable and abominable treasons' and he and three others (including two of Exeter's servants) were executed in July 1539.[16]

The year of 1540 was a bumper one for attainders. Six papists, including Richard Fetherston, Thomas Abel and Edward Powell, were attained for denying the king's supremacy. A further nine, including papists accused of adherence to the Pope and Protestant heretics, were attainted next. This is the only recorded use of attainder to convict heresy in English history. On the strength of these attainders, Fetherston, Abel and Powell were hanged at Smithfield as traitors on the same day as the three Protestants – Robert Barnes, William Jerome and Thomas Garrett – were burned there. William Bird and Walter, Lord Hungerford, were also attainted in 1540 for treasonable conversation, and, in Lord Hungerford's case, for 'the abominable and detestable vice and sin of buggery with William Maister, Thomas Smith and other his servants'.[17]

Finally, and most shockingly of all, in June 1540, Thomas Cromwell, Earl of Essex – the king's chief minister and vicegerent in spirituals – was arrested, imprisoned and convicted of high treason by attainder. The attainder, which was written in the style of a petition to the king, accused Cromwell – and simultaneously found him guilty – of being 'the most false and corrupt traitor, deceiver and circumventor against your most royal person, and the imperial crown of this your realm, that hath been known, seen, or heard of in all the time of your most noble reign'. Cromwell had, despite being 'a person of as poor and low degree as few be within this your realm', allegedly usurped 'your kingly estate, power and authority' and acted in many weighty affairs without the king's knowledge or consent. He had claimed too great an intimacy and influence with the king, 'pretending to have so great a stroke about you' and being 'sure of you; which is detestable and to be abhorred... that any subject should enterprise or take upon him so to speak of his sovereign liege lord and king'. Finally, he was a 'detestable heretic' and had caused 'damnable errors and heresies to be inculcated, impressed and infixed in the hearts' of the king's subjects. The real reason for Cromwell's fall – whether it was a result of his evangelical beliefs and support for reformed causes, his implication in heresy, the failure of Henry's marriage to Anne of Cleves or that he had simply over reached himself – is unclear. One persuasive theory suggested by Miles F. Shore is that Henry VIII relied in all but seven years of his reign on one single, trusted and idealized person of power and influence, who each in turn took an equally disproportionate amount of blame when they failed to live up to perfection. Henry's vindictiveness towards them can thus be explained by the transformation of his shame and humiliation at failure, into rage at the person he blamed for the failure. This must explain Henry's lack of pity despite Cromwell's ardent and impassioned letters of petition, even if it still does not answer the question of how Henry felt that Cromwell had let him down so badly. Under arrest, Cromwell wrote to Henry, 'prostrate at your Majesty's feet' on 12 June 1540,

> if it were in my power to make you live for ever, God knows I would; or to make you so rich that you should enrich all men, or so powerful that all the world should obey you. For your Majesty has been most bountiful to me, and more like a father than a master. I ask you mercy where I have offended.

He signed it off 'written with the quaking hand and most sorrowful heart of your most sorrowful subject and most humble servant and prisoner'. His appeal to Henry was 'Most gracious prince, I cry for mercy, mercy, mercy!' None was forthcoming. A brave letter from Cranmer to the king suggests something of the reaction to Cromwell's fall when he wrote 'who cannot be sorrowful and amazed that he should be a traitor against your majesty, he that was so advanced by your majesty... he who loved your majesty (as I ever thought) no less than God', and also neatly summed up Henry's new quandary, 'for who shall your grace trust hereafter, if you might not trust him?' For our purposes, though, it is striking that once again, someone previously so close to the king lost their footing so dramatically. Later, Henry would rue Cromwell's loss but it is terrifying that at the time, he precipitously lashed out at one of his closest confidants and paid no heed to his appeals. Henry's later regret was too little and too late. It is also conspicuous that Henry and his associates chose to stage Cromwell's downfall through parliament, rather than risk the earl's defence in a trial by jury.[18]

The last two celebrated cases of conviction by attainder involved more members of the Howard family and people particularly close to Henry VIII. On 2 November 1541, Henry VIII was told that his fifth wife, Catherine Howard, whom he had married just over a year earlier in July 1540, had committed adultery with Francis Dereham and Thomas Culpepper. Henry was shocked and horrified by this betrayal, so like his first, and after his initial disbelief had prompted further investigation, the privy council reported back their findings – that Henry Manox had been intimate with Catherine before her marriage and that Francis Dereham confessed to having known her carnally 'both in his doublet and hose between the sheets and in naked bed'. At this, 'the King's heart was pierced with pensiveness, so that it was long before he could utter his sorrow' until finally he spoke 'with plenty of tears'. The similarities between Catherine's case and that of Anne Boleyn are striking. In both, there was talk of a pre-contract before the royal marriage and of adultery with more than one man. Unlike Anne though, Catherine seems to have been sexually involved with Dereham before her marriage, and historians generally assume her guilt with Culpepper after it. Having had Anne tried before a court of her peers to his great dishonour and shame, the king was not about to repeat his mistake. Although Catherine was only imprisoned in the Tower on 10 February 1542 and executed three days later, her fate had been decided far in advance of this: on 22 November 1541, she had forfeited her title of queen; the very next day, summons had been sent to peers to attend a parliament and by 10 December, Dereham and Culpepper had been found guilty of treason (again, for an offence – consensual adultery with the queen – that was still not technically treasonous) and executed. The summons to parliament indicated Henry's intention to use the mechanism of attainder to avoid open trial and declare Catherine's guilt through parliament. In the event, the attainder was even given the king's assent by letters patent under the Great Seal (that is, *in absentia*), a decision amazingly justified on the grounds that the execution should not be delayed until the end of the parliamentary session. The text stated that Catherine and her accomplice, Jane Boleyn, Lady Rochford (widow of Anne Boleyn's brother George, who had apparently aided and abetted Catherine's infidelity), had committed abominable treasons 'to the most fearful peril and danger of the destruction of the king' and had been 'lawfully indicted... convicted and attainted of high treason' by parliament. The attainder also added to the statute book the ruling that adultery with the queen constituted treason, as did the failure of a woman to declare a previously unchaste life before marrying the king, and, additionally, convicted fifteen of Catherine's relatives and servants of misprision (or concealment) of treason (although all pleaded for the king's mercy and were eventually pardoned).[19]

The final attainder of Henry VIII's reign was in late 1546, when Parliament was summoned to deal with the offences alleged against Henry Howard, Earl of Surrey and his father, the Duke of Norfolk. Surrey was accused, not on the basis of his poetry, but for having quartered his arms with those of the kings', a clear heraldic sign of his royal blood and an apparent suggestion of the Howards' place in the line of succession – or at least, this is how the king understood it. Surrey was actually tried before a court but both he and his father were subsequently attainted through parliament without any further evidence (or details of the alleged offences) being raised in the attainder. The attainder had not even been passed by the lords when Surrey's sentence was carried out: the young poet was executed on 19 January 1547. Norfolk's fate was serendipitous – his execution was ordered on 27 January but Henry VIII died in the night and Norfolk awoke the next morning a free man. He was released by Edward VI and died aged eighty in 1554.

In total, in Henry VIII's reign, sixty-eight people were condemned without trial by common law. Thirty-four of them were executed (the others fled or their fates are unknown). Many of these had been condemned by parliamentary attainder precisely because they had either not technically committed treason or there was insufficient evidence to prove their guilt, leaving the record vague and unspecific as to their crimes. It was a legalistic way of evading the law, of acting illegally. Many attainders had also expanded the legal definition of treason – by the end of the reign, it now newly encompassed marriage to the king's relatives without royal consent, a royal bride's concealment of a previously immoral life and heresy – on top of other statutes, which, besides the attainders, had widened the definition of treason even further. These were lawful statutes but were designed to make arbitrary action possible. They were, in fact, tyrannical. Bellamy has concluded 'they were without respectable precedent and based on no principle save anything which annoyed the king was to his peril and thereby traitorous'.[20]

Some sense can, however, be made of the use of trial and attainder to convict sundry persons of high treason in Henry

VIII's reign, and this rationale further exposes the king's nature. Several cases can be categorized as genuinely perceived threats to the Crown, mostly after 1536: Buckingham, Lord Thomas Howard, the Pilgrim rebels, Exeter and Montague, Surrey and Norfolk. Nevertheless, for the most part, the evidence used to convict these men was inadequate and unconvincing or, as in the case of Lord Thomas, no actual offence had been committed but there were grounds for the king's concern that the royal succession and possibly even his person were endangered. There is a second category of people who committed treason by their failure to conform to the royal will: Barton, More, Fisher and the heretics, papists and abbots of the late 1530s and early 1540s. This was possible on the basis of a definition of treason that had expanded to include thoughts as well as words. Finally, there were those close to the king who let him down: Anne Boleyn, Rochford and Norris, Nicholas Carew, Thomas Cromwell and Catherine Howard (and the sixteen condemned with her). This group were all executed in or after 1536. The savagery of the king's reaction to their betrayal seems bound to have been linked to the deep sense of betrayal and treachery felt by Henry as a result of Anne Boleyn's alleged infidelities and cemented by the unfaithfulness of the Pilgrim rebels. For these people, treason had been unofficially expanded so that it equated to disloyalty and betrayal, personal as well as political. Their deaths were products of an injured pride from a man whose egoism no longer confined itself to showy displays in the tiltyard.

Historians are often loath to classify Henry VIII as a tyrant. This is partly to avoid the unfortunate, ahistorical hyperbole and caricature of some popular representations of Henry, but there is also another reason. The king's first biographer, William Thomas, wrote of Henry in 1547 that he was

> undoubtedly the rarest man that lived in his time. But I say not this to make him a god, nor in all his doings I will not say he hath been a saint... I will confess that he did many evil things... but not as a cruel tyrant, or as a pharisaical hypocrite... I wot [know] not where – in all the histories I have read, to find one private king equal to him.

There is a charm and charisma about Henry VIII that dissuades one from applying the dreaded epithet. I think the crux of this is that Henry VIII didn't think of himself as a tyrant. It is important to grasp that Henry believed that he had fulfilled Erasmus's instructions and he remained convinced of the lawfulness, wisdom and benevolence of his actions. Thomas More had, like Erasmus, defined the difference between a good king and a tyrant as 'a king who respects the law differs from a cruel tyrant thus: a tyrant rules his subjects as slaves, a king thinks of his subjects as his own children'. The tone of Henry's letters to the Pilgrims was strikingly like that of a father reprimanding his ungrateful and disobedient children. He reminded them of his love for them, described his 'chief charge both of your souls and bodies' and exhorted them 'in Christ, as a pitiful shepherd over his sheep' to

> offend no more so grievously your undoubted king and natural prince, which always hath shown himself most loving unto you, and remember your duty of allegiance and that ye are bound to obey us your king, both by God's commandment and law of nature.

By Henry's own estimation, he was doing the things a good king did – it was only his rebellious subjects who were deviating from the orthodox and proper way.[21]

Yet it is an inescapable conclusion that in the last decade of his reign, Henry VIII had begun to act as a tyrant. The glittering, brilliant monarch of the accession, toppled into old age by betrayal, aggravated into irascibility and suspicion as a result of ill health and corrupted by absolute power, had become a despot.

Legend has it that Thomas More, advising the young Thomas Cromwell, told him

> if you will follow my poor advice, you shall, in your counsel-giving unto his grace, ever tell him what he ought to do but never what he is able to do. So shall you show yourself a true faithful servant and a right worthy counsellor. For if a lion knew his own strength, hard it were for any man to rule him.

The old lion had learned his strength. The estimation of one priest during the Pilgrimage of Grace suggested that Wolsey's terracotta roundels had been dreadfully prescient, for he called the king

> a tyrant more cruel than Nero, for Nero destroyed but a part of Rome, but this tyrant destroyeth this whole realm.[22]

Epilogue

Hear then, you kings, take this to heart; learn your lesson, lords of the wide world; lend your ears, you rulers of the multitude, whose pride is in the myriads of your people. It is the Lord who gave you your authority; your power comes from the Most High. He will put your actions to the test and scrutinize your intentions.

Wisdom of Solomon 6 (cited in Stephen Gardiner's *In vera obedientia*, 1535)[1]

William Thomas wrote the first biography of Henry VIII in 1547 as a form of dialogue between himself and an Italian observer of Henry VIII's reign. The purpose of the book was to answer the charges of tyranny put by the Italian against Henry VIII and to offer a 'just excuse of my wrongfully slandered Prince, whose good renown, fame, and honour' Thomas recommends to his readers. One of the charges is Henry's treatment of his wives:

and not his first wife, but three or four more, did he not chop, change, or behead them, as his horse coveted new pasture, to satisfy the inordinate appetite of his lecherous will?

Were it not for the sixteenth-century language, this early assessment could pass for a modern appraisal of Henry VIII. Again and again, today's popular media represents Henry VIII as lecherous, insatiable, callous, unfeeling and self-centred. The truth is a lot more complex. The character that has emerged over these pages is of a man of strong feeling but little emotional intelligence, wilful and obstinate but also fiery and charismatic, intelligent but blinkered, attempting to rule and preserve his honour against his profound sense of duty and heavy responsibility to fulfil his divinely ordained role. This was a man who channelled great loss and hurt into physical pursuits, intense theological interest and sometimes savage anger; above all, a proud, awesome and well-intentioned but also flawed and self deceiving monarch.[2]

There was, however, a distinct difference between the Henry VIII of his first forty-odd years, and the Henry VIII that emerged in and after 1536. Many of the flaws in his character were fashioned or catalyzed by the events of this one year. It is hard to underestimate the importance of this succession of events: Henry's fall from his horse in January 1536, which brought fears for the king's mortality was to have long-lasting consequences, most of all on his health, spelling the end of an active life for this king who had heretofore been acclaimed as a man of great strength, courage and energy. It directly contributed to his famous late-life obesity, and the continual and wearying pain of his ulcer became the source of much of his later irascibility. The end of his jousting symbolized the end of his youth in the year of his forty-fifth birthday, which was considered to mark the beginning of old age. In a gerontocratic society, where men of age were considered better fitted to rule due to their calm, sedate wisdom, this aging may not have been wholly bad – but for Henry, age brought none of these things. Instead, it plunged him headlong into a wealth of anxieties and insecurities, fostering and augmenting the pre-existing angst that he felt towards his lack of an heir. Old age, for Henry, meant the onset of cynicism and suspicion.

The source of much of this cynicism was the awful, gnawing sense of betrayal that lodged itself in Henry after Anne Boleyn's alleged adultery was discovered. The treachery of this woman on whom he had staked so much, for whom he had waited so long, was devastating. It ridiculed him – not just through the comments she and her brother had made about his prowess – but by the message her actions sent about his lack of sexual dominance and patriarchal governance. As such, it had the potential to shake his sense of masculinity and potency to the core. Henry's initial reactions of hyperbolic self-pity, tears, tragedy and exaggeration show just how much the news had upset and upended his world, and how emotionally ill-equipped he was to deal with it. By the end of July 1536, over a few short months he had experienced an unbelievable catalogue of loss – two lost sons, two lost wives, the loss of his health and youth and the loss of his sense of masculinity and honour. This was suffered in the midst of threats, which looked like betrayals – the judgment of his cousin, Reginald Pole, and the sword of Damocles of the papal bull, prepared with the knowledge of his fellow monarchs. Psychologists today make clear links between loss and depression, and Henry VIII was to suffer from a depressive episode in 1541 following a serious bout of malaria, when he mourned Cromwell and remained confined at Hampton Court for a long period. But in 1536, Henry reacted as he would in fact mostly react to betrayal – he stifled the dissonance created in his mind by robustly and energetically throwing his energies into a new assertion of his power and masculinity and a new restoration of the social and patriarchal order.

Chief among these reassertions was the even-greater significance attached to a policy of which Henry was already very fond: the royal supremacy. In a variety of ways, Henry newly emphasized and exercised this role. After leniency towards his daughter's resistance for three years, Henry now insisted Mary sign in support of his supremacy and bastardize herself. His chief minister, Thomas Cromwell, was now permanently established as vicegerent in spirituals and vicar-general, and Henry issued his self-composed Ten Articles which arrogated to himself the right to define doctrine and exercise the 'care of souls' to which the Pilgrim rebels would later object. Papal authority in England was definitively abolished and royal injunctions imposed codes of practice to ensure the king's doctrine was followed. In setting out his theology, which focused around the binaries of kingship and obedience, Henry defined the core values of a system of belief to which he would hold until his death and to which he also expected others to adhere. Its central tenets reveal much about his preoccupations – his own supremacy, unity, good works and a sense of himself as a reforming king. This self-conception was an elevated one, a protestation of righteousness that put Henry on a parallel with the reforming leaders of the Old Testament and claimed a relationship similar to that of God with David, the man whom God called 'a man after my own heart'.

This belief in his own virtue combined ferociously with his reaction to dissonance – the way that perceived betrayal and treachery worked in him to produce self-justification and aggression – when his ego received its next challenge, the Pilgrimage of Grace. Such treasonous rebellion inflamed Henry into defiance, bombast and bravado. Pride and intransigence were Henry's way of quelling the panic he felt at the deceit and betrayal that rebellion represented, and the only way for him to maintain his honour in face of another huge challenge to his dominance was to quash it. His treatment of the monasteries is a classic example of how rebellion led to rage and reaction. Although in early 1536, it looked very likely that reform of the monasteries was the goal of dissolution, by late 1536, his missives about the traitorous activities of the monks suggested Henry had equated them with his existing beliefs about the dangerous power of clerics, and plans for reform had changed into plans for destruction.

Henry's reaction to rebellion was powerfully represented in the new image created for him at this time by the royal painter,

Hans Holbein. The Thyssen and Whitehall portraits exuded a magnificence, dominance and power that reaffirmed Henry's royal supremacy and asserted his pre-eminent masculinity. The confident, aggressive and domineering stance of this proto-'superman' laid claim to power and virility, precisely because these things had so recently been under attack, and just as old age was threatening to erode them.

The consequence of so many disasters in quick succession in this year was to condition Henry VIII and instil in him a morbid fear of, and obsession with, betrayal. Injuries to the king's pride became commensurate with treason, which expanded both in its legal definition and in the range of behaviours it covered in practice. Treason was no longer just a case of threats to the Crown; it also meant letting the king down or failing to conform to his will. His subjects called him the 'Mouldwarp' and covertly accused him of tyranny, and they were right; for from 1536, the use of attainder twisted the law to make arbitrary action possible. The government's attitude towards dissidents and opponents was increasingly repressive and brutal as this ailing, aging monarch sought to fight his own decline by further despotism and overreaction. The whole of 1536, and all that followed, was arguably Henry's reaction to the discomfort of holding these two different cognitions in tension.

The year 1536 marked a turning point in Henry VIII's life. And yet, when one thinks of what could have happened, it is extraordinary that its effects were so contained. If Anne Boleyn and Henry were merry together until soon before her adultery was alleged, her fall was not inevitable, and our famous king of six wives might have lived with her until his death. She may yet have borne him a son, she may have persuaded him and the country towards further reformation, or perhaps her continuing presence would have sparked the publication of the papal bull in 1536 and invasion from Europe. After Anne's death, there was a chance that Henry would have returned to Rome and brought the English Reformation, and the Anglican Church, to a swift and premature end – what is strange is that he didn't. Finally, the Pilgrims might not have accepted the December pardon, not have stood down, and have pitched battle against the king's troops, to the inevitable defeat of the royal army. 1536 could have been the year in which Henry VIII was deposed. Instead, it was the year that was to define and shape him for ever in posterity.

The terrifying and salutary thing is that, throughout, Henry VIII showed an extraordinary capacity for self-deception. He genuinely believed in the virtue of the path that he had chosen, and the story of his life after 1536 is of his ever more costly attempts to bolster his concept of himself against evidence that told him otherwise. Nevertheless, it would be hard not to feel for him in his tumultuous series of losses and misadventures. Thomas's response to the charge laid by his Italian adversary expresses this: 'the truth is he hath a great many wives, and with some of them hath as ill-luck as any other poor man'. The French ambassador, Charles de Marillac, observing Henry with Catherine Howard noted, 'the King is so fond of her that he knows not how to express his affection' – here was an emotionally inexpert, broken man but one whose sadness and rage would have devastating consequences. Perhaps an earlier French ambassador had it right when he concluded, 'he is a man to be marvelled at and has wonderful people about him… but he is an old fox, proud as the devil and accustomed to ruling'.[2]

Appendix 1
Timeline of 1536

January	7	Katherine of Aragon dies
from January		Threat of papal bull
January	24	Henry falls from his horse while jousting
January	29	Katherine of Aragon's funeral
January	29	Anne Boleyn miscarries
February	10	Jane Seymour first noted by the Spanish ambassador, Eustace Chapuys
February		End of monastic visitation
March		Act passed for Dissolution of Smaller Monasteries
March		Reginald Pole sends Henry an open letter
April	18	Spanish ambassador, Chapuys, invited to kiss Anne Boleyn's hand
April	30	Mark Smeaton arrested
May	1	Smeaton moved to the Tower May Day jousts Henry questions Henry Norris
May	2	Norris, Anne Boleyn and George, Lord Rochford arrested
May	4, 5	William Brereton, Richard Page, Sir Francis Weston, Sir Thomas Wyatt, Sir Francis Bryan detained
May	10	Grand jury indict all the accused except Page and Wyatt
May	12	Smeaton, Brereton, Weston and Norris tried and found guilty
May	15	Anne Boleyn and Rochford tried and found guilty
May	17	Archbishop Cranmer declares marriage of Anne and Henry null and Elizabeth a bastard
May	19	Anne Boleyn executed
May	19	Cranmer issues dispensation for Henry to marry Jane Seymour
May	20	Henry and Jane Seymour betrothed
May	30	Henry and Jane Seymour marry

after May		Holbein paints Thyssen portrait of Henry VIII
c. June		Second Succession Act
mid-June		Mary signs oath swearing her father's supremacy and her own illegitimacy
June		King's niece and second in line to the throne is imprisoned for marrying illegally
June	28	Henry turns 45
July	18	King makes Cromwell vicegerent over all ecclesiastical affairs
July	23	King's illegitimate son, Henry Fitzroy, Duke of Richmond and Somerset, dies, aged 17
July		King issues Ten Articles, first doctrinal statement of Anglican Church
August		Cromwell as new vicegerent issues Royal Injunctions to enforce Ten Articles
August		King proclaims that no one is to preach on controversial issues
August		King's proclamation cuts the number of holy days
August		Dissolution of monasteries begins
October	1	Lincolnshire rebellion begins at Louth
October	8	Pilgrimage of Grace (huge armed rebellion) begins in Yorkshire at Beverley
	16	Yorkshire Pilgrims march to York (10,000 men). York surrenders
	21	Pontefract Castle surrenders to Pilgrims
	21	Henry sends Lancaster Herald to Pontefract
Oct-Nov		Pole made a cardinal
	27	Pilgrim representatives sent to Henry
December	2–4	Council of Pilgrims
	6	Meeting of Pilgrims with Norfolk
	7	Pardon accepted by Pilgrims
mid-Dec		Henry asks Aske to court for Christmas

Appendix 2
Henry VIII's Wives

Katherine of Aragon (16 December 1485 – 7 January 1536)

Married Henry on 11 June 1509. He was 17, she was 23.
Princess Mary was born on 18 February 1516.
'Divorced' 23 May 1533 (married for 23 years and 11 months).
Died 7 January 1536. Likely cause of death was stomach cancer.

Anne Boleyn (c. 1500-1501 – 19 May 1536)

Married Henry on 14 November 1532 AND 25 January 1533.
He was 41, she was 31–32.
Princess Elizabeth was born on 7 September 1533.
Beheaded 19 May 1536 (married for 3 years and 3 months).

Jane Seymour (c. 1508-9 – 24 October 1537)

Married Henry on 30 May 1536. He was 44, she was 26–27.
Prince Edward was born on 12 October 1537.
Died 24 October 1537 (married for 1 year and 4 months).
Likely cause of death was puerperal sepsis ('childbed fever').

Anne of Cleves (22 September 1515 – 16 July 1557)

Married Henry on 6 January 1540. He was 48, she was 24.
'Divorced', 9 July 1540 (married for six months).
Died 16 July 1557.

Catherine Howard (c. 1518-1524 [likely 1521] – 13 February 1542)

Married Henry on 8 August 1540. He was 49, she was 17–22.
Beheaded 15 February 1542 (married for 2 years and 6 months).

Kateryn Parr (1512 – 5 September 1548)

Married Henry on 12 July 1543. He was 52, she was 31.
Survived Henry (married for 3 years and 6 months). Henry VIII died on 28 January 1547.
Died 5 September 1548. Likely cause of death was puerperal sepsis ('childbed fever').

Appendix 3
The Cost of Living in Henry VIII's Reign

In Henry VIII's reign,

> 20 shilling (s) = 1 pound sterling
> 12 pence (d) = 1 shilling

Here are some sample salaries and prices.

Salaries

Speaker of the House of Commons	£100 per annum
Master of the Jewels	£20 per annum
King's apothecary	£10 per annum
Master mason at the Tower of London	1s a day
Yeoman of the Guard	6d a day

In the army

Captain	2s a day
Archer	8d a day
Ordinary soldiers	6d a day

In the navy

Admiral	10s a day
For labourers doing a day's work (12 hours)	
Freemason, plumbers	6d a day
Agricultural labourers	4d a day

(without meat and drink, an extra 2d with)

Superior carpenters at Hampton Court	8d, 7d and 6d a day
Gardeners	6d a day
Common labourers	4d a day

Cost of goods

'The Story of David' tapestry	£1500
Gold cup and cover weighing 53 ounces	£19 7s
A coat of white and green royal livery	4s
The yearly clothing of a chief shepherd	5s
Oxen	29s 10½d each
Mutton	3s 7d
Pheasants	2s
Geese	7d
Eggs	1s per 100 eggs

Figures in this book:

Total expenditure on Field of the Cloth of Gold: £8,839 2s 4d
Cost of Westminster tournament of 1511: £4,000
Money left in Henry VIII's will for prayers for his soul: £1,266
Hans Holbein's annual salary: £30
Payment of Anne Boleyn's executioner: £23 6s 8d
Subsidy levied on men worth over: £20

Notes

Abbreviations

Aymot, 'Constantyne'	Thomas Amyot, 'A Memorial from George Constantyne to Thomas, Lord Cromwell', *Archaeologia: Or, Miscellaneous Tracts Relating to Antiquity* vol. 23 (1831), pp. 50-78
CSP, Span	G.A. Bergenroth, *Calendar of Letters, Despatches and State Papers, Relating to the Negotiations between England and Spain* (London, 1862–1954)
Baldwin Smith, *Henry VIII*	Lacey Baldwin Smith, *Henry VIII: The Mask of Royalty* (St Albans, 1971)
Bernard, *The King's Reformation*	G.W. Bernard, *The King's Reformation: Henry VIII and the Remaking of the English Church* (New Haven and London, 2005)
CSP, Ven	Brown, Rawdon (ed.), *Calendar of State Papers and Manuscripts Relating to English Affairs existing in the Archives and Collections of Venice* (1867–1873)
Bush and Bownes, *The Defeat*	Michael Bush and David Bownes, *The Defeat of the Pilgrimage of Grace: A Study of the Postpardon Revolts of December 1536 to March 1537 and their Effect* (Hull, 1999)
Cox, *Cranmer*	J.E. Cox, *Miscellaneous Writings and Letters of Thomas Cranmer* (Cambridge, 1846)
EHR	*English Historical Review*
Foxe, *Acts and Monuments*	John Foxe, *Acts and Monuments*, ed. S.R. Cattley and G. Townsend, 8 vols (London, 1837–41)
Hall, *Chronicle*	Edward Hall, *The vnion of the two noble and illustre famelies of Lancastre [and] Yorke...* (London, 1550)
HJ	*The Historical Journal*
Ives, *Life and Death*	Eric Ives, *The Life and Death of Anne Boleyn 'The Most Happy'* (Oxford, 2004)
LP	J. S. Brewer, J. Gairdner and R. H. Brodie (eds.) *Letters and Papers, Foreign and Domestic, Of the Reign of Henry VIII* (1862–1932)
MacCulloch, *Cranmer*	Diarmaid MacCulloch, *Thomas Cranmer: A Life* (New Haven and London, 1996)
Scarisbrick, *Henry VIII*	J. J. Scarisbrick, *Henry VIII* (London, 1968, 1990 reprint)
State Papers	*State Papers published under the authority of His Majesty's Commission* (1830)
Statutes	*The Statutes of the Realm*, vol. iii, 1509–1547 (London, 1817)
TRHS	*Transactions of the Royal Historical Society*
Wriothesley, *Chronicle*	Charles Wriothesley, *A Chronicle of England During the Reigns of the Tudors, From AD 1485 to 1559* ed. William Douglas Hamilton (London, 1875)
Starkey, *Six Wives*	David Starkey, *Six Wives: The Queens of Henry VIII* (London, 2003)

_1536_

Walker, _Writing_ — Greg Walker, _Writing under Tyranny: English Literature and the Henrician Reformation_ (Oxford, 2005)

Weir, _Henry VIII_ — Alison Weir, _Henry VIII: King and Court_ (London, 2001)

Shore, 'Crisis' — Miles F. Shore, 'Henry VIII and the Crisis of Generativity', _Journal of Interdisciplinary History_ 2.4 (1972)

Endnotes

Preface

1 Ives, *The Life and Death*, p. 351.

2 J.C. Flügel, 'On the Character and Married Life of Henry VIII', in *Psychoanalysis and History* ed. Bruce Mazlish (Englewood Cliffs, 1963) (reprinted from *International Journal of Psycho-Analysis*, I, 1920, 24–55); Shore, 'Crisis'; interviews with cast and crew, *Henry VIII* (ITV, 2003); Baldwin Smith, *Henry VIII*, p. 25; also see David Starkey, *Henry: Virtuous Prince* (London, 2008), which was published when this book went to press.

3 Baldwin Smith, Review article, 'Christ, What a Fright!: The Tudor Portrait as an Icon', *Journal of Interdisciplinary History* 4.1 (1973), pp. 119–127, here p. 120.

PART ONE
Setting the Scene
Prologue

1 L. P. Hartley, *The Go-Between* (New York, 1954).

2 William Shakespeare, *Troilus and Cressida*, I.i.109–110; Wilfred Hooper, 'The Tudor Sumptuary Laws', *EHR* 30 (1915), 443–49; Derek Wilson, *England in the Age of Thomas More* (Norwich, 1978), pp. 62–63.

3 Wilson, *England*, pp. 86–88.

4 Lucien Febvre, *Le problème de l'incroyance au XVIe siècle; La religion de Rabelais* (Paris, 1947); Keith Thomas, *Religion and the Decline of Magic* (Harmondsworth, 1971); Jean Delumeau, *Sin and fear: the emergence of a western guilt culture 13th–18th centuries*, trans. Eric Nicholson (New York, 1991).

5 Pieter Spierenburg, *The Spectacle of Suffering: Executions and the Evolution of Repression* (Cambridge, New York, 1984); Baldwin Smith, *A Tudor Tragedy: The Life and Times of Catherine Howard*, (London, 1961), pp. 74–78, here p. 78.

6 Susan Dwyer Amussen, '"The Part of a Christian Man": The Cultural Politics of Manhood in Early Modern England', in *Political Culture and Cultural Politics in Early Modern England. Essays presented to David Underdown* ed. Amussen and Mark A. Kishlansky (Manchester and New York, 1995), p. 215; Thomas Laqueur, *Making Sex: Body and Gender from the Greeks to Freud* (Cambridge, Mass. and London 1990), pp. 134–42; Ian Maclean, *The Renaissance Notion of Woman: A Study in the Fortunes of Scholasticism and Medical Science in European Intellectual Life* (Cambridge, 1980), pp. 16, 17, 22.

PART ONE – Chapter 1
The Change

1 Victoria Coren, 'Wilf, meet Henry, Google's top killer', *The Observer*, 15 April 2007; 'Henry VIII representation', BDRC Focus Group, April 2006.

2 LP, xiv (i), 14; xx (ii), 1030; Thomas Stapleton, *The Life and Illustrious Martyrdom of Sir Thomas More* trans. P.E. Hallett (London, 1928), p. 77.

3 Shore, 'Crisis', 361, 374, 389, 390; Sir Arthur Salisbury MacNalty, *Henry VIII: A Difficult Patient* (London, 1952), pp. 73, 95, 159ff, 183. MacNulty follows F. Chamberlin, *The Private Character of Henry VIII* (London, 1932). Although MacNulty mentions that the ulcer Henry sustained in 1527 would cause 'irritability and impatience', he foregrounds the theory of cerebral injury in explaining Henry's

change of character (compare with Weir's note to MacNulty, Weir, *Henry VIII*, p. 370); Walker, *Writing*, p. 11.

4 Flügel, 'On the Character and Married Life of Henry VIII', p. 135; Baldwin Smith, *Henry VIII*, p. 23, also see p. 106.

5 Chamberlin, *The Private Character*; Scarisbrick, *Henry VIII*, p. 485; Weir, *Henry VIII*, pp. 370, 384 – though she cites MacNulty, not Scarisbrick.

PART ONE – Chapter 2
Young Henry

1 LP, iv (iii), 5412.

2 R. A. B. Mynors and D.F.S. Thomson (trans.), *The Correspondence of Erasmus* (Toronto, 1972), 12 vols, ii, pp. 126–29.

3 Scarisbrick, *Henry VIII*, pp. 7–10.

4 Mynors and Thomson, *Correspondence of Erasmus* II, pp. 147–48; LP, i, 338; Rawdon Brown (trans.), *Four Years at the Court of Henry VIII. Selection of Dispatches Written by the Venetian Ambassador, Sebastian Giustinian* (London 1854), 2 vols, I, p. 81; CSP, Ven, iii, 1287.

5 Hall, *Chronicle*, f. 2v; *Four Years*, I, p. 76; CSP, Ven, iii, 918, 1287.

6 CSP, Ven, iii, 1053, 918; LP, I (ii) 2391; CSP, Ven, iii, 1287.

7 George Cavendish, *The Life and Death of Cardinal Wolsey* in *Two Early Tudor Lives* ed. Richard S. Sylvester and Davis P. Harding (New Haven and London, 1962), pp. 11, 12; *Four Years*, I, pp. 79–81; CSP, Ven, iii, 828, 837; *Four Years*, I, p. 232; CSP, Ven, iii, 1287; LP, i (ii), 2391; CSP, Ven, iii, 918.

8 Joycelyne G. Russell, *The Field of the Cloth of Gold: Men and Manners in 1520* (London, 1969), pp. 49, 145–46, 150–51; LP, iii (i), 919.

9 CSP, Ven, iii, 918; Four years, I, pp. 85, 90, 192; Desiderius Erasmus, *Opus Epistolarum* ed. P.S. and H.M. Allen, 11 vols (Oxford, 1906–47), VIII, 2143, p. 129; CSP, Ven, iii, 1287, 918, 1095, 1241; LP, I, (ii), 2391.

10 CSP, Span, 1509–25, 19; Cavendish, *Wolsey*, p. 12; *Four Years*, I, p. 281; CSP, Ven, iii, 875 and 894; Steven Gunn, 'Warfare in Henry's Reign', *Henry: Dressed to Kill Exhibition at the Tower of London Catalogue* (Royal Armouries, forthcoming 2009); Scarisbrick, *Henry VIII*, pp. 21–24.

11 Cavendish, *Wolsey*, p. 183.

12 CSP, Ven, iii, 839; *Four Years*, I, p. 195; Cavendish, *Wolsey*, p. 189; Scarisbrick, *Henry VIII*, p. 17.

PART ONE – Chapter 3
The Divorce

1 E. W. Ives, 'Henry VIII (1491–1547)', *ODNB*, (Oxford, 2004); with thanks to Dr Kent Rawlinson, Curator of Historic Buildings at Hampton Court Palace for his thoughts on this.

2 Cavendish, *Wolsey*, p. 32.

3 Cavendish, *Wolsey*, p. 86.

4 J. J. Scarisbrick, *Henry VIII* (London, 1969–1990 reprint), p. 163; Bernard, *The King's Reformation*, pp. 17–22.

5 Scarisbrick, *Henry VIII*, p. 287; Diarmaid MacCulloch, 'Henry VIII and the Reform of the Church', in ibid (ed.) *The Reign of Henry VIII: Politics, Policy and Piety* (Basingstoke, 1995), p. 165; William Tyndale, *The Obedience of a Christian Man* (1528), ed. R. Lovett (1888), p. 93; J.G. Nichols (ed.), *Narratives of the Days*

of the Reformation (London, 1859), p. 56.
6 *Statutes*, 24. Hen VIII, c.xii; 25 Henry VIII, c.xx; 26 Henry VIII, c.i; Peter
Marshall, *Reformation England 1480–1642* (London, 2003), p. 39.
7 *Statutes*, 28 Henry VIII, c.vii, 26 Henry VIII, c.xiii.
8 Ives, *The Life and Death*, pp. 260–62; MacCulloch, *The Reformation: A History*
(London, 2003), p. 194; CSP Span V (ii), 43; LP, x, 601.

PART ONE – Chapter 4
1536 and All That
1 Derek Wilson, *In the Lion's Court: Power, Ambition and Sudden Death in the
Reign of Henry VIII* (London, 2001), p. 382. *Annus horribilis* is Latin for 'horrible
year' and was famously used by Queen Elizabeth II to describe 1992; MacNalty,
Henry VIII, p. 95; R.W. Hoyle, *The Pilgrimage of Grace and the politics of the 1530s*
(Oxford, 2001), pp. 55–92; Wilson, *In the Lion's Court*, pp. 385, 386.

PART TWO
The Crisis of Masculinity
1 Michael Payne and John Hunter (eds.) *Renaissance Literature: An Anthology*
(Oxford, 2005).
2 LP, xi, 285; phrase from Philip D. Collington, 'Sans Wife: Sexual Anxiety and
the Old Man in Shakespeare', in *Growing Old in Early Modern Europe: Cultural
Representations* ed. Erin Campbell (Aldershot, 2006), p. 191.

PART TWO – Chapter 5
A Wife's Death
1 LP, x, 41; ix, 964, 1036, 1037; x, 60, 59.
2 MacCulloch, *Cranmer*, pp.147; CSP Span, IV (ii), 778; LP, ix, 983; N.H. Nicolas
(ed.), *Proceedings and Ordinances of the Privy Council of England, 1386–1542*, 7
vols. (London, 1830), vii, p. 347.
3 A papal bull was an edict issued by a pope, so named after the lead seal or *bulla*
that proved its authenticity.
4 LP, ix, 1036, 99, x, 70, 82, ix, 1000, x, 141.
5 LP, x, 199; Ives, *The Life and Death*, p. 295 miscalculates Elizabeth to be 16
months old, but she was born on 7 September 1533; Hall, *Chronicle*, f. 227r; see,
for example, J.J. Scarisbrick, *Henry VIII*, p. 335, 'he would mock her even in death'.
6 LP, x, 141; Starkey, *Six Wives*, p. 510; LP, x, 76, 128.

PART TWO – Chapter 6
The King's Honour
1 LP, xix (ii), 19; C.B. Watson, *Shakespeare and the Renaissance Concept of
Honour* (Princeton, 1960); Elizabeth A. Foyster, *Manhood in Early Modern
England: Honour, Sex and Marriage* (London and New York, 1999), p. 5; Lyndal
Roper, 'Stealing manhood: capitalism and magic in early modern Germany', in
Oedipus and the Devil: Witchcraft, Sexuality and Religion in Early Modern Europe
(London and New York, 1994), p. 138.
2 The term 'masculinity' dates from 1748, whereas the use of 'manhood' to
mean the qualities of manliness dates back to 1393, according to the OED. The
source of much of the detail of what follows is Alan Young, *Tudor and Jacobean*

Tournaments (London, 1987), especially pp. 14–25; Frederic J. Baumgartner, *France in the Sixteenth Century* (New York, 1995), p. 126; Hall, *Chronicle*, ff. 122v–123r; MacNalty, *Henry VIII: A Difficult Patient*, p.89.

3 Young, *Tudor and Jacobean Tournaments*, p. 23; with thanks to Dr Kent Rawlinson, Curator of Historic Buildings at Hampton Court Palace, for his thoughts on 'conspicious consumption'; Baldesar Castiglione, *The Book of the Courtier* trans. George Bull (London, 1967), p. 310; David Loades, *The Tudor Court* (London, 1986), p. 3; LP, xv, 616; Thomas Elyot, *The Book named the Governor* ed. S.E. Lehmberg (1975), Book 1, XVI.

4 *Four Years*, I, pp. 75–76, 81, see also 91; Shore, 'Crisis', 370; Raymond Lull, *Book of the Order of Chivalry* cited by Anthony Fletcher, *Gender, Sex and Subordination in England 1500–1800* (New Haven and London, 1995), p.129

5 LP, x, 200; x, 427; Robert Hutchinson, *The Last Days of Henry VIII: Conspiracy, Treason and Heresy at the Court of the Dying Tyrant* (London, 2005), p. 138; LP, x, 200, 255, 315, 427.

6 LP, x, 282, 351; Wriothesley, *Chronicle*, p. 33; Lancelot de Carles, 'Poème sur la mort d'Anne Boleyn', reprinted in *La Grande Bretagne devant l'opinion française depuis la guerre de cent ans jusqu'à la fin du XVIe siècle* ed. Georges Ascoli (Geneva, 1971), p. 242, lines 317–26. See also LP x 1036.

7 Aymot, 'Constantyne', 75; MacNalty, *Henry VIII*, pp. 67, 73, 198–9; Norman Moore, 'Vicary, Thomas (*d.* 1561)', rev. I. G. Murray, *ODNB* (Oxford, 2004); cf. Elizabeth Lane Furdell, *The Royal Doctors: 1485–1714: Medical Personnel at the Tudor and Stuart Courts* (Rochester, New York, 2001), p.33. Vicary was promised the job in 1530 and held it until his death in 1561; LP, xii (i), 1068, xii (ii), 77. This has led some commentators to suggest Henry had ulcers in both legs, but this is the only evidence to suggest it; LP xii (i), 995; xiii (ii), 800; xvi, 589 (my italics); MacNalty, *Henry VIII*, pp. 103, 160–61, 198–99.

8 MacNalty, *Henry VIII*, p.167; Maria Hayward, *Dress at the Court of King Henry VIII* (Leeds, 2007), p. 7, n.6, cf. Stephen J. Kunitz, 'Making a Long Story Short: A Note on Men's Height and Mortality in England from the First through the Nineteenth Centuries', in *Medical History* 31, (1987), p. 275; LP, xvi, 121; xvi, 589; *Four Years*, I, p. 86; Weir, *Henry VIII*, p. 2; Castiglione, *Courtier*, p. 61.

9 LP, iv (iii), 5412; Roper, 'Blood and codpieces: masculinity in the early modern German town', in *Oedipus and the Devil*, pp. 119–120.

10 These medical texts are analyzed by Alexandra Shepard in her *Meanings of Manhood in Early Modern England* (Oxford, 2003), pp. 54–55, 214–16. Cf. Alice Tobriner, 'Old Age in Tudor-Stuart Broadside Ballads', *Folklore* 102.ii (1991), 151, and Baldwin Smith, *Henry VIII*, p. 129; Prospero's age is observed by Collington, 'Sans Wife', 197; Keith Thomas, 'Age and Authority in Early Modern England', *Proceedings of the British Academy* 61 (1976), 207–8, 211–12; Collington, Sans Wife', 187, 191, 192; judgments on old age cited by Thomas, 'Age and Authority', 244.

11 John Stow, *The Annales of England faithfully collected out of the most autenticall authors, records, and other monuments of antiquitie, from the first inhabitation vntill this present yeere 1592 by Iohn Stow citizen of London* (London, 1592), p.964; Will Fisher, 'The Renaissance Beard: Masculinity in Early Modern England', *Renaissance Quarterly*, 54.1 (2001), pp. 155–188, here 156, 158, 166, 167, 173, 174; LP, x, 743.

PART TWO – Chapter 7
The Fall of Anne Boleyn

1 Having examined all the evidence, I have reached conclusions very similar to those of Greg Walker, in 'Rethinking the Fall of Anne Boleyn', *HJ* 45.1 (2002). I am also indebted to the scholarship of Eric Ives and G.W. Bernard. Those who believe it led inexorably to Anne's execution include John Guy, *Tudor England,* p. 141 and Starkey, *Six Wives,* p. 554; J.E. Neale, *Queen Elizabeth* (London, 1934), p. 17.

2 G. R. Elton suggests more than one – see *England under the Tudors* (London, 1955), p. 152, but the evidence for a miscarriage in 1535 is slim, and a series of miscarriages in 1534 does not fit with the dates; for the secret wedding, see Hall, *Chronicle,* f. 209v, cf. MacCulloch, *Cranmer,* pp. 637–38; Starkey, *Six Wives,* p. 463; LP, vii, 114, 556; Sir John Dewhurst, 'The alleged miscarriages of Katharine of Aragon and Anne Boleyn', *Medical History* 21 (1984), p. 54; LP, vii, 232, 958, see also 1013 and CSP Span V (ii), 75.

3 LP, vii, 1193, CSP Span V (i), 90; Dewhurst, 'The alleged miscarriages', p. 55; see also St Clare Byrne, *The Lisle Letters,* 1, p.240; Ives, *The Life and Death,* pp. 190–92; Starkey, *Six Wives,* p. 553; Weir, *Henry VIII,* p. 353. Chapuys does not seem to have accompanied the court, as Weir suggests; LP, x, 450, 528; Ives suggests this story was spread by Francis I, see Ives, *The Life and Death,* p. 299.

4 Wriothesley, *Chronicle,* p.33; LP, x, 282; CSP Span V (ii), 21; LP, x, 351; CSP Span V (ii), 29. Compare Ives, *The Life and Death,* p. 299; G.W. Bernard, 'The Fall of Anne Boleyn', *EHR* 106 (1991), 588 and Walker, 'Rethinking', 13. The original (in Vienna) is in French and entirely in cipher, and the translations of it in the *Letters and Papers* and the *Calendar of State Papers: Spanish* differ sufficiently to allow more than one interpretation of Henry's actions; CSP Span V (ii), 29. Walker, 'Rethinking', 11, suggests this statement about not bearing to be apart refers to Jane, not Anne, but I believe this is a misreading; LP, x, 199, 427; CSP Span V (ii) 13; LP, x, 199. George Bernard cites the original French text, in the Vienna archives, in 'The Fall', p. 585.

5 Wriothesley, *Chronicle,* I. pp. 189–91, see Randle Cotgrave, A Dictionarie of the French and English Tongues (London, 1611), which gives 'witchcraft' and 'divination' under the entry 'sortilege'; Ives, The Life and Death, p. 298, see LP, vi, 1069; Retha Warnicke, 'Sexual Heresy at the Court of Henry VIII', HJ 30 (1987), and The Rise and Fall of Anne Boleyn: Family Politics at the Court of Henry VIII (Cambridge, 1989), ch. 8, and dismissal by Bernard, 'The fall', 586, and Ives, The Life and Death, pp. 296–97; Walker, 'Rethinking', 15, note.

6 MacCulloch, *Cranmer,* p. 149; Walker, 'Rethinking', 12; LP, x, 352.

7 LP, x, 282, 495, CSP Span V (ii) 21; George Wyatt, 'Extracts from the Life of the Virtuous Christian and Renowed Queen Boleigne', in S.W. Singer, *The Life of Cardinal Wolsey* (London, 1925), p. 443; for Henry's affairs, see LP, vii, 1193; viii, 263; CSP Span V (ii), 43; LP, x, 601.

8 Ives believes Jane was coached and 'Henry discovered the new Jane at the end of March', but there is very little evidence of change; CSP Span V (ii), 43; LP, x, 601; LP, x, 901.

9 Starkey, *The Reign of Henry VIII: Personalities and Politics* (London, 2002), p. 88; Scarisbrick, *Henry VIII,* (2nd edition, London, 1997), p. xiii; Carol Tavris and Elliot Aronson, *Mistakes Were Made (but not by me): Why we justify foolish beliefs, bad decisions and hurtful acts* (London, 2008), pp. 15–17.

10 LP, x, 720, 752, 782; 'concubine' is Chapuys' ubiquitous term for Anne, LP, x,

720 (for 'she-devil'); vi, 975, 1018, 1069 (for 1533); LP, vi, 1069; vii, 1193; for 'merry', see LP, vi, 1054, 1069, vii, 126, 682, 823, 888, 1193; ix, 310, 525, 566, 571, 663; Bernard, 'The Fall', 585.

11 LP, x, 699; CSP Span V (ii), 43a; LP, x, 720; Bernard, 'The Fall', 589–590.

12 Ives, *The Life and Death,* pp. 321, 307–15; Starkey, *Six Wives*, pp. 555–61; for Anne and Cromwell on bad terms, see LP, x, 601; CSP Span V (ii), 61, LP, x, 1069. The crucial phrase is 'il se mist a fantasier et conspirer le dict affaire'. See Cotgrave, *A Dictionarie,* for a near-contemporary translation of 'fantasier'; see, for example, *Anne of the Thousand Days* (1969) and *Henry VIII* (2003).

13 de Carles, 'Poème sur la mort d'Anne Boleyn', in Ascoli, pp. 242–46, lines 339–374, 430–34, 443–44, 390–464; Bernard, 'The Fall', 596; see also Ives, *The Life and Death*, p. 333; LP, x, 953, 964, 793, Singer, *Wolsey*, p. 452; LP, x, 873.

14 LP, x, 956, 1043; LP, x, 888, 973, 956, 784, 785, 838.

15 Aymot, 'Constantyne', 64; LP, x, 908; de Carles in Ascoli, p.247, line 480; Walker, 'Rethinking', 18; Singer, *Wolsey*, p. 454.

16 Singer, *Wolsey,* p. 455, LP, x, 798; Walker, 'Rethinking', 20, Bernard, 'The Fall', 601; Walker, 'Rethinking', 20, also reflects on Smeaton's evident emotional instability. One thinks of the 2008 case of Uma Thurman's stalker, Jack Jordan, and the insight into the mind of a stalker in John Fowles's novel, *The Collector* (1963); Wyatt, 'In mourning wise', *Complete Poems* ed. Rebholz, p.255 (my italics).

17 Walker, 'Rethinking', 20.

18 CSP Foreign 1558–9, p. 527

19 de Carles in Ascoli, p.247, line 495; E. W. Ives, 'Norris, Henry (*b.* before 1500, *d.* 1536)', *ODNB* (Oxford, 2004); Singer, *Wolsey,* p. 452; LP, x, 793; Walker, 'Rethinking', 22.

20 Wriothesley, *Chronicle,* I, pp. 35–6, de Carles in Ascoli, p.247, lines 497–508, LP, x, 782; Hall, *Chronicle*, f. 227v; Amyot, 'Constantyne', 64.

21 Singer, *Wolsey*, p. 452, LP, x, 793; Ives, *The Life and Death,* pp. 70–2; Wriothesley, *Chronicle,* I, pp. 36, 189–91; LP, x, 848.

22 Aymot, 'Constantyne', 66, Wriothesley, *Chronicle,* I, pp. 37–39; LP, x, 876, 908; CSP Span, V (ii), 55, LP, x, 908: 'nestoit habile en cas de soy copuler avec femme, et quil navoit ne vertu ne puissance', my translation; Bernard, 'The Fall', 603, Wyatt, 'In mourning wise', *Complete Poems* ed. Rebholz.

23 *Circa Regna tonat* means 'around thrones he thunders' (a classical reference to Jupiter, King of the gods, but likely to be here a veiled reference to Henry himself, who had often been equated in literature with Jupiter). CSP Span, V (ii), 54, Wriothesley, *Chronicle,* I, pp. 40–41; LP, x, 911; Wyatt, 'V. Innocentia Veritas viat Fides circumdederunt me inimici mei' or 'Who list his wealth and ease retain' *Complete Poems* ed. Rebholz, p. 155; Walker, *Writing*, pp. 290–291, see, for example, John Heywood's *The Play of the Weather*.

24 Bernard, see 'The Fall', 606; LP, x, 873, 866; Thomas, *The Pilgrim*, p. 56; MacCulloch, *Cranmer,* pp. 157–58; LP, x, 792, Cox, *Cranmer*, pp. 323–3; CSP Foreign 1558–9, 1303.

25 Wriothesley, *Chronicle,* I, p. 36; Singer, *Wolsey,* pp.451, 457, 458, 461; LP, x, 793, 797, 876, 910; CSP Span V (ii), 55; Ives, *The Life and Death,* pp. 342–43. 345, 357; Ives, 'Debate: The Fall of Anne Boleyn Reconsidered', *EHR* 107 (1992), 652. I disagree with Bernard, 'The Fall of Anne Boleyn: A Rejoinder', *EHR* 107 (1992), 668, note, as the evidence for Anne's oath seems sufficient; Walker, 'Rethinking', 7–8, 25.

26 Ives, 'Debate', 664; Ives, *The Life and Death*, p. 351; LP, x, 902; LP, xi, 381; LP, x,

908; CSP Span, V (ii), 54, 55; Hall, *Chronicle*, f. 228r; LP, x, 915, 926, 993, 1000, cf. Wriothesley, *Chronicle*, I, pp. 43–44; LP, x, 888.

27 Cox, *Cranmer*, pp. 323–24 and LP, x, 792 (the texts differ slightly and I quote both); LP, x, 1033; Foyster, *Manhood*, pp. 4–9, here 5; Roper, *The Holy Household: Women and Morals in Reformation Augsburg* (Oxford, 1989), p.86; see also Fletcher, *Gender, Sex and Subordination*, p.101; LP, xiii (i), 493; Collington, 'Sans Wife', 187, Tobriner, 'Old Age', 163; John Dod and Robert Cleaver, *A Godlie Form of Householde Government* (London, 1612), p.16; CSP Foreign 1558–9, 1303.

PART TWO – Chapter 8
A Dearth of Heirs

1 Beverley A. Murphy, *Bastard Prince: Henry VIII's Lost Son* (Stroud, 2001), pp. ix, 37–38, 122–24, 154; LP, iv (iii), 6307, v, 1485; Venetian ambassador cited by Murphy, *Bastard Prince*, p. 126 – I have been unable to find the original.

2 *State Papers*, I, pp. 457–459; LP, x, 1137, xi, 7; CSP Span, V (ii), 61, 70, 77; see Ives, 'Tudor dynastic problems revisited', *Historical Research* 81 (2008), 255–279, esp. 262–63.

3 *Statutes*, 28 Henry VIII, c.xxiv; CSP Span, V (ii), 77; LP, xi, 147, 293; Wriothesley, *Chronicle*, I, p. 54

4 There seems to be some uncertainty over whether he died on 22 or 23 July; LP, xi, 148 says 23 July; Wriothesley, *Chronicle*, I, p.53 says 22 July; LP, xi, 285; *Statutes*, 28 Henry VIII, c. vii.

5 LP, xi, 233, 221, 236; Hayward, *Dress*, p. 68; Murphy, *Bastard Prince*, p. 179.

6 Cited by Collington, 'Sans Wife', pp. 190-1; LP, xi, 285, 479; MacNaulty reaches a similar conclusion, *Henry VIII*, p. 95; Aristotle, *On Rhetoric*, trans. W. Rhys Roberts in *The Rhetoric and the Poetics of Aristotle* ed. Edward P. J. Corbett (New York, 1954), Book II, Ch. 12, pp. 123–24, cited by Collington, 'Sans Wife', p. 189; LP, xviii (i), 873; xvii, 1334, 177.

PART TWO – Chapter 9
Masculinity and Image

1 Derek Wilson, *Hans Holbein: Portrait of an Unknown Man* (London, 1996), p.242; Susan Foister, *Holbein in England* (London, 2006), p. 93; Xanthe Brooke and David Crombie, *Henry VIII Revealed: Holbein's Portrait and Its Legacy* (London, 2003), p. 13.

2 N. Wolf, cited by Tatiana C. String, *Art and Communication in Henry VIII's Reign* (Aldershot, 2008), p. 56.

3 Brooke and Crombie, *Henry VIII Revealed*, p. 9; Christopher Lloyd and Simon Thurley, *Henry VIII: Images of a Tudor King* (Oxford, 1990), p. 28. For debate about whether 1536 marked a complete change in image and iconography of Henry VIII, see Roy Strong, *Holbein and Henry VIII* (London, 1967), p. 4; Lloyd and Thurley, *Henry VIII*, pp. 20, 24; John N. King, 'The Royal Image, 1535–1603', in *Tudor Political Culture* ed. Dale Hoak (Cambridge, 1995), p. 104, and *Tudor Royal Iconography: Literature and Art in an age of Religious Crisis* (Princeton, 1989), p. 4; Sydney Anglo, *Images of Tudor Kingship* (London, 1992), pp. 1, 3, 112; Greg Walker, 'Henry VIII and the Politics of the Royal Image', in *Persuasive Fictions: Faction, Faith and Political Culture in the Reign of Henry VIII* (Aldershot, 1996), pp. 73, 76, 78, 84, 93; String, *Art and Communication*, pp. 10, 14, 87–88.

4 Walker, 'Henry VIII', pp. 74, 88; String, *Art and Communication*, p. 83.

5 Brooke and Crombie, *Henry VIII Revealed*, p. 9.

6 David Starkey, 'Introduction', in *Lost Faces: Identity and Discovery in Tudor Royal Portraiture* (Catalogue of an exhibition held at the galleries of Philip Mould Ltd, London 2007), ed. Bendor Grosvenor, p. 7. Also see Greg Walker, *The Private Life of Henry VIII* (The British Film Guide 8, London 2003), pp. 18–20.

7 Howarth, *Images of Rule*, p. 82; String, 'Projecting Masculinity: Henry VIII's Codpiece', in *Henry VIII and his Afterlives: Literature, Politics and Art* ed. Christopher Highley, John N. King, and Mark Rankin (forthcoming Cambridge, 2009). My thanks go to Dr String for allowing me to see this chapter in draft.

8 Strong, *Holbein,* pp. 39, 41–2; String, 'Projecting Masculinity' and String, *Art and Communication*, pp. 72–3; Brooke and Crombie, *Henry VIII Revealed*, pp. 28, 34, citing Jodochim Willich (1501–1522)'s treatise on gesture; Lloyd and Thurley, *Henry VIII*, p. 69.

9 String, 'Projecting Masculinity'; this is by eye; Crombie notes that the measurements for the cartoon, Walker Art Gallery copy and Petworth copy, for the width at the top of the braid at the left edge of the coat to the right edge of the coat under the dagger, are 945mm, 906mm and 935mm respectively, Brooke and Crombie, *Henry VIII Revealed*, p. 113; Grosvenor and Philip Mould, *Lost Faces*, p. 53; van Mander cited by Brooke and Crombie, *Henry VIII Revealed,* p. 27.

10 Roper, 'Blood and codpieces', pp. 119–120; String, 'Projecting Masculinity'; Brooke and Crombie, *Henry VIII Revealed*, pp. 84, 113, 34, 24–27; String, *Art and Communication*, p. 71; Grosvenor and Mould, *Lost Faces*, p. 53.

11 Walker, *Private Life,* p. 22; Richard Woods, 'It's fun, it's sexy – but is this really history?', *The Sunday Times*, 27.07.08; Anglo, *Images of Tudor Kingship*, p. 1; String, 'Projecting Masculinity'.

12 Cited by Collington, 'Sans Wife', pp. 190–91; LP, xi, 285, 479; MacNalty reaches a similar conclusion, *Henry VIII*, p.95; Aristotle, *On Rhetoric*, trans. W. Rhys Roberts in *The Rhetoric and the Poetics of Aristotle* ed. Edward P.J Corbett (New York, 1954), Book II, Ch. 12, pp. 123–24, cited by Collington, 'Sans Wife', p.189; LP, xviii (i), 873; xvii, 1334, 177.

PART THREE
The King's Religion

1 LP, xvi, 106.

2 W.G. Naphy, *The Protestant Revolution* (London, 2007), p. 96.

PART THREE – Chapter 10
The Reformation in England

1 Foxe, *Acts and Monuments*; A.G. Dickens, *The English Reformation* (London, 1964).

2 Eamon Duffy, *The Stripping of the Altars* (New Haven, 1992); Christopher Haigh, *The English Reformation Revisited* (Cambridge, 1987), p. 6 and *English Reformations: Religion, Politics, and Society under the Tudors* (Oxford, 1991), p. 142; Ryrie, *The Gospel and Henry VIII*, p. 1; Susan Brigden, *London and the Reformation*, (Oxford, 1989), p. 383.

PART THREE – Chapter 11
1536: The Church Established

1 LP, x, 315, 575.

2 LP, x, 956 (see also x, 450 and 1162), 1043, 792; MacCulloch, *Cranmer,* p.157; Cox, *Cranmer,* pp. 323–3; LP, xi, 210; LP, x, 1212 (see also xi, 54); LP, xi, 860, 1250; x, 909, 1069, 1212.

3 Thomas F. Mayer, *Reginald Pole: Prince and Prophet* (New York and Cambridge, 2000), pp. 13–28; Bernard, *The King's Reformation,* p. 220.

4 LP, x, 1137; xi, 7; F. Donald Logan, 'Thomas Cromwell and the Vicegerency in Spirituals: a revisitation', *EHR* 103 (1988), 658–667, especially 666–7; Robert Hutchinson, *Thomas Cromwell: The Rise and Fall of Henry VIII's Most Notorious Minister* (London, 2007), p. 105; *Statutes,* 28 Henry VIII, c.x.

5 Marshall, *Religious Identities in Henry VIII's England* (Aldershot, 2006), pp. 13–14; MacCulloch, 'Henry VIII', p. 161.

6 *Statutes,* 27 Henry VIII, c.xxviii; J.H. Bettey, *The Suppression of the Monasteries in the West Country* (Gloucester and New Hampshire, 1989), pp. 23, 43; LP, x, 92, 721; G.W. Bernard, *The King's Reformation: Henry VIII and the Remaking of the English Church* (New Haven and London, 2005), pp. 249–251, 255, 258; LP, x, 858, 364 (see also x, 1191). Bernard compares the abbreviations in LP with the original PRO, SP1/102.

7 Henry Gee and William John Hardy (ed.), *Documents Illustrative of English Church History* (London, 1914), pp. 257–68; *Statutes,* 27 Henry VIII, c.xxviii, c.xxvii; LP, x, 601, 216, 552, 1211, 484; xi, 42; x, 335, 385, 741.

8 MacCulloch, 'Henry VIII', p. 162; Hutchinson, *Thomas Cromwell,* p. 104.

9 LP, xi, 1110, 59; C. Lloyd (ed.), *Formularies of Faith Put Forth by Authority During the Reign of Henry VIII* (Oxford, 1825), pp. xiii–xxxii, 2–20; Gilbert Burnet, *The History of the Reformation of the Church of England* ed. Nicholas Pocock (Oxford, 1865), Vol IV, pp. 272–285; for the king's central involvement in the process, see Bernard, *The King's Reformation,* pp. 281–82.

10 Burnet, *The History of the Reformation,* Vol IV, pp. 272–285 (my italics).

11 Bernard, *The King's Reformation,* p. 291.

12 Burnet, *The History of the Reformation,* Vol IV, p. 308; LP, xi, 377; Wriothesley, *Chronicle,* p. 55; LP, vii, 750 (misdated, see Bernard, 'The Making', 324); LP, x, 45; Marshall, *Reformation England,* p. 9; LP, xi, 270, 271; Duffy, *Stripping of the Altars,* pp. 394–95.

PART THREE – Chapter 12
The Role of Henry VIII in Later Reformation

1 This is the point of view argued by Bernard, *The King's Reformation* and his 'The Making of Religious Policy, 1533–1546: Henry VIII and the Search for the Middle Way', *HJ* 41.2 (1998). This chapter adopts a version of this, modified by particular reference to the work of Peter Marshall, Alec Ryrie, and Diarmaid MacCulloch.

2 Including Elton, Starkey, Duffy and Haigh, see Haigh, *English Reformations,* p. 125.

3 For firm direction, see Bernard, 'The Making', 139 and Glyn Redworth, 'Whatever happened to the English Reformation?', *History Today* (October, 1987), 36; MacCulloch, 'Henry VIII', p. 178 and Andrew Pettegree, 'Protestant English; Henry pushed, and history shoved, toward Reformation (book review of *The King's Reformation Henry VIII and the Remaking of the English Church*)', *The Weekly Standard* 5.01.2006; for the *via media,* see Bernard, Redworth and Walker, *Persuasive Fictions,* p. 139; Scarisbrick, *Henry VIII,* p. 304; Marshall, *Reformation*

England, p. 25 and *Religious Identities*, p. 14.

4 MacCulloch, 'Henry VIII', pp. 165, 162–63; Bernard, 'The Making', 322–23; LP, xi, 1110; Scarisbrick, *Henry VIII*, p. 403; Henry's Psalter is now in the British Library, MS Royal 2, AXVI; Walker, 'Henry VIII', p. 82; LP, xxi (ii), 634.

5 Shore, 'Crisis', 370; Scarisbrick, *Henry VIII*, p. 248.

6 LP, xi, 780, 783; xii (i) 479; Greg Walker, *Writing*, pp. 339–40; Bernard, 'The Tyranny of Henry VIII', in *Authority and Consent in Tudor England: Essays Presented to C.S.L. Davies* ed. G.W. Bernard and S.J. Gunn (Aldershot, 2002), pp. 122–23; Bettey, *The Suppression*, pp. 70–85, 102–4; Hall, *Chronicle*, f. 237v; LP, xiv, (ii), 206, 272, 399.

7 *Statutes*, 31 Henry VIII, c.xiii.

8 Bernard, *The King's Reformation*, pp. 525, 496; String, 'Henry VIII's Illuminated 'Great Bible',' *Journal of the Warburg and Courtauld Institutes*, 59 (1996), 315–324; John N. King, *Tudor Royal Iconography: Literature and Art in an Age of Religious Crisis* (Princeton, 1989), p. 70–74; Christopher Lloyd and Simon Thurley, *Henry VIII: Images of a Tudor King* (Oxford, 1990), p. 36; String, *Art and Communication in Henry VIII's Reign* (Aldershot, 2008), pp. 54, 97; Walker, 'Henry VIII', p. 92; Haigh, *English Reformations*, p. 134; compare with Margaret Aston, *England's Iconoclasts (Oxford, 1988), v. 1 Laws Against Images*, pp. 226–28; Marshall, *Reformation England*, p. 54; see also R. B. Merriman, *The Life and Letters of Thomas Cromwell* 2 vols (Oxford, 1902), ii, pp. 156–57.

9 Hall, *Chronicle*, f. 233v; Foxe, *Acts and Monuments*, v, p.234.

10 *Statutes*, 31 Henry VIII, c.xiv; Ryrie, *The Gospel and Henry VIII*, pp.27–28, 31–32; Hall, *Chronicle*, f. 234r; MacCulloch, 'Henry VIII', p. 175, in fact, suggests that the Act contained a few distinct compromises for evangelicals.

11 Lloyd, *Formularies of faith*, pp. 213–377, especially 263, 364–65, 375–77, 215–216.

12 *Statutes*, 34 and 35 Henry VIII, c.i; Hall, *Chronicle*, f. 261v–262r.

13 LP, xvi, 106.

PART THREE – Chapter 13
Henry VIII's Theology

1 See Lloyd, *Formularies of faith*, pp. 215–16; Felicity Heal, *Reformation in Britain and Ireland* (Oxford, 2003), p. 138.

2 Pamela Tudor–Craig, 'Henry VIII and King David', *Early Tudor England: Proceedings of the 1987 Harlaxton Symposium* ed. Daniel Williams (Woodbridge, 1989); Heal, *Reformation*, p. 134; John Guy, 'The Tudors: Henrician Reformation: An Agenda', www.tudors.org; Marshall, *Religious Identities*, p.13; Richard Rex, *Henry VIII and the English Reformation* (Basingstoke, 1993), p. 24.

3 Burton, *Three Primers*, p. 441, 514; LP, xv, 345; xv, 411, 576; Brigden, 'Popular disturbance and the fall of Thomas Cromwell and the reformers 1539–40', *HJ* 24.2 (1981), 257–278, here 264; Wriothesley, *Chronicle*, p. 114; Marshall, *Religious Identities*, p. 157; LP, xx (ii), 1030; MacCulloch, 'Henry VIII', p. 175; Bernard, 'The Making', 175.

4 Ryrie, *The Gospel and Henry VIII*, p. 23.

5 LP, xv, 345, 411; Bernard, 'The Making', 326.

6 Letter cited by Bernard, 'The Making', 327; Burton, *Three Primers*, p. 481; Tudor–Craig, 'Henry VIII and King David'; Heal, *Reformation*, pp. 134, 150; Marshall, *Reformation England*, pp. 48, 26.

7 Heal, *Reformation*, p. 150; quote from January 1536 cited by Bernard, 'The Making', 331; Marshall, 'Mumpsimus and Sumpsimus: The Intellectual Origins of a Henrician Bon Mot', *Journal of Ecclesiastical History* 52 (2001), 512–20; Hall, *Chronicle*, ff. 243r–v; Thomas, *Pilgrim* (original letters are reprinted), p. 152; Haigh, *English Reformations*, p. 154.

PART THREE – Chapter 14
The Aftermath of the Reformation
1 Ryrie, *The Gospel and Henry VIII*, pp. 23–24; Barbara Diefendorf, 'Prologue to a Massacre: Popular Unrest in Paris, 1557–72', *American Historical Review* (1991.)
2 Winthrop S. Hudson, *The Cambridge Connection and the Elizabeth Settlement of 1559* (Durham, North Carolina, 1980), pp. 92, 136, 126–27, 98, 129; CSP Span 1558–67, 89, 29; William P. Haugaard, *Elizabeth and the English Reformation: The Struggle for a Stable Settlement of Religion* (Cambridge, 1968), pp. 140, 262, 107, 250, 200; Haigh, *Elizabeth I* (London and New York, 1988) 2nd edn., pp. 34–35.
3 MacCulloch, 'Henry VIII', p. 178.

PART FOUR
Henry the Tyrant
1 *The Oxford Book of Renaissance Verse 1509–1659* ed. David Norbook and H.R. Woudhuysen (London, 1992), pp. 527–28.
2 Sir Walter Raleigh, *History of the World* (London, 1614); *Statutes*, 26 Henry VIII, c.xiii.

PART FOUR – Chapter 15
The Pilgrimage of Grace
1 LP, xi, 828 i and iii.
2 LP, xi, 569, 782, 826, 828; xii (i), 380; R.W. Hoyle, 'Thomas Master's Narrative of the Pilgrimage of Grace', *Northern History* 21 (1985), 70; Anthony Fletcher and Diarmaid MacCulloch, *Tudor Rebellions* (5th edn. Harlow, 2004), p. 26; LP, xii (i), 201.
3 LP, xi, 533, 580; Fletcher and MacCulloch, *Rebellions*, pp. 27–28; Hoyle, *The Pilgrimage of Grace and the Politics of the 1530s*, (Oxford, 2001), pp. 102–118
4 LP, xi, 705.
5 Hoyle, 'Master's Narrative', 64; Michael Bush, *The Pilgrimage of Grace: a Study of the Rebel Armies of October 1536* (Manchester, 1996), p. 119; 'Aske's Proclamation to the City of York, 15–16 October 1536', reprinted in Hoyle, *The Pilgrimage*, pp. 456–7; LP, xi, 705, 761.
6 LP, xi, 826; *State Papers*, v.1, pp. 485–87.
7 Hoyle, 'Master's Narrative', 72; Ethan Shagan, 'Politics and the Pilgrimage of Grace Revisited', in *Popular Politics and the English Reformation* (Cambridge, 2003), p. 98.
8 The terms can be extrapolated from LP, xi, 1271, xii (i), 98, 302, Shagan, 'Politics', pp. 112–114. See also the written pardon, reprinted in Bush and Bownes, *The Defeat*, pp. 415–17; Bernard, *The King's Reformation*, pp. 349–52; Scarisbrick, *Henry VIII*, p. 342.
9 Shagan, 'Politics', p. 90.
10 Shagan, 'Politics', p. 106; C.S.L. Davies, 'The Pilgrimage of Grace Reconsidered', *Past and Present* xli (1968), 57–60; LP, xi, 598, see also LP, xi, 569.

11 See Aske's address to York in Hoyle, *The Pilgrimage*, p. 456; LP, xi, 780; Bernard, *The King's Reformation,* pp. 297–299; Davies, 'Popular Religion and the Pilgrimage of Grace', in *Order and Disorder in Early Modern England* eds. Fletcher and John Stevenson (Cambridge, 1985), p.85; Shagan, 'Politics', p. 91.

12 Hoyle, *The Pilgrimage,* p. 456; Eamon Duffy, *The Stripping of the Altars: Traditional Religion in England 1400–1580* (New Haven and London, 1992), pp. 238–48; Hall, *Chronicle,* ff. 228r–v; Hoyle, 'Master's Narrative', 76; 'The Pontefract articles', reprinted in Hoyle, *The Pilgrimage,* pp. 46–3; Shagan, 'Politics', p. 105; Bateson, 'Aske's examination', 565; This was, for example, affirmed in his intended proclamation to the rebels by Lancaster Herald (LP, xi, 826) and the pardon (Bush and Bownes, *The Defeat,* p. 415).

13 LP, xii (i), 6; Bateson (ed.), 'The Pilgrimage of Grace' (includes the text of 'The manner of the taking of Robert Aske') *EHR* v (1890), and 'Aske's examination', 342, 558, also 559; Davies, 'The Pilgrimage', 66.

14 LP, xi, 576.

15 Bernard, *The King's Reformation,* p. 372; LP, xi, 598, 816; Hall *Chronicle,* f.229v; Madeleine Hope Dodds and Ruth Dodds, *The Pilgrimage of Grace 1536–7, And The Exeter Conspiracy 1538* (Cambridge, 1915), 2 vols, vol I, p. 137; LP, xi, 826; also Hall, *Chronicle,* f. 229v; LP, xi, 780, 783, 956.

16 LP, xi, 569, 783; Bernard, *The King's Reformation,* p. 374; Bush and Bownes, *The Defeat,* p. 9 [citing LP, xi, 1224, 1227, 1228, 1232, 1239, 1251]; LP, xi, 1227, 1236.

17 Barnes, *Supplication unto the most gracious Prince, King Henry VIII*, cited by Allen, *Political Thought,* p. 127; Cox, *Cranmer,* p.188; Tyndale, *Obedience of a Christian Man* (1528), ed. R. Lovett (1888), p. 93; LP, xi, 1110, 1175.

18 Erasmus, *Education,* pp. 22, 28, 54; John Guy, 'The rhetoric of counsel in early modern England', in *Tudor Political Culture* ed. Dale Hoak (Cambridge, 1995), pp. 292–310; David Starkey, 'The Court: Castiglione's ideal and Tudor reality', *Journal of Warburg and Courtauld Institutes 45* (1982), pp. 232–239, here 233; Walker, *Writing,* p. 8.

19 Cited by Bernard, 'The Tyranny', p. 113 (see LP, xiv (i), 402 and xiv (ii), 454); LP, xi, 841.

20 Bernard, *War, Taxation, and Rebellion in Early Tudor England: Henry VIII, Wolsey and the Amicable Grant of 1525* (Brighton, 1986); Bernard and Hoyle, 'The Instrument for the Levying of the Amicable Grant, March 1525', *Bulletin of the Institute of Historical Research* 68 (1994), 190–202.

21 Bush and Bownes, *The Defeat,* pp. i, 12–19, 73; LP, xi, 569, 956 where he boasted of armies of 100,000 and 50,000 men.

22 LP, xi, 1175, 1306; *State Papers,* v.1, pp. 523–24; Bernard, *The King's Reformation,* p. 377; Hall, *Chronicle,* f. 231r; LP, xii (i), 43.

23 Bernard, *The King's Reformation,* p. 378; Bush and Bownes, *The Defeat,* p. 36. This seems to me to jar with their other image of Henry as a humiliated king; LP, xii (ii), 133, 156.

24 Hoyle, *The Pilgrimage*, p. 366; LP, xi, 1410, xii (ii), 292.iii; Bernard, *The King's Reformation,* p. 390.

25 LP, xi, 1410.

26 LP, xii (i), 43, 45, 136.

27 LP, xii (i), 98, 302; Bernard is insistent the pardon did not allow re–suppression; Bush and Bownes are equally adamant that it did; I think Shagan's reading of

the equivocality of the pardon explains the potential for different understandings exhibited by the Pilgrims and the king; LP, xi, 780, Dodds, *The Pilgrimage of Grace,* I, p. 137; LP, xii (i), 479.

28 LP, xii (ii), 498, 479, 156, 166, 229, xi (i), 846; Bush and Bownes, *The Defeat,* pp. 73, 314, 364, 365, 411–22; K.J. Kesselring, *Mercy and Authority in the Tudor State* (Cambridge, 2003), p.177.

29 LP, xi, 1271; Bush and Bownes, *The Defeat,* pp. 366–67; Greg Walker, Writing: *English Literature and the Henrician Reformation* (Oxford, 2005), pp. 339–40, Bernard, 'The Tyranny of Henry VIII', in *Authority and Consent in Tudor England: Essays Presented to C.S.L. Davies* ed. G. W. Bernard and S. J. Gunn (Aldershot, 2002), pp. 122–23.

30 Howarth, *Images of Rule,* p. 80; Foister, *Holbein in England,* p. 94, following Buck; Brooke and Crombie, *Henry VIII Revealed,* p. 29; Starkey, 'Holbein and Henry VIII', *Lost Faces,* pp. 49–50.

31 Howarth, *Images of Rule,* p. 82; String, 'Projecting Masculinity'.

32 Adapted from a translation by Margot Eates, Strong; *Holbein,* p. 57.

33 Brooke and Crombie, *Henry VIII Revealed,* p. 32.

34 Hall, *Chronicle,* f. 244v; LP, xvi, 1130, 1131.

PART FOUR – Chapter 16
The Mouldwarp Prophecy

1 Sharon L. Jansen, *Political Protest and Prophecy under Henry VIII* (Woodbridge, 1991), p.15; T.M. Smallwood, 'The Prophecy of the Six Kings', *Speculum* 60.3 (1985), 571 592, here 575; James C. Scott, *Domination and the Arts of Resistance: Hidden Transcripts* (New Haven and London, 1990), p. xi, 137. See also Jansen, *Political Protest,* p. 18.

2 Keith Thomas, *Religion and the Decline of Magic,* p. 467; Jansen, *Political Protest,* pp. 5, 13, 14; William Shakespeare, *Henry IV, part 1,* III.i.142–49.

3 Smallwood, 'The Prophecy', 571, 575, 582–5. The text is preserved in the British Library MS Cotton Galba E.Ix, f. 49r 50v and reproduced by Smallwood; Madeleine Hope Dodds, 'Political Prophecies in the Reign of Henry VIII', *The Modern Language Review* 11.3 (1916), 279; Thomas, *Religion,* pp. 473–74.

4 LP, viii, 565, 609, 567, 791.

5 LP, xii (i), 318, xi, 790; Jansen, *Political Protest,* pp. 1, 39, 42, 44–45; LP, xii (i), 1087, 1212; Thomas, *Religion,* p. 474; LP, xii (ii), 800, 1231.

6 Text cited in Jansen, *Political Protest,* p. 57 (the word 'elderly' read 'helderly'); LP, xiv (i) 794 (April 1539); the case of John Bonnefant in Thomas, *Religion,* p. 474; *Statutes,* 33 Henry VIII, c.xviv; LP, xvii, 28; Alexandra Walsham, *Providence in Early Modern England* (Oxford, 1999), p. 175; Thomas, *Religion,* p. 477; LP, xii (ii), 602; xiii (ii), 829; xiv (i), 186; xiv (i), 794; xiv (ii), 124; xviii (ii), 546; xix (i), 444 (v); xx (i), 282 (xxv).

PART FOUR – Chapter 17
Courtly Dissent

1 Walker, *Writing,* pp. 286; LP, x, 840; see chapter 7. Historians have debated whether Wyatt could see the executions on Tower Hill and Tower Green from his cell in the Bell Tower. Jane Spooner, the Curator of Historic Buildings at the Tower of London, tells me he could almost certainly have seen the former, and may have seen the latter depending on whether or not the previous lieutenant's lodging was lower than the present one (built 1540). Surrey, 'Wyatt resteth here', *Oxford Book*

1536

of Renaissance Verse, pp. 627–28.

2   For the full text, see Wyatt, *Complete Poems,* ed. Rebholz, pp. 186–9; H.A. Mason, *Humanism and Poetry in the Early Tudor Period* (London, 1959), pp. 203, 222; Stephen Greenblatt, *Renaissance Self-Fashioning: From More to Shakespeare* (Chicago, 2005), p. 115; Wyatt, 'Stand so who list', *Complete Poems*, ed. Rebholz, p. 94; Walker, *Writing,* pp. 301–7; Stephen Gardiner, *De vera obedientia*, reprinted in *Obedience in Church and State: Three Political Tracts by Stephen Gardiner* ed. P. Janelle (London, 1930), p. 89; *The Complete Works of Thomas More* vol 3 (New York, 1984), p. 165, cited by Walker, *Writing,* p.7.

3   Walker, *Writing,* p. 355; Susan Brigden, 'Henry Howard, Earl of Surrey and the 'Conjured League', *HJ* 37 (1994), 507–537, here 508, 510.

PART FOUR – Chapter 18
Did Henry VIII Become a Tyrant?
1   CSP, Ven, iii, 1287.
2   Elton, 'The Rule of Law in Sixteenth-Century England', in *Studies in Tudor and Stuart Politics and Government* (Cambridge, 1974), v.1, pp. 261, 262, 274, 282–83. See also his *Policy and Police: The Enforcement of the Reformation in the Age of Thomas Cromwell* (Cambridge, 1972), p. 399; Ellis, 'Henry VIII', 531; Shore, 'Crisis', 359–390, here 375; Joel Hurstfield, 'Was There a Tudor Despotism After All?', *TRHS* (1966) 5th series, pp. 83–108; John Bellamy, *The Tudor Law of Treason: An Introduction* (London, Toronto and Buffalo, 1979), p.7; Davies, 'The Cromwellian Decade', 194; Bernard, 'The Tyranny', p. 125
3   William Thomas, *The Pilgrim: A Dialogue. on the Life and Actions of King Henry VIII* ed. J.A. Froude (London, 1861), pp. 9–10. In fact, the entire book is a dialogue designed to answer various charges of tyranny against Henry VIII, as p. 81 suggests.
4   Maurice Latey, *Tyranny: A Study in the Abuse of Power* (1972), p.18.
5   Davies, 'The Cromwellian Decade', 180, 185; Kesselring, *Mercy and Authority*, pp. 25, 37; *Statutes,* 25 Henry VIII, c.xxii; Walker, *Writing*, p. 24; Bernard, 'The Tyranny', p.119; Hall, *Chronicle*, f. 232v.
6   Bellamy, *Tudor Law of Treason*, pp. 153, 97; LP, xiv (ii), 494; Seymour Baker House, 'More, Sir Thomas (1478–1535)', *ODNB* (Oxford, 2004); LP, viii, 895, 846; Bernard, 'The Tyranny'; Kesselring, *Mercy and Authority*, pp. 60–64; Baldwin Smith, *Henry VIII*, pp. 31–35, 64–67; William Huse Dunham Jr., 'Regal Power and the Rule of Law: A Tudor Paradox', *Journal of British Studies* III (1964), 24–56; Hurstfield, 'Was There a Tudor Despotism'; Elton, 'The Rule of Law'; Latey, *Tyranny*, p. 184.
7   LP, xvi, 183, 590; Foxe, *Acts and Monuments,* V, p. 554, VI, p. 36; LP, xvi, 590, 589.
8   LP, xv, 954; Walker, *Writing*, p. 6; William Thomas, *The Pilgrim*.
9   This wonderful anecdote is cited by Latey, *Tyranny*, p.97; Derek Wilson, *In the Lion's Court: Power, Ambition and Sudden Death in the Reign of Henry VIII* (London, 2001), pp. 385–86.
10 Bellamy, *Tudor Law of Treason*, p. 29; Sean Cunningham, 'Pole, Edmund de la, Eighth Earl of Suffolk (1472?–1513)', *ODNB* (Oxford, 2004); *Statutes*, 14 and 15 Henry VIII, c.xx.
11 Ives, *The Life and Death of Anne Boleyn*, p. 345; Bellamy, *Tudor Law of Treason*, p.41; *Statutes*, 33 Henry VIII, c.xxi.

230

12 Dodds, *Pilgrimage of Grace*, vol 2, pp. 277–327.

13 Stanford E. Lehmberg, 'Parliamentary Attainder in the Reign of Henry VIII', *The Historical Journal* 18.4 (1975), 675–702 – my debt of scholarship to Dr Lehmberg is apparent from what follows; William R. Stacy, 'Richard Roose and the Use of Parliamentary Attainder in the Reign of Henry VIII', *The Historical Journal* 29.1 (1986), 1–15; Bernard, 'The Tyranny', p. 125.

14 Stacy, 'Richard Roose', 2–3; Bellamy, *Tudor Law of Treason*, pp. 28–29.

15 Lehmberg, 'Parliamentary Attainder', 685, 692, 679; Ellis, 'Henry VIII', 522–526; *Statutes*, 28 Henry VIII. c.xxiv, 27 Henry VIII. c. lviii and c.lix; Stacy, 'Richard Roose', 10.

16 Lehmberg, 'Parliamentary Attainder', 685–687; *Statutes*, 31 Henry VIII, c.xv; Walker, *Writing*, p. 340.

17 Lehmberg, 'Parliamentary Attainder', 688–689; *Statutes*, 32 Henry VIII, c.lix, c.lx, c.lxi; Hall, *Chronicle*, f. 243r.

18 Burnet, *The History of the Reformation*, Vol. IV, pp. 415–432; Shore, 'Crisis', 366, 372, 376; R.B. Merriman, *The Life and Letters of Thomas Cromwell* 2 vols (Oxford, 1902), ii pp. 264–67, 268–73; LP, xv, 776, 823; Cox, *Cranmer*, p. 401.

19 LP, xvi, 1334; Lehmberg, 'Parliamentary Attainder', 695, 697; Bellamy, *Tudor Law of Treason*, p. 41; *Statutes*, 33 Henry VIII, c.xxi ; Retha M. Warnicke, 'Katherine Howard'; Retha M. Warnicke, 'Katherine [Katherine Howard] (1518x24–1542)', *ODNB* (Oxford, 2004).

20 Stacy, 'Richard Roose', 67–68; Bellamy, *Tudor Law of Treason*, p. 44.

21 For something of a caricature of Henry VIII, see Jasper Ridley, *Henry VIII: The Politics of Tyranny* (New York, 1985) and review by Baldwin Smith, *American Historical Review* 91.2 (1986), 391–392; Thomas, *The Pilgrim*, p. 79; *The Complete Works of Thomas More* vol 3 (New York, 1984), p. 163 (cited by Walker, *Writing*, p.7); Dodds, *The Pilgrimage*, I, pp. 136–38; Hall, *Chronicle*, f. 229v; LP, xi, 780, 826; see also Henry's speech to parliament in 1535, Hall, *Chronicle*, ff. 260v–262r.

22 William Roper, *The Life of Sir Thomas More* reprinted in *Two Early Tudor Lives* ed. Richard S. Sylvester and Davis P. Harding (New Haven and London, 1962), p. 228; LP, xii (ii), 908.

Epilogue

1 Stephen Gardiner, *De vera obedientia*, reprinted in *Obedience in Church and State: Three Political Tracts* by Stephen Gardiner ed. P. Janelle (London, 1930), p. 113.

2 Thomas, *The Pilgrim*, pp. 81, 11.

3 Thomas, *The Pilgrim*, pp. 11, 55; Marillac, 3 September 1540, in Thomas, *The Pilgrim*, p. 155; Jean Kaulek (ed.), *Correspondance politique de Castillon et de Marillac* (1885) (LP, xiii (i), 56).

Further Reading

Henry VIII

Lacey Baldwin Smith, *Henry VIII: The Mask of Royalty* (St Albans, 1971)
Robert Hutchinson, *The Last Days of Henry VIII: Conspiracy, Treason and Heresy at the Court of the Dying Tyrant* (London, 2005)
Sir Arthur Salisbury MacNalty, *Henry VIII: A Difficult Patient* (London, 1952)
J. J. Scarisbrick, *Henry VIII* (London, 1968)
Miles F. Shore, 'Henry VIII and the Crisis of Generativity', *Journal of Interdisciplinary History* 2.4 (1972), pp. 359–390
David Starkey, *Henry: Virtuous Prince* (London, 2008)
Alison Weir, *Henry VIII: King and Court* (London, 2001)
Derek Wilson, *In the Lion's Court: Power, Ambition and Sudden Death in the Reign of Henry VIII* (London, 2001)

Masculinity

Will Fisher, 'The Renaissance Beard: masculinity in early modern England', *Renaissance Quarterly* 54.1 (2001), pp. 155–187
Elizabeth A. Foyster, *Manhood in Early Modern England: Honour, Sex and Marriage* (London, 1999)
Alexandra Shepard, *Meanings of Manhood in Early Modern England* (Oxford, 2003)
Tatiana C. String, 'Projecting Masculinity: Henry VIII's Codpiece', in *Henry VIII and his Afterlives: Literature, Politics and Art* ed. Christopher Highley and John N. King, Mark Rankin *(forthcoming*, Cambridge, 2009)

Anne Boleyn's fall

G. W. Bernard, 'The fall of Anne Boleyn', *EHR* 106 (1991), pp. 584–610
G. W. Bernard, 'The fall of Anne Boleyn: a rejoinder', *EHR* 107 (1992), pp. 665–74
E. W. Ives, 'Faction at the court of Henry VIII: the fall of Anne Boleyn', *History,* 57 (1972), pp. 169–88
E. W. Ives, 'Debate: The Fall of Anne Boleyn Reconsidered', *EHR* 107, (1992), pp. 651–664
Greg Walker, 'Rethinking the Fall of Anne Boleyn', *HJ*, 45.1 (2002), 1–29

Image

Xanthe Brooke and David Crombie, *Henry VIII Revealed: Holbein's Portrait and Its Legacy* (London, 2003)
Susan Foister, *Holbein in England* (London, 2006)
Christopher Lloyd and Simon Thurley, *Henry VIII: Images of a Tudor King* (Oxford, 1990)

Tatiana C. String, *Art and Communication in Henry VIII's Reign* (Aldershot, 2008)

The Reformation

G. W. Bernard, *The King's Reformation: Henry VIII and the Remaking of the English Church* (New Haven and London, 2005)
Susan Brigden, *London and The Reformation* (Oxford, 1989)
A. G. Dickens, *The English Reformation* (London, 1964)
Christopher Haigh, *English Reformations: Religion, Politics, and Society under the Tudors* (Oxford, 1991)
Peter Marshall, *Religious Identities in Henry VIII's England* (Aldershot, 2006)
Alec Ryrie, *The Gospel and Henry VIII: Evangelicals in the Early English Reformation* (Cambridge, 2003)

The Pilgrimage of Grace

Michael Bush and David Bownes, *The Defeat of the Pilgrimage of Grace: A Study of the Postpardon Revolts of December 1536 to March 1537 and their Effect* (Hull, 1999)
Madeleine Hope Dodds and Ruth Dodds, *The Pilgrimage of Grace 1536–7 and the Exeter Conspiracy 1538* (Cambridge, 1915), 2 vols
Anthony Fletcher and Diarmaid MacCulloch, *Tudor Rebellions*, 5th edn. (Harlow, 2004)
R.W. Hoyle, *The Pilgrimage of Grace and the Politics of the 1530s* (Oxford, 2001)
Ethan Shagan, 'Politics and the Pilgrimage of Grace Revisited', in *Popular Politics and the English Reformation* (Cambridge, 2003)

Tyranny

John Bellamy, *The Tudor Law of Treason: An Introduction* (London, Toronto and Buffalo, 1979)
G. W. Bernard, 'The Tyranny of Henry VIII' in *Authority and Consent in Tudor England: Essays Presented to C.S.L. Davies* ed. G.W. Bernard and S. J. Gunn (Aldershot, 2002)
Sharon L. Jansen, *Political Protest and Prophecy under Henry VIII* (Woodbridge, 1991)
K. J. Kesselring, *Mercy and Authority in the Tudor State* (Cambridge, 2003)
Maurice Latey, *Tyranny: A Study in the Abuse of Power* (Harmondsworth, 1972)
Stanford E. Lehmberg, 'Parliamentary Attainder in the Reign of Henry VIII', *HJ* 18.4 (1975), pp. 675–702
Greg Walker, *Writing under Tyranny: English Literature and the Henrician Reformation* (Oxford, 2005)

_1536_

Other important works

Antonia Fraser, _The Six Wives of Henry VIII_ (London, 1992)
Maria Hayward, _Dress at the Court of Henry VIII_ (Leeds, 2007)
Eric Ives, _The Life and Death of Anne Boleyn 'The Most Happy'_ (Oxford, 2004)
Diarmaid MacCulloch, _Thomas Cranmer: A Life_ (New Haven and London, 1996)
David Starkey, _Six Wives: The Queens of Henry VIII_ (London, 2003)
Alan Young, _Tudor and Jacobean Tournaments_ (London, 1987)

Index